To contact the publisher:
HeartBeat Productions Inc.
Box 633
Abbotsford, BC V2T 6Z8 Canada
tel: 604 852.3761
email: win@heartbeat1.com

YOU
CAN UNDERSTAND
THE BIBLE

An introduction to and application of the contextual/textual method
of Biblical Interpretation (Hermeneutics)

TEXTBOOK

Dr. Bob Utley
Professor of Hermeneutics (Retired) Bible Lessons International

Bob & Peggy Utley

The Great Commission (cf. Matt. 28:18-20; Luke 24:46-47; Acts 1:8) mandates both evangelism and discipleship. Bob has been involved in both of these for more than 35 years. He has participated in at least 45 international evangelistic crusades where thousands of people trusted Christ. Although these crusades were wonderful evangelistic experiences, a lack of follow-up materials for discipleship was evident to him.

God's will is for disciples, not decisions only! He saw the absence of Bible studies resources in other countries that were affordable and of good quality. This was a burden on his heart and he was willing to help remedy this problem.

While teaching hermeneutics in an OMS seminary in Haiti, God spoke to Bob's heart about providing his Bible studies free to the world. He structured his commentaries to provide an in-depth resource for churches, pastors and lay people. The Bible studies emphasize the original author's intent, by means of: (1) context, (2) history, (3) word studies, (4) grammar, (5) genre and (6) parallel passages.

Several years ago Bob's commentaries were included in the Logos Bible Study Software. Soon after, Logos contacted Bob on behalf of Dr. Bill Bright (Founder of Campus Crusade for Christ) to include Bob's NT commentaries on a CD-Rom of training material for CCC ministers. They planned to translate them into 50 languages and give them away free of charge. However, Bill Bright went home to heaven before the project was finished. Because of his experience in Haiti and the anticipation of the project with CCC, Bob felt this was Divine direction for him to pursue this new Great Commission task!

Bible Lessons International now produces:
1. a free Bible study website in 44 languages (www.freebiblecommentary.org)
2. a free CD-Rom which includes all written commentaries in the 44 languages and a DVD of Bob's Bible Interpretation Seminar

Bible Lessons International distributes these CD's and DVD's worldwide, free of charge. We have sent over 150,000 thus far!

TABLE OF CONTENTS

THE INTERPRETER

THE CONTEXTUAL METHOD OF BIBLICAL INTERPRETATION

SOME POSSIBLE INTERPRETIVE PITFALLS

PRACTICAL PROCEDURES FOR INTERPRETATION

C.	Write down your observations
	1. main purpose of the passage
	2. genre of the passage
D.	Check other Bible study resources on these points
E.	Re-read the entire book or literary unit and outline the major literary units (i.e., truths) and look for historical issues (i.e., author, date, recipient, occasion)
F.	Check other Bible study resources
G.	Check the significant parallel passages
H.	Eastern people present truth in tension-filled pairs
I.	Systematic Theology
J.	Use of parallel passages

SAMPLE CATEGORIES FOR NOTE TAKING

A SELECTED LIST OF RECOMMENDED RESEARCH TOOLS BY CATEGORY

A GUIDE TO GOOD BIBLE READING:
A PERSONAL SEARCH FOR VERIFIABLE TRUTH

BRIEF DEFINITIONS OF HEBREW VERBAL FORMS WHICH IMPACT EXEGESIS

	A.	VERBS

DEFINITIONS OF GREEK GRAMMATICAL FORMS WHICH IMPACT EXEGESIS

SAMPLES OF NOTE-TAKING

APPENDICES

ABBREVIATIONS USED IN THIS COMMENTARY

AB	Anchor Bible Commentaries, ed. William Foxwell Albright & David Noel Freedman
ABD	Anchor Bible Dictionary (6 vols.), ed. David Noel Freedman
AKOT	Analytical Key to the Old Testament by John Joseph Owens
ANET	Ancient Near Eastern Texts, James B. Pritchard
BDB	A Hebrew and English Lexicon of the Old Testament by F. Brown, S. R. Driver, C. A. Briggs
BHS	Biblia Hebraica Stuttgartensia, GBS, 1997
IDB	The Interpreter's Dictionary of the Bible (4 vols.), ed. George A. Buttrick
ISBE	International Standard Bible Encyclopedia (5 vols.), ed. James Orr
JB	Jerusalem Bible
JPSOA	The Holy Scriptures According to the Masoretic Text: A New Translation (The Jewish Publication Society of America)
KB	The Hebrew and Aramaic Lexicon of the Old Testament by Ludwig Koehler and Walter Baumgartner
LAM	The Holy Bible From Ancient Eastern Manuscripts (the Peshitta) by George M. Lamsa
LXX	Septuagint (Greek-English) by Zondervan, 1970
MOF	A New Translation of the Bible by James Moffatt
MT	Masoretic Hebrew Text
NAB	New American Bible Text
NASB	New American Standard Bible
NEB	New English Bible
NET	NET Bible: New English Translation, Second Beta Edition
NRSV	New Revised Standard Bible
NIDOTTE	New International Dictionary of Old Testament Theology and Exegesis (5 vols.), ed. Willem A. VanGemeren
NIV	New International Version
NJB	New Jerusalem Bible
OTPG	Old Testament Parsing Guide by Todd S. Beall, William A. Banks, and Colin Smith
REB	Revised English Bible
RSV	Revised Standard Version
SEPT	The Septuagint (Greek-English) by Zondervan, 1970
TEV	Today's English Version from United Bible Societies
YLT	Young's Literal Translation of the Holy Bible by Robert Young
ZPBE	Zondervan Pictorial Bible Encyclopedia (5 vols), ed. Merrill C. Tenney

A WORD FROM THE AUTHOR:
A BRIEF SUMMARY OF THIS INTERPRETIVE METHOD

Biblical interpretation is a rational and spiritual process that attempts to understand an ancient inspired writer in such a way that the message from God may be understood and applied in our day.

The spiritual process is crucial but difficult to define. It does involve a yieldedness and openness to God. There must be a hunger (1) for Him, (2) to know Him, and (3) to serve Him. This process involves prayer, confession, and the willingness for lifestyle change. The Spirit is crucial in the interpretive process, but why sincere, godly Christians understand the Bible differently is a mystery.

The rational process is easier to describe. We must be consistent and fair to the text and not be influenced by our personal, cultural, or denominational biases. We are all historically conditioned. None of us are objective, neutral interpreters. This commentary offers a careful rational process containing three interpretive principles structured to help us attempt to overcome our biases.

First Principle

The first principle is to note the historical setting in which a biblical book was written and the particular historical occasion for its authorship (or when it was edited). The original author had a purpose and a message to communicate. The text cannot mean something to us that it never meant to the original, ancient, inspired author. His intent—not our historical, emotional, cultural, personal, or denominational need—is the key. Application is an integral partner to interpretation, but proper interpretation must always precede application. It must be reiterated that every biblical text has one and only one meaning. This meaning is what the original biblical author intended through the Spirit's leadership to communicate to his day. This one meaning may have many possible applications to different cultures and situations. These applications must be linked to the central truth of the original author. For this reason, this study guide commentary is designed to provide a brief introduction to each book of the Bible.

Second Principle

The second principle is to identify the literary units. Every biblical book is a unified document. Interpreters have no right to isolate one aspect of truth by excluding others. Therefore, we must strive to understand the purpose of the whole biblical book before we interpret the individual literary units. The individual parts—chapters, paragraphs, or verses—cannot mean what the whole unit does not mean. Interpretation must move from a deductive approach of the whole to an inductive approach to the parts. Therefore, this study guide commentary is designed to help the student analyze the structure of each literary unit by paragraphs. Paragraph and chapter divisions are not inspired, but they do aid us in identifying thought units.

Interpreting at a paragraph level—not sentence, clause, phrase, or word level—is the key in following the biblical author's intended meaning. Paragraphs are based on a unified topic, often called the theme or topical sentence. Every word, phrase, clause, and sentence in the paragraph relates somehow to this unified theme. They limit it, expand it, explain it, and/or question it. A real key to proper interpretation is to follow the original author's thought on a paragraph-by-paragraph basis through the individual literary units that make up the biblical book. This study guide commentary is designed to help the student do that by comparing the paragraphing of modern English translations.

These translations have been selected because they employ different translation theories:

A. The New King James Version (NKJV) is a word-for-word literal translation based on the Greek manuscript tradition known as the Textus Receptus. Its paragraph divisions are longer than the other translations. These longer units help the student to see the unified topics.

B. The New Revised Standard Version (NRSV) is a modified word-for-word translation. It forms a midpoint between the following two modern versions. Its paragraph divisions are quite helpful in identifying subjects.

C. The Today's English Version (TEV) is a dynamic equivalent translation published by the United Bible Society. It attempts to translate the Bible in such a way that a modern English reader or speaker can understand the meaning of the original text.

D. The Jerusalem Bible (JB) is a dynamic equivalent translation based on a French Catholic translation. It is very helpful in comparing the paragraphing from a European perspective.

E. The printed text is the 1995 Updated New American Standard Bible (NASB), which is a word for word translation. The verse by verse comments follow this paragraphing.

Third Principle

The third principle is to read the Bible in different translations in order to grasp the widest possible range of meaning (semantic field) that biblical words or phrases may have. Often a phrase or word can be understood in several ways. These different translations bring out these options and help to identify and explain the manuscript variations. These do not affect doctrine, but they do help us to try to get back to the original text penned by an inspired ancient writer.

Fourth Principle

The fourth principle is to note the literary genre. Original inspired authors chose to record their messages in different forms (e.g., historical narrative, historical drama, poetry, prophecy, gospel [parable], letter, apocalyptic). These different forms have special keys to interpretation (see Gordon Fee and Doug Stuart, *How to Read the Bible for All Its Worth*, D. Brent Sandy and Ronald L. Giese, Jr., *Cracking Old Testament Codes,* or Robert Stein, *Playing by the Rules*).

This Textbook offers a quick way for the student to check his interpretations. It is not meant to be definitive, but rather informative and thought-provoking. Often, other possible interpretations help us not be so parochial, dogmatic, and denominational. Interpreters need to have a larger range of interpretive options to recognize how ambiguous the ancient text can be. It is shocking how little agreement there is among Christians who claim the Bible as their source of truth.

These principles have helped me to overcome much of my historical conditioning by forcing me to struggle with the ancient text. My hope is that it will be a blessing to you as well.

Bob Utley
East Texas Baptist University
June 27, 1996

INTRODUCTION

I. A Word About the Trend in Biblical Interpretation Toward Specializations in Hermeneutics

I can remember, as a new believer, how excited I was about understanding more about Christ, the Christian life, and the Bible. I was told that it was the joy and job of every believer to study the Bible. I can remember how frustrating it was when I began reading the Bible. What I thought would be an exciting adventure turned into a confusing nightmare.

> "The thought of personal Bible study frightens most Christians. It seems to be so difficult without any formal training. Yet Psalm 119 persistently beckons every Christian to feed on the spiritual nourishment of Scripture" (Mayhue 1986, 45).

But there was hope. I was told that religious training would provide the tools and techniques necessary to understand the Bible for myself, but this turned out to be a half truth. It was true that religious training opened the Bible to me in many wonderful ways. However, very quickly it was evident to me that more education and specialization were needed to really understand the Bible. Suddenly I realized that years of linguistic, semantic, exegetical, hermeneutical, and theological expertise were needed to fully understand the Bible. By this time, my level of education was such that I recognized that the specialists who were training me did not interpret the Bible with uniformity either (Silva 1987, 2-3). They each claimed that educational acumen in their particular field was crucial to proper biblical interpretation and yet they continued to disagree on how to interpret certain difficult passages.

These comments are not meant to be strongly critical of Christian education, but a recognition that it could not deliver all it promised. Somehow, somewhere, someway there had to be more than education.

> "The Bible is so simple that the least educated can understand its basic message and yet so profound that the best scholar can never exhaust its full meaning" (Schultz and Inch 1976, 9).

Somehow we have turned the interpretation of the Bible into the exclusive domain of the academic specialists. We have taken the Bible, which was written for the common person, and given it to the privileged, highly-trained expert.

> Wycliffe wrote: "Christ and His apostles taught the people in the language best known to them. It is certain that the truth of the Christian faith becomes more evident the more faith itself is known. Therefore, the doctrine should not only be in Latin, but in the vulgar tongue and, as the faith of the church is contained in the Scripture, the more these are known in a true sense the better. The laity ought to understand the faith, and as doctrines of our faith are in the Scriptures, believers should have the Scriptures in a language which they fully understand" (Mayhue 1986, 106).

What we have done with the principles of interpretation parallels what
    (1) the Jews did with their legal experts, the scribes;
    (2) the Gnostics did with their intellectual emphasis and secret knowledge, which only they
        dispensed; and
    (3) the Roman Catholic Church of the Middle Ages did with the clergy vs. laity dichotomy,
        which continues until today.

We have again taken the Bible from the grasp of the common person only to make its truths available to the specialist. We have done to biblical interpretation what medicine has done to physicians: a specialist for every system of the human body, yet these specialists often disagree on diagnosis and treatment. The same tendency has occurred in almost every area of modern life, including the academic disciplines of the Christian college and seminary.

With the glut of information available today, the specialists cannot even keep up in their own fields. So, how can the average Christian be expected to keep up with biblical scholarship when even "the experts" cannot do so? Gordon Fee, in a book entitled *Interpreting the Word of God*, made this statement:

> "The suggestions offered in this paper may seem so staggering to the common man, to whom the Bible was originally addressed, that interpretation becomes an affair only of the expert. Fortunately, the Spirit, as the wind, 'bloweth where it listeth' (John 3:8), and in this instance, He has a wonderful way of graciously bypassing the expert and addressing us directly" (Schultz and Inch 1976, 126).

I think we would agree that in this area of hermeneutics (the principles of biblical interpretation) and exegesis (the practice of interpretation) we have inadvertently taken the Bible from the very ones to whom it was given. Daniel Webster commented in this area.

> "I believe that the Bible is to be understood and received in the plain, obvious meaning of its passages, since I cannot persuade myself that a book intended for the salvation and conversion of the whole world should cover its meaning in any such mystery and doubt that none but critics and philosophers discover it" (Mayhue 1986, 60).

It seems that the insistence on advanced education as a necessity to interpret the Bible must surely be wrong by the very fact that the vast majority of the world never has had, and never can have, the level of theological training enjoyed by Europe and America since the Enlightenment.

> "Most people probably think that reference books, like commentaries and Bible dictionaries, are necessary tools for Bible study. No doubt they are helpful, for they give us the insights of Bible scholars. But many Christians, especially those in poorer circumstances, cannot have these helps. Must they wait to study the Bible until they can get them? If so, many would have to wait forever" (Sterrett 1973, 33).

> "One can be confident that the vernacular will convey most of the grammatical factors necessary for understanding Biblical writing. If this were not true, the bulk of Christendom would be unqualified for Bible study, and the Bible would be accessible to only a few privileged few" (Traina 1985, 81).

The church must return to a balanced position between (1) education and (2) supernatural giftedness. There are many factors involved in a proper understanding of the Bible's message, not the least of which is the spiritual motivation, commitment, and giftedness of the interpreter. Obviously, a trained person will be more adept at some aspects of the task, but not necessarily the crucial ones.

> "The presence of the Holy Spirit and the ability of language to communicate truth combine to give all you need to study and interpret the Bible for yourself" (Henricksen 1973, 37).

Could it be that biblical interpretation is a spiritual gift, as well as a learned discipline? This is not to imply that all Christians do not have the right and responsibility to interpret the Scriptures for themselves, but could it be there is that which is beyond education? A good analogy might be the gift of evangelism. In witnessing situations it is obvious when this gift is present. Its effectiveness and fruitfulness is apparent. However, this surely does not remove or lessen the biblical responsibility for witnessing to a select, gifted few. All believers can learn to do a better, more effective job of sharing our faith through training and personal experience. I believe this is true of Bible interpretation also. We must combine our dependence on the Spirit (Silva 1987, 24-25) with the insight from education and the benefit of practical experience.

> "It might seem up to this point that I am advocating a non-intellectual approach to Bible interpretation. This is certainly not the case. Spurgeon warns us of this when he says, 'It seems odd that certain men who talk so much of what the Holy Spirit reveals to them should think so little of what He revealed to others'" (Henricksen 1973, 41).

This brings us to the question of how we balance these two obvious truths: God's ability to communicate through His Word to the uneducated and how education can facilitate the process.

First, I would like to assert that our opportunities for education surely must be taken into consideration. To whom much is given, much is required (Luke 12:48). Many Christians lack the motivation for improvement, not the opportunities. For not only are we stewards of our opportunities, but of our motivation and attitude as well.

> "God is His own interpreter, but the student of Scripture must bring to his task a disciplined mind as well as a warm heart. Faith offers no shortcuts to a responsible reading of the Bible. Nor can we leave the task of biblical interpretation to a few experts. None of us can avoid the task of interpretation. Every time we listen to someone speak, or whenever we read what someone has written, we interpret what is being said. It is no different when we open the Bible. The question is not whether we need to interpret, but how well or how badly we do it" (Jansen 1968, 17).

To the need of a warm heart, I would like to add that though our hearts might be warm they are still sinful (Silva 1987, 23, 118). We need to be careful of linking our understanding of the Bible with God's understanding. We have all been, and continue to be, affected by sin. In the last analysis neither the best hermeneutical principles or exegetical procedures nor a warm heart can overcome our propensity toward sin. Humility must accompany our interpretations.

"Proper hermeneutics demands a stance of humility. This includes not only the humility of learning from others, but more significantly, the humility of coming under the judgment of the Word one is interpreting. Although the task of the interpreter requires study and judgment, his ultimate task is to let the Word he is studying address him and call him to obedience" (Gordon Fee quoted in Schultz and Inch 1976, 127).

Another possible solution is the concept of varying degrees or levels of interpretation. It seems obvious to me that untrained lay people will not have the depth of insight that a trained interpreter might have. However, this does not imply that incomplete knowledge is faulty knowledge.

"Saying that we understand God's Word does not mean we can understand everything in it, solve all problems of interpretation and get answers to all our questions. The precise meaning of some things seems to be still secret" (Sterrett 1973, 16).

If so, all human knowledge is in the same category. The Spirit's task of leading God's children into truth (John 14:26; 16:13-14; I John 2:20-21) is only expanded by our intellectual skills. The basics of the Christian faith can be known by anyone by means of a simple reading of the Bible in a translation he/she understands. It is in the area of maturity and balance that Christian education becomes an invaluable aid. We can trust the Spirit in the area of interpretation. Surely there will be misinterpretations and theological problems, but are these absent from scholars?

The crucial need for the modern church is that we begin to involve all believers in meaningful, personal, daily Bible study for themselves. This involves the church training them in interpretive techniques which they can comprehend and implement.

"The challenge to the church is to stress individual study of the Bible among those who believe the Bible" (Osborne and Woodward 1979, 13).

This is further stressed:

"In-depth Bible study, as we have seen, is meant for every believer, whether a lay student of the Word or a professional Christian worker. We must remember that God does not require us to be brilliant, but He does require us to be faithful. Spending an extensive amount of time in detailed study of Scripture does not take a genius, but it does take a disciplined believer. Faithfulness and discipline are two sides of the same coin" (Osborne and Woodward 1979, 82).

The hermeneutical techniques must be reduced to common sense concepts, for really they should involve nothing more than the normal application of human reason and language skills (Fee 1982, 16; Sire 1980, 51). God wants to communicate to us as badly as believers want to understand His message. The techniques need to balance the individual's own analytical processes while providing good, reliable reference material as quickly as possible to the process. This is particularly true of historical and cultural background material. Gordon Fee offers these helpful suggestions.

"Let the non-expert not despair; but let him also be prepared to study, not simply to devotionalize. To study he should use these basic tools: (a) More than one good contemporary translation. This should point out at times where some of the problems lie. He should be sure to use translations which recognize the differences between prose and poetry and are aware of paragraphs. (b) At least one good commentary, especially one that takes into account the hermeneutical principles offered in this paper (e.g., C. K. Barrett, on I Cor.; F. F. Bruce, on Hebrews; R. D. Brown on John). Again, consulting several will usually apprise one of various options. (c) His own common sense. Scripture is not filled with hidden meanings to be dug out by miners in dark caves. Try to discover what is plainly intended by the biblical author. This intention usually lies close to the surface and needs only a little insight into grammar or history to become visible. Very often it lies right on the surface and the expert misses it because he is too prone to dig first and look later. At this point the nonexpert has much to teach the expert (Gordon Fee in *Interpreting the Word of God*," quoted in Schultz and Inch 1976, 127).

A Word to the Laity

For many laypersons there is a growing apathy and indifference to personal Bible study. Many are willing for someone else to interpret the Bible for them. This flies in the face of the biblical principle of "the priesthood of the believer," which was so enthusiastically reinforced by the Reformation. We are all responsible to know God through Christ and to understand for ourselves His will for our lives (i.e., soul competency). We dare not delegate this awesome responsibility to another, no matter how much we respect that person. We will all give an account to God for our understanding of the Bible and how we have lived it (cf. II Cor. 5:10).

Why is the prevalence toward pre-digested Bible study (sermons, commentaries) so evident today? First, I think the large number of interpretations so readily available in western culture has caused great confusion. It seems that no one agrees about the Bible. This is certainly not the case. However, one must distinguish between major, historical Christian truths and peripheral issues. The major pillars of the Christian faith are shared by all Christian denominations. By this I mean the doctrines related to the person and work of Christ, God's desire to save, and the central place of the Bible and other similar truths which are common to all Christians. Laypeople must be trained to distinguish between the wheat and the chaff. Just because there are so many interpretations does not relieve us of the responsibility of choosing the ones which are most in line with an inspired biblical author's intent expressed in a biblical context.

Not only is the variety of interpretations a barrier, but also the interpreter's denominational traditions. Often, laypeople think they know what the Bible means before they study it or even read it for themselves. Often, we become so comfortable in a theological system that we forget the problems these man-made systems have caused throughout the history of the Church. Also, we forget how many different, often seemingly conflicting, systems there are in the Christian community. We dare not limit ourselves to that with which we are familiar! We must force ourselves to remove the glasses of denominational and cultural tradition and view the Bible in light of its own day. Denominational and cultural traditions can be helpful, but they must always be subject to the Bible, not vice versa. It is painful to reexamine what we have been told, but it is crucial that we do so, individually, apart from parents, pastor, teacher, spouse, or friends.

We must realize that we have all been affected, not only by our parents, our place of birth, our time of birth, but also by our personal experiences and personality type. These all greatly influence how we interpret the Bible. We cannot change or eliminate these factors, but we can recognize their presence, which will help us not to be unduly influenced by them. We are all historically conditioned.

There was a time in America when the laity knew the Bible as well as the preachers, but in our day of specialization and the encroachment of mass media on our time, we have opted for the expert. However, in biblical interpretation we must do it for ourselves. This does not mean that we do not consult the gifted, called, and trained Christian leaders, but we must not allow their interpretation to become ours without prayerful, personal, biblical analysis. We are all affected by sin, even after we are saved. This affects every aspect of our understanding about God and His purposes. We must recognize the major truth that our understanding is never God's understanding. We must cling to the major pillars of Christianity, but allow maximum expression of interpretation and practice in peripheral or non-essential areas. We must each decide where the boundaries are located and live appropriately, by faith, by love, in the light we have from Scripture.

In summary, it seems to me that the church must devote more energy to communicating the principles for adequately understanding the Bible's ancient, inspired author's intent. We as Bible readers must also reduce our experiential, parochial, denominational, tradition-bound presuppositions in order to truly seek the message of the inspired biblical writers, even when these might violate our personal biases or denominational traditions. We must leave our popular "proof texting" techniques for a true contextual interpretation of the original biblical authors. The only inspired person in biblical interpretation is the original author(s).

Believers must reexamine their goals and motives in light of Eph. 4:11-16. May God help us move into the fullness of His Word in thought and deed.

II. The Author's Experiences in Teaching Hermeneutics in Local Churches, Classrooms, and Seminars

As a pastor for fifteen years, a university professor for sixteen, I have had ample opportunity to observe and discuss hermeneutical issues with Christians from several denominational groups. I have pastored in Southern Baptist churches and taught at three Southern Baptist schools (Wayland Baptist University extension, Lubbock, Texas; The Hispanic School of Theology, Lubbock, Texas; and East Texas Baptist University, Marshall, Texas), and a charismatic junior college level Bible school (Trinity Bible Institute, Lubbock, Texas). Since retirement I have taught courses for several years at the OMS Emmaus Seminary in Cap Haitian, Haiti; the Baptist Armenian Seminary in Yerevan, Armenia, and the interdenominational seminary in Novi Sod, Serbia. Also, I am an associate member of the United Methodist Church and the Presbyterian Church of America. I did my doctoral work at an interdenominational seminary, Trinity Evangelical Divinity School in the Chicago area. This has allowed me to minister across denominational lines for several years. One common theme has developed in these discussions and that is the obvious lack of training in hermeneutical concepts and procedures.

Most Christians, in interpreting the Bible, rely on

1. proof-texting
2. literalizing
3. allegory/moralizing
4. denominational indoctrination
5. personal experience
6. cultural conditioning

There is a desperate need for a consistent, verifiable, textually-oriented hermeneutical approach to biblical interpretation. It is crucial that the hermeneutical principles be presented in (1) non-technical language; (2) simply stated principles; and (3) principles that can be demonstrated with several relevant biblical examples.

Laypersons readily respond to a simplified hermeneutical approach which can be demonstrated to provide a more consistent, verifiable procedure for personally interpreting the Scriptures. Most laypersons sense the relativity of much of the Bible study with which they are presented, from local churches, Christian literature and also from broadcast media (radio and television).

I have taught hermeneutics in several settings.
1. citywide seminars
2. local church seminars
3. Sunday School classes
4. junior college classrooms
5. university classrooms

In each of these settings I have found laypersons to be open and eager to respond to a consistent, verifiable approach to Bible study. There is a real hunger to understand the Bible and live in light of its teachings.

There is also a real frustration because of
1. the multiplicity of interpretations
2. the relativity of interpretations
3. the denominational arrogance connected with certain interpretations
4. the lack of ability to verify what they have been told in God's name

This Textbook is not designed to be a technical, exhaustive, academic presentation of hermeneutics, but an introduction to the average believer to the Contextual/Textual approach of the textually-oriented school of interpretation (i.e., Antioch of Syria) and the personal application of these principles into daily study and life.

The Introduction will focus on five specific areas.
1. the need for hermeneutical training
2. the Contextual/Textual principles of biblical hermeneutics
3. some major pitfalls in contemporary hermeneutics
4. some guiding methodological procedures, and
5. the Bible study resources which are available to the modern English speaking layperson

This Textbook is designed to raise the interest and desire of Christians to interpret the Scriptures for themselves. It is admittedly only a beginning step, but a crucial step nevertheless. The Bibliography provides numerous additional sources for further study in Bible study techniques. The recognition that there is a problem in our current popular methods of biblical interpretation and that there is a more consistent, verifiable approach available to laypersons is the major goal of this Textbook. Because the journey of a thousand miles begins with one step, hopefully this Introduction will start laypersons on the right path of the exciting and fulfilling task of lifestyle, daily, personal Bible study.

III. The Issue of Authority

The question of whether or not there is a God has never really been an issue for me personally. I, following the biblical writers, have assumed the existence of God. I have never felt the need for a philosophical argument to bolster my faith at this point. Thomas Aquinas' five proofs for God are helpful to those who seek evidence from rationalism. However, even the philosophical necessity arguments do not really prove the existence of the God of the Bible, the Father of our Lord Jesus Christ. At best they posit a logical necessity, an unmoved mover, or a prime cause.

Also, the question about whether we can know God (Greek philosophy) has never been a major concern for me. I have assumed that God is trying to communicate to us. This is not only true in natural revelation: (1) God's witness in creation (Ps. 19:1-6; Rom. 1:19-20) and (2) mankind's inner moral witness (Rom. 2:14-15), but uniquely in God's written revelation (II Tim. 3:15-17). God has spoken to us through events, laws, and prophets (cf. Matt. 5:17-19). He has spoken supremely in His Son (John 1:1-14; Heb. 1:1-3; Matt. 5:21-48).

The major question for me has revolved around <u>what</u> God is saying. This concern developed very early in my Christian life. Desiring to know the Bible I was appalled at all the different interpretations of Scripture. It seemed that everyone had his own opinion about the Bible, often based on individual personality type, denominational background, personal experience, or parental training. They were all so convinced and convincing. I began to wonder if one could really know, with any degree of certainty, what God was saying.

In seminary I was finally introduced to the concept of "biblical authority." It became clear to me that the Bible was the only basis for faith and practice. This was not just a cliche to defend one's traditional methodologies and theologies. It was really a specific answer to the issue of authority.

Even after accepting the authority of the Bible as properly interpreted, there still remains the difficult issue of which hermeneutical system is best. The same bewilderment that I felt in the maze of interpretations I found to be present in the area of hermeneutics. As a matter of fact, the divergence of expressed or unexpressed, conscious or unconscious, principles of hermeneutics may really be the cause for the multiplicity of interpretations. Hermeneutical principles were extremely difficult to analyze because they themselves were not inspired, but were developed within differing theological traditions and through historical crises. There are godly interpreters in all of the different systems. How does one decide which system to use? The basic issue for me came down to "verifiability" and "consistency." I am sure that this is because I live in a day which is dominated by the scientific method. However, there must be some boundaries placed on interpretation. Ambivalence does exist within hermeneutics because it is both a gift (art) and a set of logical guidelines for understanding human languages (science). Whatever one's principles of interpretation, they must balance these two perspectives.

The Antiochian (Syrian) school of interpretation offered the best available balance. Its contextual/textual focus allows at least some measure of verifiability. There will never be unanimity, but at least it stressed the importance of interpreting the Scriptures in their obvious, normal sense.

It must be admitted that the approach is basically a historical reaction to the allegorical school of Alexandria (Egypt). This is an oversimplification (Silva 1987, 52-53), but it is still helpful to use it in analyzing the two basic approaches of the church to biblical interpretation. The Antiochian school, with its Aristotelian methodology, did provide an adequate rationale for Reformation/ Renaissance interpretation, which set the stage for our modern scientific orientation.

The Contextual/Textual approach to interpretation allows the Bible to speak first to its day (one meaning) and then to our day (many applications). It bridges the gap of time and culture in a methodology acceptable to the intellectual community of our day. They accept it because it is basically the same method that is used to interpret all ancient literature and it fits the thought forms of our modern academic mindset.

As hermeneutics became a major concern of my ministry, I began to analyze preaching, teaching, and religious writing more carefully. It was appalling to see the abuses that were occurring in God's name. The church seemed to be praising the Bible and then perverting its message. This was not only true of the layperson, but also the church's leadership. It was not an issue of piety, but true ignorance of the basic principles of interpretation. The joy I found in knowing the Bible by means of the original author's purpose (intent) was simply a non-entity to many wonderful, committed, loving believers. I decided to develop a Textbook in order to introduce laypersons to the basic principles of the Antiochian, contextual/textually-focused method. At that time (1977) there were not very many books available on hermeneutics. This was especially true for the laity. I tried to develop interest by exposing our faulty interpretations as well as our conscious biases. This was combined with a brief explanation of the contextual/textual method and a list of common theological errors encountered in interpretation. Finally, a procedural order was proposed to help someone walk through the different hermeneutical tasks and the appropriate time to consult research tools.

IV. The Need for Non-technical Hermeneutical Procedures

A. Apathy Among Believers

This problem has been on my heart as a pastor and professor for several years. I have been made painfully aware of the decline in general biblical knowledge among believers in our day. This lack of knowledge has been the root cause of many of the problems in the contemporary church. I know that modern believers love God as much as past generations have loved Him and His Word, so what is the cause of the degeneration in our understanding, not only of the content of Scripture, but what it means and how it is applicable today?

In my opinion a sense of frustration has caused the majority of Christians to become indifferent and apathetic about studying and interpreting the Bible. This apathy is discernible in several areas of modern life. One of the major problems is our cultural attitude of consumerism. We as a people are accustomed to instant gratification of our every need. Our culture has turned the "fast food" industry's mentality into a cultural norm. We are accustomed to a product being readily available and instantaneously consumed. Christian maturity based on Bible knowledge and daily lifestyle cannot accommodate this cultural expectation. Bible knowledge is only available by paying a personal price of prayer, persistence, training, regular study, and personal application. In reality, most modern believers are on the fast track of twenty-first century, materialistic America and are not willing to pay such a personal price.

Also, the non-biblical dichotomy between clergy and laity has accentuated the problem. It almost seems that our "hired gun" mentality has relieved most lay persons of the sense of need to study and understand the Bible personally. "Let the preacher do it" has become our mind set. The problem with this mentality is, "What if the pastor misinterprets?" or "What if you change pastors?" This apathetic attitude circumvents the biblical truth and the Reformation reemphasis (Luther) of the doctrine of "soul competency" (I Pet. 2:5,9; Rev. 1:6). It reinforces our "herd society" tendency. It tends to focus spiritual responsibility away from ourselves and onto others. Church leaders become intermediaries or gurus instead of "player coaches" (Eph. 4:11-12). Not only have we as a culture divided life into the secular and the sacred, but we have delegated the sacred to surrogates.

Another major cause for apathy among the majority of modern believers in the area of Bible study is our growing modern trend toward specialization. Bible study has become the technical domain of trained specialists. The principles and procedures are so complicated and involved that one feels incompetent unless he has several PhD. degrees: linguistics, Greek, Hebrew, hermeneutics, and theology. This introduces the danger of "modern gnosticism," which is spiritual truth available only from an intellectual elite. Of course, even the elite do not agree. It seems that even technical skills do not bring consensus.

This brings us to the next reason for apathy, which is the multiplicity of interpretations. Not only is one confronted with denominational differences, but even within denominations there is a divergence of opinion. It is no wonder that the majority of believers are confused in the face of such disagreement, which is usually presented in such a forceful, dogmatic fashion.

B. Dogmatism Among Believers

Is it any wonder that there is confusion and reluctance to become involved in the interpretive process? Besides these previously mentioned external factors, there are several internal ones. If there is an apathy about getting involved in Bible study, it almost seems that once the decision is made to overcome that apathy, immediate polarization and exclusivism results. The level of dogmatism among modern western Bible students is very high.

This seems to involve several factors. The first is often related to the spiritual tradition in which one is raised. Often dogmatism is a learned response from our parents or church teachers. This can be either a complete identification with their views and practices or the complete rejection of their position. This transference, assimilation, or negative reaction is usually unrelated to personal Bible study. Often our biases, presuppositions, and á priories are passed on through families.

If parents do not stamp us with their spiritual views, then most assuredly our denomination will. Much that we believe is not a result of personal Bible study, but of denominational indoctrination. Today very few churches systematically teach what they believe and why. This problem is affected not only by denominationalism, but by the geographical location of the denominational church. As it is obvious that the age (post-modernity) in which we live affects our belief system, so too, does our geographical location. Parochialism is as significant as parental or denominational tradition. For over thirty years I have been involved in Partnership Evangelism and have taken church members and students on mission trips to work with my denomination's churches in foreign countries. I have been amazed how differently churches from the same denominational tradition practice their faith! This really opened my eyes to the denominational, parochial indoctrination (not Bible reading) that has affected all of us.

The second major cause of dogmatism among believers is related to personal factors. As we are affected by time, place, and parents, so too, are we equally impacted by our own personhood. This concept will be developed in some detail in a later section of this Textbook, but it needs to be mentioned at the beginning how much our personality type, personal experience, and spiritual gift affect our interpretations. Often our dogmatism could be expressed by "if it happened to me it ought to happen to you" and "if it has never happened to me, it should never happen to you either." Both are false!

V. Basic Presuppositions About the Bible

At this point I need to be as transparent as possible and try to spell out my own operating assumptions. If we are so affected by non-biblical factors, why is this Textbook not just one more in the series? I am not attempting to get you to agree with me, but to provide a more consistent, verifiable methodology for personal, non-technical Bible study. The methodology is not inspired, but it is a developed ancient Christian model.

My basic presuppositions are

A. The Bible, both Old and New Testaments, is from the one and only Creator, Redeemer God. He gave it to us through human instrumentality so that we might know and understand Him and His will for our lives (cf. II Tim. 3:15-17). It is absolutely authoritative.

B. The Bible, like hermeneutics, is not an end in itself, but a means to a personal encounter with God (Grant and Tracy 1984, 177; Carson 1984, 11; Silva 1987, vi). God has clearly spoken to us in the Bible and even more clearly in His Son, Jesus Christ (Heb. 1:1-3). Christ is the focus of all Scripture. He is its crowning fulfillment and goal. He is Lord of Scripture. In Him revelation is complete and final (John 1:1-18; I Cor. 8:6; Col. 1:13-20).

C. The Bible is written in normal, non-technical human language. Its focus is the obvious, normal meaning of words, clauses, sentences (Silva 1987, 42). The Holy Spirit gave simple statements of truth. This is not to say that the Bible is unambiguous, that it does not contain cultural idioms, or that it does not contain difficult passages and, at this point in time, scribal errors. However, it does not have hidden or secret meanings. It is not contradictory (analogy of faith) although it does contain paradoxical or dialectical tension between truths.

D. The message of the Bible is primarily redemptive and is meant for all humans (Ezek. 18:23,32; John 4:42; I Tim. 2:4; 4:10; II Pet. 3:9). It is for the world, not exclusively for Israel (Gen. 3:15; 12:3; Exod. 19:5-6). It is for the "lost" (fallen) world, not only for the church. It is for the common, average human being, not only for the spiritually or intellectually gifted.

E. The Holy Spirit is an indispensable guide to proper understanding.
   1. There must be a balance between human effort and piety (II Tim. 2:15) and the leading of the Spirit (John 14:26; 16:13-14; I John 2:20-21,27).
   2. Biblical interpretation is possibly a spiritual gift (like evangelism, giving, or prayer), yet it is also the task of every believer. Although it is a gift, by analyzing the gifted, all of us can do a better job.
   3. There is a spiritual dimension beyond human intellectual reach. The original authors often recorded more than they understood (future events, aspects of progressive revelation, and multiple fulfillment prophecy). The original hearers often did not comprehend the inspired message and its implications. The Spirit illumines us to comprehend the basic message of the biblical writers. We may not understand every detail, but then, who does? The Spirit is the true author of all Scripture.

F. The Bible does not speak directly to every modern question (Spire 1980, 82-82). It is ambiguous in many areas. Some of it is locked into the original historical setting (e.g., I Cor. 15:29) and other parts are hidden behind the "not yet" of history (e.g., Dan. 12:4). It must be remembered that the Bible is analogous truth, not exhaustive truth. It is adequate for faith and life. We cannot know everything, either about God or a specific doctrine of Scripture, but we can know what is essential (Silva 1987, 80).

VI. General Statements About the Contextual/Textual Method

This Textbook is basically an introduction to the **Contextual/Textual** or **Literal** method of interpreting the Bible. This method developed in the third century A.D. in Antioch, Syria, in reaction to the **Allegorical** method, which had previously developed in Alexandria, Egypt. The historical development and explanation of this ancient methodology will be developed in a later session.

In this introductory session let me make some general statements about the Antiochian method.

A. It is the only methodology available which provides controls on interpretation which enables others to verify, from the text, a given interpretation. This provides a measure of consistency and assurance that one has interpreted the passage properly in light of the original inspired author's intent. As Gordon Fee says, "A Bible that can mean anything, means nothing."

B. This is not a method for scholars or church leaders only, but a means of getting back to the original hearers. These original hearers would have understood the message in their own existential context and cultural milieu. Because of time, language, and culture the task of understanding the original setting and message becomes increasingly difficult (Virkler 1981, 19-20). That which was readily apparent is often lost in history, culture, or idiom. Therefore, knowledge of history and culture becomes crucial. Knowledge of the original language, its structure, and its idioms becomes very helpful. Because of the cultural and linguistic gap we become researchers, or at least, readers of competent researchers.

C. Our first and final task in interpretation is to understand as clearly as possible what the biblical authors were saying to their day, what the original hearers would have understood, and how these truths are applicable to our culture and our personal lives. Apart from these criteria there is no meaningful interpretation!

At this point let me spell out several context and content questions that one should ask every biblical text.

1. What did the original author say? (textual criticism)
2. What did the original author mean? (exegesis)
3. What did the original author say elsewhere on the same subject? (parallel passages)
4. What did the other biblical authors say on the same subject? (parallel passages)
5. How did the original hearers understand the message and respond to it? (original application)
6. How does the original message apply to my day? (modern application)
7. How does the original message apply to my life? (personal application)

VII. Some General Comments to the Reader

A. Sin affects everyone's interpretation (even after salvation), education, prayer, and systematization. I know it affects mine, but I do not always understand where and how. Therefore, each of us must filter our study through the indwelling Holy Spirit. Look at my examples, ponder my logic, allow me to stretch your concepts.

B. Please do not judge or react to this Textbook based solely on what you have always heard or believed. Allow me the opportunity to at least challenge your traditional understandings. I often tell my classes, "Just because I say something you have never heard does not automatically mean I am weird!"

C. The examples I use are controversial. They are meant to make you think and reexamine your personal theology and Bible study techniques. Please do not become so involved in the illustrations of these hermeneutical principles or exegetical procedures that you miss the methodology I am trying to present.

The examples are meant to

1. show alternate interpretations
2. show inappropriateness of interpretations
3. illustrate hermeneutical principles
4. get and keep your attention

D. Please remember that I am not trying to impart to you my personal theology, but to introduce an ancient Christian hermeneutical methodology and its application. I am not seeking your agreement, but am attempting to challenge you into implementing interpretive procedures which may not always answer all of our questions, but which will help in recognizing when one is trying to say too much or too little about a passage of Scripture.

E. This Textbook is not primarily designed for new Christians. It is for believers who are struggling with maturity and are seeking to express their faith in biblical categories. Maturity is a tension-filled process of self-examination and lifestyle faith. It is a pilgrimage that never ceases.

THE BIBLE

I. The Canon

Because this Textbook is basically an introduction to contextual and textual principles for interpreting the Bible, it seems obvious that we need to first look at the Bible itself. For the purpose of this study we are going to assume the Spirit's guidance in canonization (the greatest presupposition).

A. The Author's General Presuppositions
   1. God exists and He wants us to know Him.
   2. He has revealed Himself to us.
      a. He acted in history (revelation)
      b. He chose certain people to record and explain His acts (inspiration)
      c. His Spirit helps the reader (hearer) of this written revelation understand its main truths (illumination)
   3. The Bible is the only trustworthy source of truth about God (I know about Jesus' life and teachings only through the Bible). It is collectively our only source for faith and practice. OT and NT books written to specific occasions and times are now inspired guides for all occasions and ages. However, they do contain some cultural truths that do not transcend their own time and culture (i.e., polygamy, holy war, slavery, celibacy, place of women, wearing veils, holy kiss, etc.).

B. I realize that the canonization process is a historical process with some unfortunate incidents and events, but it is my presupposition that God led its development. The early church accepted the recognized books of the OT that were accepted within Judaism. From historical research it seems that the early churches, not the early councils alone, decided the New Testament canon. Apparently the following criteria were involved, either consciously or subconsciously.
   1. The Protestant Canon contains all the inspired books; the canon is closed! (i.e., "the faith," Acts 6:7; 13:8; 14:22; Gal. 1:23; 6:10; Jude vv. 3,20)
      a. accepted OT from Jews
      b. twenty-seven books in NT (a progressive historical process)
   2. New Testament authors are connected to Jesus or an Apostle (a progressive historical process)
      a. James and Jude to Jesus (His half brothers)
      b. Mark to Peter (turned his sermons at Rome into a Gospel)
      c. Luke to Paul (missionary partner)
      d. Hebrews traditionally to Paul
   3. Theological unity with Apostolic training (later called "rule of faith"). The Gospels were written after most of the other NT books.
      a. because of the rise of heresy (i.e., adoptionism, Gnosticism, Marcionism, and Montanism)
      b. because of the delayed Second Coming
      c. because of the death of the twelve Apostles

4. The permanently and morally changed lives of hearers where these books were read and accepted

5. The general consensus of the early churches and later church councils can be seen in the early lists of canonical books

   a. Origen (A.D. 185-254) asserts that there were four Gospels and the Epistles of the Apostles in circulation among the churches.

   b. the Muratorian Fragment dates between A.D. 180-200 from Rome (the only copy available today is a damaged, late Latin text). It lists the same 27 books as the Protestant NT (but adds Apocalypse of Peter and Shepherd of Hermas).

   c. Eusebius of Caesarea (A.D. 265-340) introduced a threefold designation (as did Origen) to describe Christian writings: (1) "received" and thereby accepted; (2) "disputed" and thereby meaning some churches, but not all, accepted them; and (3) "spurious" and thereby unaccepted in the vast majority of churches and not to be read. The ones in the disputed category which were finally accepted were: James, Jude, II Peter, and II and III John.

   d. the Cheltenham list (in Latin) from North Africa (A.D. 360) has the same 27 books (except for Hebrews, James, and Jude [Hebrews is not specifically mentioned, but may be included in Paul's letters]), as the Protestant NT, but in an unusual order.

   e. Athanasius' Easter Letter of A.D. 367 is the first to list exactly the same 27 books (no more, no less) as the Protestant NT.

   f. The concept and contents of an authoritative list of unique books was a historical and theological development.

6. Suggested reading

   a. *The Canon of the New Testament* by Bruce Metzger, published by Oxford Press

   b. Articles on canon in *Zondervan Pictorial Bible Encyclopedia*, Vol. 1, pp. 709-745

   c. *Introduction to the Bible* by William E. Nix and Norman Geisler, published by Moody Press, 1968 (esp. the chart on p. 22)

   d. *Holy Writings – Sacred Text: The Canon in Early Christianity* by John Barton, published by Westminster John Knox Press.

7. The Old and New Testaments are the only literary productions of the Ancient Near East that were "canonized" as especially coming from and revealing divine purposes. There are no other religious lists which differentiate between canonical (i.e., authoritative) vs. non-canonical religious writings.

How, why, and when did this historical process happen?

   a. Was it by the decisions of the church councils of the 3rd and 4th centuries A.D.?

   b. Was it by the use of Christian writers of the second century?

   c. Was it by the churches of the late first through fourth centuries?

II. Claims of Inspiration

In our day of conflicting claims and statements about the Bible, biblical authority, and interpretation, it becomes extremely important that we focus on what the Bible claims for itself. Theological and philosophical discussions and their claims are interesting, but not inspired. Human categories and formulations have always been guilty of overstatement. It is crucial that we allow the Bible to speak for itself.

Since Jesus is the focus of our faith and doctrine, if we could find Him speaking on this subject it would be very informative. He did this in Matt. 5:17-19 in an opening section of the so-called "Sermon on the Mount" (Matthew 5-7). He spells out clearly His view of the body of sacred literature which we call the Old Testament. Notice His emphasis on its eternality and significance for the life and faith of believers. Also notice His central place in its purpose and fulfillment. This passage not only supports a divinely inspired Old Testament, but a supreme focusing of that revelation in Himself (Christocentric typology). However, it is also readily noticeable that in vv. 21-26, 27-31, 33-37, and 38-40 that He completely reorients the traditional interpretation of the Old Testament among rabbinical Judaism of His day. The Scripture itself is inspired, eternal, and Christocentric, but our human interpretations are not. This is an extremely valuable foundational truth. The Bible, not our understanding of it, is what is eternal and inspired. Jesus intensified the traditional, rule-focused application of the Torah and raised it to the impossible level of attitude, motivation, and intent.

The classical statement of biblical inspiration comes from the Apostle to the Gentiles, Saul of Tarsus. In II Timothy 3:15-16 Paul specifically states the "God-givenness" (literally, God-breathed) of Scripture. At this point it is textually uncertain if he would have included all the New Testament writings that we know in this statement. However, by implication, they are surely included. Also, II Pet. 3:15-16 includes Paul's writings in the category of "Scripture."

Another supporting Scripture passage from Paul concerning inspiration is found in I Thess. 2:13. Here, as before, the focus is on God as the real source of the Apostle's words. This same truth is echoed by the Apostle Peter in II Pet. 1:20-21.

Not only are the Scriptures presented as divine in origin, but also in purpose. All Scripture is given to believers for their faith and life (Rom. 4:23-24; 15:4; I Cor. 10:6, 11; I Pet. 1:10-12).

III. The Bible's Purpose

A. Not a Rule Book

Much of our misunderstanding concerning Scripture begins in our mistaken notions concerning its purposes. One way to establish what a thing is is to state what it is not. The fallen human tendency toward legalism, so evident among the Pharisees, is alive and well and lives in your home church. This tendency turns the Bible into an extensive set of rules. Modern believers have almost turned the Scriptures into a legalistic rule book, a kind of "Christian Talmud." It must be stated forcibly that the Scriptures' primary focus is redemptive. It is meant to confront, convince, and turn wayward mankind back to God (McQuilkin 183, 49). The primary focus is salvation (II Tim. 3:15), which issues in Christlikeness (II Tim. 3:17). This Christlikeness is also a major goal (Romans 8:28-29; II Cor. 3:18; Gal. 4:19; Eph. 1:4; I Thess. 3:13; 4:3; I Pet. 1:15), but it is a result of the first goal. At least one possibility for the structure and nature of the Bible is its redemptive purpose and not a systematized rule book or doctrine book (i.e., not a Christian Talmud).

The Bible does not address all of our intellectual questions. Many issues are addressed in ambiguous or incomplete ways. The Bible was not designed primarily as a systematic theology book, but as a selective history of God's dealing with His rebellious creation. Its purpose is not merely rules, but relationship. It leaves areas uncovered so that we are forced to walk in love (I Corinthians 13), not rules (Col. 2:16-23). We must see the priority of people made in His image (cf. Gen. 1:26-27), not rules. It is not a set of rules, but a new character, a new focus, a new life that is presented.

This is not to imply that the Bible does not contain rules, because it does, but they do not cover every area. Often rules become barriers instead of bridges in mankind's search for God. The Bible provides us with enough information to live a God-pleasing life; it also provides us some guidelines or boundaries. Its primary gift, however, is the "Guide," not the guidelines. Knowing and following the Guide until you become like Him is the second goal of Scripture.

B. Not a Science Book

Another example of modern mankind's attempt to ask questions of Scripture which it is not designed to answer is in the area of modern scientific inquiry. Many want to force the Scriptures onto the philosophical grid of natural law, particularly in relation to the "scientific method" of inductive reasoning. The Bible is not a divine textbook on natural law. It is not anti-scientific; it is pre-scientific! Its primary purpose is not in this area. Although the Bible is not speaking directly to these questions it does speak about physical reality, however, it does so in the language of description (i.e., phenomenological language), not science. It describes reality in terms of its own day. It presents a "world view" more than a "world picture." This means that it focuses more on "the who" than on "the how." Things are described as how they appear (i.e., the five senses) to the common person. Some examples are

1. Do the dead really live in the ground? The Hebrew culture, like our own, buries their dead. Therefore, in the language of description, they were in the earth (Sheol or Hades).
2. Does the land really float on water? This is often connected to the three-storied universe model. The ancients knew that water was present underground (i.e., oasis). Their conclusion was expressed in poetic language.
3. Even we, in our day, speak in these categories.
   a. "the sun rises"
   b. "dew falls"

Some books which have really helped me in this area are
1) *Religion and the Rise of Modern Science* — R. Hooykaas
2) *The Scientific Enterprise and the Christian Faith* — Malcolm A. Jeeves
3) *The Christian View of Science and Scripture* — Bernard Ramm
4) *Science and Hermeneutics* — Vern S. Poythress
5) *Darwinism on Trial* — Phillip Johnson
6) Several good books — Hugh Ross, Pensacola Bible Church, Pensacola, FL
7) *Science and Faith: An Evangelical Dialogue* — Henry Poe and Jimmy Davis
8) *The Battle of Beginnings* — Del Ratzsch
9) *Coming to Peace with Science* — Daniel Falk
10) *Mere Christianity: Science and Intelligent Design* — William Demoski

C. Not a Magic Book

Not only is the Bible not a rule book or a science book, but it is not a magic book either. Our love for the Bible has caused us to handle it in some very strange ways. Have you ever sought God's will by praying and then letting your Bible fall open to a page and then put your finger on a verse? This common practice treats the Bible as if it were a crystal ball or divine "Ouija board." The Bible is a message, not a modern Urim and Thummim (Exod. 28:30). Its value is in its message, not in its physical presence. As Christians, we take our Bible into the hospital with us, not so we can read it, because we are too sick. We do so because it represents God's presence to us.

For many modern Christians the Bible has become a physical idol. Its physical presence is not its power, but its message about God in Christ. Placing your Bible on your surgical incision will not help it heal faster. We do not only need the Bible beside our bed; we need its message in our hearts.

I have even heard people get upset if someone drops a Bible or if someone writes in it. The Bible is nothing more than cow skin (if you have an expensive one), tree pulp, and ink. It is only holy in its connection to God. The Bible is useless unless it is read and followed. Our culture is reverent toward the Bible and rebellious toward God. Earlier in our court system one had to swear to tell the truth while holding his hand on the Bible. If one is a believer he would not lie anyway. If one is swearing on an ancient book in which he did not believe and whose content he did not know, what makes us think that he would not lie?

The Bible is not a magical charm. It is not a detailed, complete, unabridged textbook on natural phenomena and it is not "Hoyle's" rule book on the game of life with detailed instructions in every area. It is a message from the God who acts within human history. It points toward His Son and it points its finger at our rebellion.

IV. Author's Presuppositions About the Bible

Even though the Bible has been abused by mankind's expectations and usages, it is still our only guide for faith and practice. I would like to state my presuppositions about the Bible.

I believe the Bible, both Old and New Testaments, is the only clear self-revelation of God. The New Testament is the perfect fulfillment and interpreter of the Old Testament (we must view the OT through the new revelations of Jesus and the NT, which radically universalize the promises to Israel).

I believe the one and only Eternal, Creator, Redeemer God initiated the writing of our canonical Scriptures by inspiring certain chosen persons to record and explain His acts in the lives of individuals and nations.

The Bible is our only clear source of information about God and His purposes (I know about Jesus only from the pages of the NT). Natural revelation (cf. Job 38-39; Ps. 19:1-6; Rom. 1:19-20; 2:14-15) is valid, but not complete. Jesus Christ is the capstone of God's revelation about Himself (cf. John 1:18; Col. 1:14-16; Heb. 1:2-3).

The Bible must be illuminated by the Holy Spirit (cf. John 14:23; 16:20-21; I Cor. 2:6-16) in order to be correctly understood (in its spiritual dimension). Its message is authoritative, adequate, eternal, infallible, and trustworthy for all believers. The exact mode of its inspiration has not been revealed to us, but it is obvious to believers that the Bible is a supernatural book, written by natural people under special leadership.

V. Evidence for a Supernaturally Inspired and Authoritative Bible

Although the above statement is presuppositional, as is all human knowledge, it does not mean that there is no credible supportive evidence. At this point let us examine some of this evidence.

A. The Bible contains very precise predictions (historical, not typological [Hosea 11:1] or apocalyptic [Zechariah 9]) about future events, not in vague formulations, but in specific and often shocking preciseness. Two good examples follow.

   1. The area of Jesus' ministry was predicted to be in Galilee, Isa. 9:1. This was very unexpected by Judean Jewry because Galilee was not considered to be quite Kosher because of its physical distance from the Temple. Yet, the majority of Jesus' ministry was spent in this geographical area.

   2. The place of Jesus' birth is specifically recorded in Micah 5:2. Bethlehem was a very small village whose only claim to fame was that the family of Jesse lived there. Yet, 750 years before the birth of Jesus the Bible specifically pinpoints this as the birthplace of the Messiah. Even the rabbinical scholars of Herod's court knew this (Matt. 2:4-6). Some may doubt the 8th century B.C. date for both Isaiah and Micah, however, because of the Septuagint (which is the Greek translation of the Hebrew Scripture, which was begun about 250-200 B.C.), even at the very minimum these prophecies were made over 200 years before their fulfillment.

B. Another evidence relates to the modern scientific discipline of archaeology. The last few decades have seen a tremendous amount of archaeological discovery. To my knowledge there have not been any finds that have repudiated the Bible's historical accuracies (Nelson Glueck, *Rivers in the Desert*, p. 31, "No archaeological discovery has ever been made that contradicts or controverts historical statements of Scripture"), quite the contrary. Archaeology has facilitated confidence in the historicity of the Bible over and over again.

   1. One example is the use of Mesopotamian names in the Nuzi and Mari Tablets of the second millennium B.C., which also occur in Genesis. Now these are not the same people, but the same names. Names are characteristic of a particular time and place. The names "Terah" and "Nahor" are common to the biblical record and in these ancient tablets.

   2. The existence of a Hittite civilization in Asia Minor is another example. For many years (19th century) secular history had no references to the stable, highly developed culture known by this name (Archer 1982, 96-98, 210). However, Genesis 10 and the historical books of the Bible mention them many times (II Kings 7:6,7; II Chr. 1:17). Archaeology has since confirmed, not only their existence, but their longevity and power (i.e., 1950 archeologists found royal library of 2,000 cuneiform tablets where the nation was called both Anatolia and Hittite).

   3. The existence of Belshazzar, the last Babylonian king (Daniel 5), has often been denied. There are ten lists of Babylonian kings in secular history taken from Babylonian documents, but none contain Belshazzar's name. With further archaeological finds it became obvious that Belshazzar was co-regent and the official in charge during that period of time.

His father, Nabonidus, whose mother was the high priestess of the moon goddess, *Zin*, had become so involved in the worship of *Zin* (Nana) that he had moved to Tema (Arabia), her holy city, while on a ten-year military campaign against Egypt. He left his son, Belshazzar, to reign in the city of Babylon in his absence.

C. A further evidence for a supernatural Bible is the consistency of its message. This is not to say that the Bible does not contain some paradoxical material, but it also does not contradict itself. This is amazing when one considers that it was written over a 1600/1400 year period (depending on the date of the Exodus, i.e., 1495, 1290 B.C.) by authors of radically different educational and cultural backgrounds from Mesopotamia to Egypt. It is composed of various literary genres and is written in three separate languages (Hebrew, Aramaic, and Koine Greek). Yet, even with all of this variety, a unified message (i.e., plot line) is presented.

D. Finally, one of the most marvelous evidences for the Bible's unique inspiration is the permanently morally changed lives of men and women from different cultures, different educational levels, and different socio-economic levels through history. Wherever the Bible has simply been read, radical, permanent lifestyle changes have occurred. The Bible is its own best apologist.

VI. Problems Related to Our Interpretation of the Bible

The above does not mean to imply that it is easy to understand or that there are not some problems connected with the Bible. Because of the nature of human language, hand copied manuscripts combined with the problem of translation, our modern Bibles must be interpreted in an analytical fashion.

The first problem to confront the modern Bible reader is the manuscript variations which exist. This is not only true of the Hebrew Old Testament, but also the Greek New Testament. This subject will be discussed in a more practical manner in a later chapter, but for now let us look at the problem.

It is often called **Textual Criticism**. It basically tries to decide the original wording of the Bible. Some good books concerning this problem are:

A. *Biblical Criticism: Historical, Literary and Textual* — B. K. Walke, D. Guthrie, Gordon Fee, and R. H. Harrison
B. *The Text of the New Testament: Its Transmission, Corruption and Restoration* — Bruce M. Metzger
C. *Introduction to New Testament Textual Criticism and Scribes, Scrolls, and Scriptures* — J. H. Greenlee
D. *The Books and the Parchments* — F. F. Bruce
E. *The Early Versions of the New Testament* — Bruce Metzger
F. *The New Testament Documents: Are They Reliable?* — F. F. Bruce
G. *The King James Version Debate: A Plea for Realism* — D. A. Carson
H. *Ancient Orient and Old Testament* — K. A. Kitchen
I. *The Orthodox Corruption of Scripture* — Bart D. Ehrman
J. *Rethinking New Testament Textual Criticism* — ed.David Alan Beach

VII. The Major Textual Sources of Our Modern Bible

The modern text of the Old Testament in Hebrew is called the Masoretic Text (the consonantal text set by Rabbi Aquiba in A.D. 100). It was probably the text used by the Pharisees of Jesus' day, who were the only religious group that survived the destruction of Jerusalem by Titus in A.D. 70. Its name comes from a group of Jewish scholars who put vowel points, punctuation marks, and some textual comments into the ancient, unpointed (no vowels) Hebrew text (finished in the 9th century A.D.). Following is a brief outline of OT and NT sources.

A. Old Testament

1. **Masoretic Text** (MT) – The Hebrew consonantal textual form was set by Rabbi Aquiba in A.D. 100. The addition of vowel points, accents, marginal notes, punctuation, and apparatus notes was finished in the 9th century A.D. by Masoretic scholars. This textual form is quoted in the Mishnah, Talmud, Targums (Aramaic translation), Peshitta (Syriac translation), and Vulgate (Latin translation).

2. **Septuagint** (LXX) – Tradition says it was produced by 70 Jewish scholars in 70 days for the library of Alexandria, Egypt. It was supposedly requested by a Jewish leader of King Ptolemy II living in Alexandria (285-246 B.C.). The Ptolemy rulers of Egypt boasted of the largest library in the world. This tradition comes from "Letter of Aristeas." The LXX provides a differing Hebrew textual tradition from the text of Rabbi Aquiba (MT). Both traditions are represented in the Dead Sea Scrolls.

   The problem comes when these two texts do not agree. And, in books like Jeremiah and Hosea, they are radically different. Since the finding of the Dead Sea Scrolls in 1947, it has become obvious that both the Masoretic Text and the Septuagint have ancient manuscript attestation. Usually the Masoretic Text is accepted as the basic text for the Old Testament and the Septuagint is allowed to supplement it in difficult passages or corrupted readings.

   a. The LXX has helped in the understanding of the MT (one example):
      (1) the LXX of Isa. 52:14, "as many shall be amazed at him"
      (2) the MT of Isa. 52:14, "just as many were astonished over you"
   b. The DSS have helped in the understanding of the MT (one example):
      (1) the DSS (IQ Isaiah) of Isa. 21:8 – "then the seer cried, upon a watchtower I stand. . ."
      (2) the MT of Isa. 21:8 – "and I cried a lion! My Lord, I always stand on the watchtower by day. . ."
   c. Both the LXX and DSS have helped our understanding of Isa. 53:11
      (1) LXX and DSS – "after the travail of his soul he will see light, he will be satisfied"
      (2) MT – "he shall see of the travail of his soul. He shall be satisfied" (The MT doubled the VERB, but left out the first OBJECT).

We do not have the autographs or original manuscripts of any of the original biblical authors, only copies of copies of copies.

3. **Dead Sea Scrolls** (DSS) – Written in the Roman B.C. period, close to New Testament times by a sect of Jewish separatists (they left temple worship because the current high priest was not of the line of Aaron), called "Essenes." The Hebrew manuscripts (MSS) were found in 1947 in several cave sites around the Dead Sea. They contain the Hebrew textual family behind both the MT and the LXX.

   Another problem in this area is the discrepancy between the Masoretic Text and the Old Testament quotes in the New Testament. One good example would be a comparison of Num. 25:9 and I Cor. 10:8. The OT reference states that 24,000 died, while Paul states that 23,000 died. Here we are faced with the problem of an ancient text which was copied by hand. This could be a scribal error in transmission or it could be a quotation from memory by Paul or a rabbinical tradition. I know it is painful to us (because of our presuppositions about inspiration) to find discrepancies such as this, but the truth of the matter is that our modern translations of the Bible have some minor problems of this type.

   A similar problem is found in Matt. 27:9, where an OT quote is referred to Jeremiah, when it seems to come from Zechariah.

   To show you how much disagreement this has caused let me give you some of the supposed reasons for this discrepancy.

   1. The 5th century Syriac version called the Peshitta simply removes the name "Jeremiah."
   2. Augustine, Luther, and Keil assert an error in Matthew's text.
   3. Origen and Eusebius assert an error by a copyist.
   4. Jerome and Ewald assert that it is a quote from an apocryphal work attributed to Jeremiah which was lost and that it was not a quote from Zechariah at all.
   5. Mede asserts that Jeremiah wrote Zechariah 9-11.
   6. Lightfoot asserts that Jeremiah was listed as the first of the prophets; in this designation all other prophets were implied.
   7. Hengstenberg asserts that Zechariah quoted Jeremiah.
   8. Calvin asserts that an error has crept into the text in an unknown way.

With so many theories from learned, godly men it is obvious that we simply do not know. To deny the problem (#1) is not an answer either. To hide behind cliches or presuppositions also does not solve the problem. Our modern translations of the Bible have some problems which we must try to sort out. For the layperson this can often be done by comparing modern translations. A simple practical suggestion would be, if in the margin of your modern study Bible it says, "not in the oldest and best Greek manuscripts," just do not build a doctrine on this text. Find the parallel passages where the doctrine is clearly taught.

B. New Testament

Over 5,300 manuscripts (whole or fragmentary) of the Greek New Testament are in existence today. About 85 of these are written on papyri. There are 268 (uncial) manuscripts written in all capital letters. Later, about the ninth century A.D., a running script (minuscule) was developed. The Greek manuscripts written in this form number about 2,700. We also have about 2,100 copies of lists of Scripture texts used in worship that are called lectionaries. The following is a brief outline of NT sources.

1. **The Papyri** – About 85 Greek manuscripts containing parts of the New Testament are extant, written on papyrus, dating from the second century A.D., but most are from the third and fourth centuries A.D. None of these manuscripts contain the whole New Testament. Some are done by professional scribes, but many of them are hastily copied by less exacting copyists. Just being old does not, in and of itself, make it more accurate.
2. **Codex Sinaiticus** – is known by the Hebrew "A" (*aleph*), ℵ, or (01). It was found at St. Catherine's monastery on Mt. Sinai by Tischendorf. It dates from the fourth century A.D. It contains both the Old and New Testaments. It is of "the Alexandrian Text" type, as is Codex B.
3. **Codex Alexandrinus** – is known as "A" (*alpha*) or (02). It is a fifth century A.D. manuscript which was found at Alexandria, Egypt. Only the Gospels are of "the Alexandrian text" type.
4. **Codex Vaticanus** – is known as "B" or (03), was found in the Vatican's library in Rome and dates from the middle of the fourth century A.D. It contains both the Old and New Testaments. It is of "The Alexandrian Text" type, as is Codex ℵ. Its roots go back into the second century from P^{75}.
5. **Codex Ephraemi** – is known as "C" or (04), is a fifth century A.D. manuscript which was partially destroyed. Its roots go back to the third century P^{45}. Codex W, from the fifth century is also of this textual family.
6. **Codex Bezae** – is known as "D" or (05), is a fifth or sixth century A.D. manuscript. Its roots, according to Eldon Jay Epp, go back into the second century, based on the Old Latin and Old Syriac translations, as well as many papyri fragments. However, Kurt and Barbara Eland do not list any papyri connected to this textual family and they put it to the fourth century and no earlier, but they do list a few precursor papyri (i.e., P^{38}, P^{48}, P^{69}). It is the chief representative of what is called "The Western Text." It contains many additions and was the main Greek witness behind the third edition of Erasmus' Greek New Testament, which was the Greek witness for the King James translation.

The NT manuscripts can be grouped into three, possibly four, families of manuscripts that share certain characteristics.

1. **Alexandrian** "local" text, which includes
    a. P^{75}, P^{66} (about A.D. 200) the Gospels
    b. P^{46} (about A.D. 225) Paul's letters
    c. P^{72} (about A.D. 225-250) Peter and Jude
    d. Codex B, called Vaticanus (about A.D. 325), which includes the entire OT and NT
    e. quoted by Origen
    f. other manuscripts which show this text type are ℵ, L, W, 33
2. **Western text** from North Africa which includes
    a. quotes from North Africa: Tertullian, Cyprian, and the Old Latin
    b. quotes from Irenaeus
    c. quotes from Tatian and Old Syriac
    d. Codex D "Bezae"

3. **Byzantine text**
   a. reflected in over 80% of the 5,300 manuscripts (mostly minuscules)
   b. quoted by leaders from Antioch of Syria: Cappadoceans, Chrysostom, and Therdoret
   c. Codex A in the Gospels only
   d. Codex E (eighth century) for the full NT
4. the fourth possible type is **"Caesarean"**
   a. primarily seen in Mark
   b. some witnesses to it are P^{45}, W, H

C. Brief explanation of the problems and theories of "lower criticism," also called "textual criticism."
   1. How did the variants occur?
      a. inadvertent or accidental (vast majority of occurrences)
         (1) slip of the eye
             (a) in hand copying, which reads the second instance of two similar words and, thereby, omits all of the words in between (homoioteleuton)
             (b) in omitting a double letter word or phrase (haplography)
             (c) in hand copying, a mental error in repeating a phrase or line of a Greek text (dittography)
         (2) slip of the ear in hand copying by oral dictation, where a misspelling occurs (itacism) in similar sounding words. Often the misspelling implies or spells another Greek word
         (3) the earliest Greek texts had no chapter or verse divisions, little or no punctuation, and no division between words. It is possible to divide letters into different words

      b. intentional
         (1) changes were made to improve the grammatical form of the text copied
         (2) changes were made to bring the text into conformity with other biblical texts (harmonization of parallels)
         (3) changes were made by combining two or more variant readings into one long combined text (conflation)
         (4) changes were made to correct a perceived problem in the text (cf. Bart Ehrman, *The Orthodox Corruption of Scripture*, pp. 146-50, concerning Heb. 2:9)
         (5) changes were made to make the text more doctrinally orthodox (cf. I John 5:7-8)
         (6) some additional information as to the historical setting or proper interpretation of the text was placed in the margin by one scribe, but placed into the text by a second scribe (cf. John 5:4)

D. The basic tenets of textual criticism (transcriptional probabilities)

1. the most awkward or grammatically unusual text is probably the original because the scribes tended to make the text smoother
2. the shortest text is probably the original because scribes tended to add additional information or phrases from parallel passages (this has recently been challenged by papyrus comparative studies)
3. the older text is given more weight because of its historical proximity to the original, everything else being equal
4. manuscripts that are geographically diverse usually have the original readings
5. attempts to explain how variants could have occurred. This is considered the most important tenet by most scholars.
6. analysis of a given biblical author's literary style, vocabulary, and theology is used to decide probable original wording.
7. doctrinally weaker texts, especially those relating to major theological discussions during the period of manuscript changes, like the Trinity in I John 5:7-8, are to be preferred. At this point I would like to quote from J. Harold Greenlee's book, Introduction to New Testament Textual Criticism.

    "No Christian doctrine hangs upon a debatable text; and the student of the New Testament must beware of wanting his text to be more orthodox or doctrinally stronger than is the inspired original" (p. 68).

8. W. A. Criswell told Greg Garrison of THE BIRMINGHAM NEWS that he (Criswell) doesn't believer every word in the Bible is inspired, "at least not every word that has been given to the modern public by centuries of translators." Criswell further said,

    "I very much am a believer in textual criticism. As such, I think the last half of the 16th chapter of Mark is heresy: it's not inspired, it's just concocted. . .when you compare those manuscripts way back yonder, there was no such thing as that conclusion of the Book of Mark. Somebody added it. . ."

    The patriarch of the SBC inerrantists also claimed that "interpolation" is also evident in John 5:4, the account of Jesus at the pool of Bethesda. And he discusses the two different accounts of the suicide of Judas (cf. Matt. 27 and Acts 1),

    "It's just a different view of the suicide," Criswell said.

    "If it is in the Bible, there is an explanation for it. And the two accounts of the suicide of Judas are in the Bible." Criswell added, "Textual criticism is a wonderful science in itself. It is not ephemeral, it's not impertinent. It's dynamic and central..."

An additional problem with our modern English copies of the Bible is that from the time of the original authors until the invention of the printing press, the Bible was copied by hand. Often these copyists added their own thoughts or "corrected" the manuscript they were copying. This has caused several non-original additions to the New Testament.

E. Some examples of the problem of hand-copied manuscripts in the Greek New Testament.

1. Mark 16:9ff – In the Greek manuscripts of Mark there are four different endings. The longest ending of twelve verses found in King James is missing in manuscripts ℵ and B. The Greek texts used by Clement of Alexandria, Origen, Eusebius, and Jerome also lack this long ending. The long ending is present in manuscripts A, C, D, K, U, and ℵ c. The earliest witness to this long ending in the Fathers is Irenaeus (ministered from A.D. 177-190) and the Diatessaron (A.D. 180).   The passage is obviously non-Markian (i.e., uninspired).

   These verses contain terms and theology not found elsewhere in Mark. They even contain heresy (i.e., drinking of poison and handling snakes).

2. John 5:4 – This verse is not in P66, P75, nor the uncial manuscripts ℵ, B, C, or D. However, it is found in A. It was obviously added by a scribe to explain the historical setting. This is likey Jewish folklore answering the question why there were so many sick people around this pool. God does not heal by angels stirring water with the first to enter being rewarded with physical healing.

3. John 7:53-8:11 – This passage does not appear in any of the ancient Greek manuscripts or early church Fathers until the sixth century A.D. in manuscript "D" called Bezae. No Greek church Father, until the twelveth century A.D., comments on this passage. The account is found in several other places in the Greek manuscripts of John, after 7:36, after 7:44, and after 21:25. It also appears in Luke's Gospel after Luke 21:38. It is obviously non-Johannine (i.e., uninspired). It is probably an oral tradition from the life of Jesus. It sounds so much like Him, but it is not from the pen of an inspired Apostle, therefore, I reject it as Scripture.

4. Matthew 6:13 – This verse is not found in manuscripts ℵ, B, or D. It is present in manuscripts K, L, and W, but with variations. It is also absent from the early church Father's comments on the Lord's Prayer (i.e., Tertullian [A.D. 150-230], Origen [A.D.182-251], and Cyprian [A.D. ministered 248-258]). It is found in the King James translation because it was included in Erasmus' third edition Greek text.

5. Luke 22:43-44 – These verses are found in the ancient Greek uncial manuscripts ℵ*, ℵ2, D, K, L, X, and Delta. They are also found in the quotations of Justin Martyr, Irenaeus, Hippolytus, Eusebius, and Jerome. However, they are omitted in MSS P69[probably],75, ℵc, A, N, T, and W, as well as the manuscripts used by Clement of Alexandria and Origen. The UBS4 ranks their omission as "certain" (A).

   Bart D. Ehrman, The Orthodox Corruption of Scripture, pp. 187-194, assumes these verses are an early second century addition to refute docetic (agnostic) Christologists who denied Christ's humanity and suffering. The church's conflict with Christological heresies was the source of many of the early manuscript changes.

   The NASB and NRSV bracket these verses, while NKJV, TEV, and NIV have a footnote which says, "some ancient manuscripts omit verses 43 and 44."   This information is unique to Luke's Gospel.

6. I John 5:7-8 – These verses are not found in manuscripts ℵ, A, or B nor any other Greek manuscript except four dating from the twelveth century A.D. This text is not quoted by any of the Greek Fathers, even in their defense of the concept of the deity of Christ or the Trinity. They are absent from all ancient translations including Jerome's Vulgate.

They were apparently added later by well-meaning copyists in order to bolster the doctrine of the Trinity. They are found in the King James translation because of their inclusion in Erasmus' third edition (and only this edition) of the Greek New Testament.

Our modern translations of the Bible do have some textual problems. However, these do not affect a major doctrine. We can trust these modern translations of the Bible for all that is necessary for faith and practice. One of the translators of the RSV, F. C. Grant, said, "No doctrine of the Christian faith has been affected by the revision, for the simple reason that, out of thousands of variant readings in the manuscripts, none has turned up thus far that requires a revision of Christian doctrine."

> "It is noteworthy that for most scholars over 90% of all the variants of the NT text are resolved, because in most instances the variant that best explains the origins of the others is also supported by the earliest and best witnesses" (Gordon Fee, *The Expositor's Bible Commentary*, Vol. 1, p. 430).

I have cited these examples to show you that we must analyze our English translations (Fee and Stuart 1982, 30-34). They do have textual problems. I do not feel comfortable with these textual variants, but they are a reality. It is reassuring to realize that they are rare and do not affect any major Christian doctrine. Also, in comparison to other ancient literature, the Bible has remarkably few variations.

F. The problem of translating from one language to another.

Besides the problem of manuscript variations there is the added problem of translating one language into anther. In reality all translations are concise commentaries. Possibly an understanding of translation theory will
      (1) encourage us to use more than one translation in our study and
      (2) help us know which different translations to compare.

There are three basic methods available to translators.
1.   A literal approach tries to use a word-for-word correspondence.
2.   An idiom-for-idiom approach tries to use clauses or phrases, not words, as the basis to communicate the ancient text.
3.   A thought-for-thought approach tries to use concepts instead of actual terms and phrases of the originals.

We can see this more clearly on the following graph.

KJV	NIV	Amplified Bible
ASV	NAB	Phillips Translation
NASB	TEV	LB
RSV	JB	
	NEB	
	Williams Translation	

Literal	Idiom-for-idiom	Idea-for-idea
Word-for-word	Clause-for clause	Free Rendering
Formal Correspondence	Dynamic Equivalent	Paraphrase

A good discussion of translation theory is found in Gordon Fee and Douglas Stuart's *How To Read the Bible for All Its Worth*, pp. 34-41. Also, tremendous help in this area is found in the United Bible Societies' publications by Eugene A. Nida on translation theory and practice.

G. The problem of human languages in describing God.

Not only do we face an uncertain text at some places, but also, if we are not fluent in ancient Hebrew and Koine Greek, we face a variety of English translations. Complicating the problem even more is our own human finitude and sinfulness. Human language itself limits and determines the categories and scope of divine revelation. God has spoken to us in analogies. Human language is adequate to speak about God, but it is not exhaustive or ultimate. We can know God, but with some limits.

One good example of this limitation is anthropomorphism, that is, speaking about God in human, physical, or psychological terms. We have nothing else to use. We assert that God is a person and all we know about personhood is in human categories. Some examples of this difficulty follow.

1. Anthropomorphism (God described in human terms)
   a. God with human body
      (1) walking - Gen. 3:8; 18:33; Lev. 26:12; Deut. 23:14
      (2) eyes - Gen. 6:8; Exod. 33:17
      (3) man on a throne - Isa. 6:1; Dan.7:9
   b. God as female
      (1) Gen. 1:2 (Spirit as female bird)
      (2) Deut. 32:18 (God as mother)
      (3) Exod. 19:4 (God as mother eagle)
      (4) Isa. 49:14-15; 66:9-13 (God as nursing mother and also possibly Hos. 11:4)
   c. God as advocating lying (cf. I Kgs 22:19-23)
   d. NT examples of "God's right hand" (cf. Luke 22:69; Acts 7:55-56; Rom. 8:34; Eph. 1:20; Col. 3:1; Heb. 13:1; 8:1; 10:12; 12:2; I Pet. 3:22)
2. Human titles used to describe God
   a. Shepherd (cf. Psalm 23)
   b. Father (cf. Isaiah 63:16; Psalm 103:13)
   c. Go'el – kinsman redeemer (cf. Exod. 6:6)
   d. Lover – husband (cf. Hosea 1-3)
   e. Parent, father, and mother (cf. Hos. 11:3-4)
3. Physical objects used to describe God
   a. Rock (cf. Psalm 18)
   b. Fortress and stronghold (cf. Psalm 18)
   c. Shield (cf. Gen. 15:1; Psalm 18)
   d. Horn of salvation (cf. Psalm 18)
   e. Tree (cf. Hos. 14:8)
4. Language is part of the image of God in mankind, but sin has affected all aspects of our existence, including language.
5. God is faithful and communicates to us adequately, if not exhaustively, knowledge about Himself. This is usually in the form of negation, analogy, or metaphor.

The biggest problem we face in interpreting the Bible, along with the others mentioned, is our sinfulness. We twist everything, including the Bible, to fit and meet our wants. We never have an objective, unaffected view of God, our world, or ourselves. Yet, even with all of these handicaps, God is faithful. We can know God and His Word because He wants us to do so (Silva 1987, 118). He has provided all that we need by the illumination of the Holy Spirit (Calvin). Yes, there are problems, but there are also abounding provisions. The problems should limit our dogmatism and increase our thanksgiving through prayerful, diligent Bible study. The road is not easy, but He walks with us. The goal is Christlikeness, not only a correct interpretation. Interpretation is a means to the goal of knowing, serving, and praising Him who called us out of darkness through His Son (Col. 1:13).

BIBLICAL AUTHORITY

I. Author's Presuppositional Definition

Many Christians would agree that the Bible is the only source for faith and practice. If this is so, why are there so many different interpretations? So many are speaking seemingly conflicting interpretations in God's name. How do we know who is to be believed? These questions reflect the confusion of the modern Christian community and are a critical issue. How can average believers evaluate what they hear or read—all of which claims to be God's truth? For me, the answer has come in my presuppositional definition of what "biblical authority" involves. I realize that I am reacting to my own existential circumstances, yet I have no other option. It may bother you that I speak of "presuppositions." Yet, most, if not all, of the significant questions of life are dealt with in this manner because of the very nature of our human situation. Total objectivity is impossible. One hopes we have not uncritically assimilated our cultural "givens." In an attempt to limit, not only my own "givens," but also those of others, I have tried to put some boundaries on the interpretation of the Bible. I realize that this may mean that I will not be able to receive some truth, but I feel it will protect me from cultural, denominational, and experiential misinterpretations. In truth, the contextual/textual method will force us to say less about the Bible, but should help us become more committed to the major pillars of the Christian faith.

For me, "biblical authority" is normally defined as the belief in the God-givenness of the Bible, and thereby, its authority. For me it is also understanding what the biblical author was saying to his day and then applying that truth to my day. This means that I must try to put myself into his day, his reasoning, and his purpose(s). I must try to hear as the original hearers heard. I must struggle with the "then" of the biblical author, book, event, parable, etc. I must be able to show others, from the text of the Bible itself, the how, why, and where of my interpretation. I am not free to let it, or make it, say what I want it to say (Liefeld 1984, 6). It must be free to speak; I must be ready to hear and pass this truth on to the people of my day. Only if I have understood the original author and only if I have transferred the eternal truth to my day and to my life have I participated in true "biblical authority." There will surely be some disagreements on the "then" and the "now" aspects of interpretation, but we must limit our interpretations to the Bible and verify our understanding from its pages.

II. Need for Verifiable Interpretations

One of the plagues of the Protestant Reformation is the multiplicity of interpretations (resulting in modern denominationalism), which resulted from its "back to the Bible" movement. I have no real hope of unanimity on this side of heaven, but we must return to the Scriptures, consistently and verifiably interpreted. We all must walk in our own light, but hopefully we will be able to defend our doctrine (faith) and practice (life) from the Scriptures. The Scriptures must be allowed to speak; speak in light of their literary, grammatical, and historical context. We must defend our interpretations in the light of
   A. **the normal usage of human language**
   B. **the original author's intent in the passage**
   C. **the balance of all Scripture**
   D. **Christlikeness**

The contemporary curse of proof-texting and spiritualizing has devastated the church. The cults have learned our techniques and how to use them with great effectiveness (Sire, 1980, *Scripture Twisting*; Carson 1984, *Exegetical Fallacies*; Silva 1983, *Biblical Words and Their Meanings*).

The hope of this Textbook is not only to give a methodology for interpretation, but also to give you the ability to evaluate other interpretations. We must defend our own interpretations and be able to analyze other's interpretations. Here is how we do this.

A. The writers of Scripture used normal human language and expected to be understood.
B. Modern interpreters seek the original author's intent by documenting several types of information.
   1. historical and cultural setting of their day
   2. literary context (whole book, literary unit, paragraph)
   3. genre (historical narrative, prophecy, law, poetry, parable, apocalyptic)
   4. textual design (e.g., John 3 - Mr. Religious and John 4 - Ms. Irreligious)
   5. syntax (grammatical relationships and forms)
   6. original word meanings
      a. Old Testament
         (1) cognate languages (Semitic languages)
         (2) Dead Sea Scrolls (DSS)
         (3) Samaritan Pentateuch
         (4) rabbinical writings
      b. New Testament
         (1) the Septuagint (the NT writers were Hebrew thinkers writing in street Greek)
         (2) papyri finds from Egypt
         (3) Greek literature
C. The balance of all of Scripture (parallel passages) because it has one divine author (the Spirit).
D. Christlikeness (Jesus is the goal and fulfillment of Scripture. He is both the perfect revelation of Deity and the perfect example of true humanity).

It is a basic presupposition that every text has one and only one proper interpretation and that is the original author's intent. This authorial meaning had an original application. This application (significance) can be multiplied to different situations, but each one must be inseparably linked to the original intent (cf. *The Aims of Interpretation* by E.D. Hirsch).

III. Examples of Interpretative Abuse

To illustrate my point concerning the pervasiveness of improper hermeneutics (even among evangelicals), consider the following selected examples.

A. Deuteronomy 23:18 is used to prove that believers should not "sell" their dogs. Dogs in Deuteronomy are male prostitutes of the Canaanite fertility cult.
B. II Samuel 9 is used as a metaphor of grace covering our sins as Mephibosheth's crippled feet are allegorized as "our sin" and David's table is allegorized as God's grace covering them from sight (ancient people did not sit with their feet under a table).
C. John 11:44 is used to speak of "things that bind" to refer to inappropriate habits, motives, and actions.

D. I Corinthians 13:8 is used to prove that tongues will cease first and of themselves, when in context, anything but love will cease.
E. Colossians 2:21 is used to prove total abstinence, when it is a quote from the false teachers!
F. Revelation 3:20 is used as an evangelistic passage, when it is addressed to one of the seven churches.

The plague of proof-texting and spiritualizing abounds.

A. "The practice of isolating sentences, thoughts, and ideas from their immediate context is nearly always fatal when applied to Paul. 'Solitary proof-texts,' says Professor H. A. A. Kennedy, 'have wrought more havoc in theology than all the heresies,'" *A Man in Christ* by James Steward, p. 15.

B. "The proof-text method of interpreting Paul's letters, which views them as direct revelations of the supernatural will of God conveying to men eternal, timeless truths that need only to be systematized to produce a complete theology, obviously ignores the means by which God has been pleased to give to men his Word," G. E. Ladd, *Theology of the NT*, p. 379.

So, what can be done? We must all reexamine our working definition of biblical authority.

If our interpretation would have surprised the original author or hearers, it probably surprises God. If we speak in His name, we surely should have paid the price of personal confession, prayer, and diligent study. We do not all need to be scholars, but we do need to be serious, regular, capable students of the Bible (i.e., good Bible readers, see Table of Contents, "*A Guide to Good Bible Reading*"). Humility, teachableness, and a daily walk of faith will protect us from many a pitfall. Remember, every paragraph has one main truth (words have meaning only in sentences; sentences have meaning only in paragraphs; paragraphs must relate to a specific literary unit). Be careful of overconfidence in interpreting the details (the Spirit will help believers find the main truths of paragraphs)!

THE INTERPRETER

I. Presuppositional Conditioning

We are all historically conditioned. Total objectivity is not possible (Carson, *Biblical Interpretation and the Church* 1984, 12). However, if we can identify our biases, or at least areas in which they may be found, we are better able to control their influence. There is an excellent discussion of our pre-understanding in Duncan Ferguson's *Biblical Hermeneutics*, pp. 6-22.

> "Because we all have our prejudices and misconceptions it is all too easy to see in Scripture only what we want to see, and to miss the new and edifying revelation of fuller truth which is God's purpose for us. It is all too easy to read our own ideas into Scripture instead of getting out of the Scripture what it teaches, which might quite possibly overthrow our ideas (Stibbs 1950, 10-11).

There are many areas from which our presuppositions may come.

A. One major factor is our personality type. This causes many confusions and disagreements among believers. We expect everyone to think and analyze as we do. A very valuable book in this area is *Why Christians Fight Over the Bible* by John Newport and William Cannon. Some believers are very logical and structured in their thought processes, while others are much more emotional and less prone to details and systems. Yet all believers are responsible to interpret the Bible and live in light of its truths.

B. Another factor is our personal perception of our world and our experience of it. Not only do personality factors affect us, but also our maleness and femaleness. We are learning from the study of brain function how differently men and women perceive their worlds. This will affect how we interpret the Bible. Also, our personal experiences, or the experiences of those close to us, can affect our interpretations. If a unique spiritual experience has happened to us, we will surely look for it on the pages of the Bible and in the lives of others.

C. Closely related to personality difference is spiritual giftedness (I Corinthians 12-14; Rom. 12:3-8; Eph. 4:7,11-12). Often our giftedness is directly related to our personality type (Ps. 139:13-16). Giftedness comes at salvation (I Cor. 12:4,7,11), not physical birth. However, they may be related. Spiritual giftedness is meant to be gracious service (I Cor. 12:7) to our fellow believers, but it often turns into conflict (I Cor. 12:12-30), especially in the area of biblical interpretation. Our personality type also affects how we approach the Scriptures. Some approach the Scriptures looking for systematic categories, while others approach it in a more existential, devotional fashion. Our reason for coming to the Bible often affects our understanding. There is a difference between teaching a Sunday School class for five year olds and preparing a lecture series for a university. However, the process of interpretation should be the same.

D. Another significant factor is our place of birth. There are so many cultural and theological differences even within the United States and this is multiplied by other cultures and nationalities. Often we learn strong biases from our culture, not the Bible. Two good contemporary examples of this are American individualism and capitalism.

E. As the place of our birth affects us, so too, the time of our birth. Culture is a fluid factor. Even those from the same culture and geographical area can be affected by "the generation gap." If one multiplies this generation gap over centuries and cultures back to the Bible days, the potential for error becomes significant. We are affected by the twenty-first century scientific mindset and our societal form and norms. Every age has "flavor" all its own. However, when we come to the Bible, we must understand its cultural setting for the purpose of interpretation.

F. It is not only geography, time, and culture which affect us, but also our parental training. Parents are so influential and sometimes it is in a negative sense. Their biases are often passed on to their children or else the children totally reject the teachings and lifestyle of the parents. When one adds denominational factors to this mixture, it is clear how presuppositional we can become. The sad division of Christendom into splinter groups, each claiming authority and preeminence over all others, has caused great problems in interpreting the Bible. Many know what they believe the Bible says before they ever read or study it personally, because they have been indoctrinated by a particular perspective. Tradition is neither good nor bad. It is neutral and can be very helpful. However, every generation of believers must be allowed to analyze it in light of the Bible; tradition can protect us or bind us (the movie "Fiddler on the Roof").

G. Every one of us has been, and continues to be, affected by sin and rebellion, both overtly and inadvertently, knowingly and unknowingly. Our interpretations are always impacted by our spiritual maturity or lack thereof. Even the most Christlike believers are affected by sin and the most carnal believers have the light of the indwelling Spirit. All of us, hopefully, are going to continue to grow in our relationship with God through Christ by means of the Spirit. We must walk in the light we have, always being open to more light from the Scriptures by means of the Spirit. Our interpretations will surely change and modify the longer we live, the more contact we have with God's people and God Himself.

If you have not had a new thought about God in several years, you are "brain dead"!

II. Some Examples of Evangelical Conditioning

At this point I would like to give some concrete examples of the relativity that results from the above mentioned factors.
A. Mixed swimming (boys and girls swimming together) is a real issue in some churches, usually those geographically removed from places where swimming can take place easily.
B. Use of tobacco is a real issue in some churches (especially South America), usually in those geographical places where it is not a major cash crop (believers, often physically out of shape themselves, use tobacco as an excuse to accuse others of hurting their bodies).
C. Use of alcohol in America is an important issue in many church groups, while in parts of Europe and South America it is not an issue. America is more affected by the 1920's temperance movement than by the Bible. Jesus surely drank fermented wine. Are you more "spiritual" than Jesus?

The following is a Special Topic taken from Dr. Utley's commentaries. You can view and download all of them free at www.freebiblecommentary.org.

SPECIAL TOPIC: ALCOHOL (FERMENTATION) AND ALCOHOLISM (ADDICTION)

I. **Biblical Terms**
   A. Old Testament
   1. *Yayin* - This is the general term for wine (BDB 406), which is used 141 times. The etymology is uncertain because it is not from a Hebrew root. It always means fermented fruit juice, usually grape. Some typical passages are Gen. 9:21; Exod. 29:40; Num. 15:5,10.
   2. *Tirosh* - This is "new wine" (BDB 440). Because of climatic conditions of the Near East, fermentation started as soon as six hours after extracting the juice. This term refers to wine in the process of fermenting. For some typical passages see Deut. 12:17; 18:4; Isa. 62:8-9; Hos. 4:11.
   3. *Asis* - This is obviously alcoholic beverages ("sweet wine" BDB 779, e.g., Joel 1:5; Isa. 49:26).
   4. *Sekar* - This is the term "strong drink" (BDB 1016). The Hebrew root is used in the term "drunk" or "drunkard." It had something added to it to make it more intoxicating. It is parallel to *yayin* (cf. Prov. 20:1; 31:6; Isa. 28:7).

   B. New Testament
   1. *Oinos* - the Greek equivalent of *Yayin*
   2. *Neos oinos* (new wine) - the Greek equivalent of *tirosh* (cf. Mark 2:22).
   3. *Gleuchos vinos* (sweet wine, *asis*) - wine in the early stages of fermentation (cf. Acts 2:13).

II. **Biblical Usage**
   A. Old Testament
   1. Wine is a gift of God (Gen. 27:28; Ps. 104:14-15; Eccl. 9:7; Hos. 2:8-9; Joel 2:19,24; Amos 9:13; Zech. 10:7).
   2. Wine is a part of a sacrificial offering (Exod. 29:40; Lev. 23:13; Num. 15:7,10; 28:14; Deut. 14:26; Judg. 9:13).
   3. Wine is used as medicine (II Sam. 16:2; Prov. 31:6-7).
   4. Wine can be a real problem (Noah- Gen. 9:21; Lot- Gen. 19:33,35; Samson- Judg. 16:19; Nabal- I Sam. 25:36; Uriah- II Sam. 11:13; Ammon- II Sam. 13:28; Elah- I Kin. 16:9; Benhadad- I Kin. 20:12; Rulers- Amos 6:6; and Ladies- Amos 4).
   5. Wine can be abused (Prov. 20:1; 23:29-35; 31:4-5; Isa. 5:11,22; 19:14; 28:7-8; Hosea 4:11).

6. Wine was prohibited to certain groups (Priests on duty, Lev. 10:9; Ezek. 44:21; Nazarites, Num. 6; and Rulers, Prov. 31:4-5; Isa. 56:11-12; Hosea 7:5).
7. Wine is used in an eschatological setting (Amos 9:13; Joel 3:18; Zech. 9:17).

B. Interbiblical
1. Wine in moderation is very helpful (Ecclesiasticus 31:27-30).
2. The rabbis say, "Wine is the greatest of all medicine, where wine is lacking, then drugs are needed." (BB 58b).

C. New Testament
1. Jesus changed a large quantity of water into wine (John 2:1-11).
2. Jesus drank wine (Matt. 11:18-19; Luke 7:33-34; 22:17ff).
3. Peter accused of drunkenness on "new wine" at Pentecost (Acts 2:13).
4. Wine can be used as medicine (Mark 15:23; Luke 10:34; I Tim. 5:23).
5. Leaders are not to be abusers of alcohol. This does not mean total abstainers (I Tim. 3:3,8; Titus 1:7; 2:3; I Pet. 4:3).
6. Wine used in eschatological settings (Matt. 22:1ff; Rev. 19:9).
7. Drunkenness is deplored (Matt. 24:49; Luke 11:45; 21:34; I Cor. 5:11-13; 6:10; Gal. 5:21; I Pet. 4:3; Rom. 13:13-14).

III. Theological Insight
    A.   Dialectical tension
1. Wine is the gift of God.
2. Drunkenness is a major problem.
3. Believers in some cultures must limit their freedoms for the sake of the gospel (Matt. 15:1-20; Mark 7:1- 23; I Cor. 8-10; Rom. 14).

    B.   Tendency to go beyond given bounds
1. God is the source of all good things.
2. Fallen mankind has abused all of God's gifts by taking them beyond God-given bounds.

    C.   Abuse is in us, not in things.
There is nothing evil in the physical creation (cf. Mark 7:18-23; Rom. 14:14,20; I Cor. 10:25-26; I Tim. 4:4; Titus 1:15).

IV. First Century Jewish Culture and Fermentation
    A.   Fermentation begins very soon, approximately 6 hours after the grape is crushed.
    B.   Jewish tradition says that when a slight foam appeared on the surface (sign of fermentation), it is liable to the wine-tithe (*Ma aseroth* 1:7). It was called "new wine" or "sweet wine."
    C.   The primary violent fermentation was complete after one week.
    D.   The secondary fermentation took about 40 days. At this state it is considered "aged wine" and could be offered on the altar (*Edhuyyoth 6:1*).
    E.   Wine that had rested on its lees (old wine) was considered good but had to be strained well before use.

F.   Wine was considered to be properly aged usually after one year of fermentation. Three years was the longest period of time that wine could be safely stored. It was called "old wine" and had to be diluted with water.

G.   Only in the last 100 years with a sterile environment and chemical additives has fermentation been postponed. The ancient world could not stop the natural process of fermentation.

V. **Closing Statements**

A.   Be sure your experience, theology, and biblical interpretation does not depreciate Jesus and first century Jewish/Christian culture! They were obviously not total-abstainers.

B.   I am not advocating the social use of alcohol. However, many have overstated the Bible's position on this subject and claim superior righteousness based on a cultural/ denominational bias.

C.   For me, Romans 14 and I Corinthians 8-10 have provided insight and guidelines based on love and respect for fellow believers and the spread of the gospel in our cultures, not personal freedom or judgmental criticism. If the Bible is the only source for faith and practice, then maybe we must all rethink this issue.

D.   If we push total abstinence as God's will, what do we imply about Jesus, as well as those modern cultures that regularly use wine (e.g., Europe, Israel, Argentina)?

D. Tithing is often proclaimed as
   (1) a way to personal wealth, but only in cultures where wealth is possible or
   (2) a way to avoid God's judgment.

The following is a Special Topic taken from Dr. Utley's commentaries.

SPECIAL TOPIC: TITHING

Matthew 23:23 and Luke 11:42 are the only NT references to tithing. I do not believe the NT teaches tithing because this entire setting is against "nit-picking" Jewish legalism and self-righteousness.

I believe the NT guidelines for regular giving (if there are any) are found in II Cor. 8 and 9, which go far beyond tithing! If a Jew with only the information of the OT was commanded to give ten to thirty percent (there are two, possibly three, required tithes in the OT), then Christians should give far beyond and not even take the time to discuss the tithe!

NT believers must be careful of turning Christianity into a legal performance-oriented code (Christian Talmud). Their desire to be pleasing to God causes them to try to find guidelines for every area of life.

However, theologically it is dangerous to pull old covenant rules which are not reaffirmed in the NT (cf. Acts 15) and make them dogmatic criteria, especially when they are claimed (by modern preachers) to be causes of calamity or promises of prosperity (cf. Malachi 3).

Here is a good quote from Frank Stagg, *New Testament Theology*, pp. 292-293:

"The New Testament does not once introduce tithing into the grace of giving. Tithes are mentioned only three times in the New Testament: (1) in censoring the Pharisees for neglect of justice, mercy, and faith while giving meticulous care to the tithing of even garden produce (Matt. 23:23; Luke 11:42); (2) in the exposure of the proud Pharisee who 'prayed to himself,' boasting that he fasted twice each week and tithed all his possessions (Luke 18:12); and (3) in arguing for the superiority of Melchizedek, and hence of Christ, to Levi (Heb. 7:6-9)

It is clear that Jesus approved tithing as a part of the Temple system, just as in principle and practice he supported the general practices of the Temple and the synagogues. But there is no indication that he imposed any part of the Temple cultus on his followers. Tithes were chiefly produce, formerly eaten at the sanctuary by the one tithing and later eaten by the priests. Tithing as set forth in the Old Testament could be carried out only in a religious system built around a system of animal sacrifice.

Many Christians find the tithe to be a fair and workable plan for giving. So long as it is not made to be a coercive or legalistic system, it may prove to be a happy plan. However, one may not validly claim that tithing is taught in the New Testament. It is recognized as proper for Jewish observance (Matt. 23:23; Luke 11:42), but it is not imposed upon Christians. In fact, it is now impossible for Jews or Christians to tithe in the Old Testament sense. Tithing today only faintly resembles the ancient ritual practice belonging to the sacrificial system of the Jews.

Paul Stagg has summed it up:

"While much may be said for adopting the tithe voluntarily as a standard for one's giving without rigidly imposing it upon others as a Christian requirement, it is clear in adopting such a practice that one is not carrying on the Old Testament practice. At most one is doing something only remotely analogous to the tithing practice of the Old Testament, which was a tax to support the Temple and the priestly system, a social and religious system which no longer exists. Tithes were obligatory in Judaism as a tax until the destruction of the Temple in A.D. 70, but they are not thus binding upon Christians.

"This is not to discredit tithing, but it is to clarify its relationship to the New Testament. It is to deny that the New Testament supports the coerciveness, legalism, profit motive, and the bargaining which so often characterize the tithing appeals today. As a voluntary system, tithing offers much; but it must be redeemed by grace if it is to be Christian. To plead that 'it works' is only to adopt the pragmatic tests of the world. Much 'works' that is not Christian. Tithing, if it is to be congenial to New Testament theology, must be rooted in the grace and love of God."

III. What Can Be Done?

The above list could go on and on. Obviously, it needs to be stated that these personality factors usually affect only peripheral areas. It is helpful for each of us to analyze what we believe to be the irreducible minimums of the Christian faith. What are the major pillars of the church in every age and any culture? This is not an easy question, but I think it is a necessary one. We must be committed to the essential core of historical Christianity, but discuss in love our cultural and individual differences in areas that are not crucial (cf. Rom. 14:1-15:13; I Corinthians 8-10). The more I understand myself and the Bible, the smaller my irreducible core has become. Primarily,

for me, it involves the person and work of the Triune God and how one comes into fellowship with Him. All else becomes less crucial in light of these major issues. Maturity will tend to make us less dogmatic and judgmental!

All of us have presuppositions, but few of us have ever defined, analyzed or categorized them. However, we must recognize their presence. We all wear glasses or filters of one kind or another. The book that has helped me to differentiate between the eternal and cultural aspects recorded in Scripture has been Gordon Fee and Doug Stuart, *How To Read the Bible For All Its Worth*, especially chapters 4 and 5. The Bible records some things it does not advocate.

IV. The Responsibility of the Interpreter

In light of the above discussion, what is our responsibility as an interpreter? It involves the following.

1. Christians are personally responsible to interpret the Bible for themselves. This has often been called the priesthood of the believer (soul competency). This phrase never appears in the Bible in the SINGULAR, but always PLURAL (cf. Exod. 19:5; I Pet. 2:5,9; Rev. 1:6). Interpretation is a community of faith's task. Be careful of an over-emphasis on western individualism. We dare not relegate this responsibility to another person (I Cor. 12:7).

2. The Bible is a book that demands interpretation (i.e., Matt. 5:29-30). It cannot be read as if it were the morning newspaper. Its truth is historically conditioned, just as we are. We must bridge the gap between "the then" and "the now."

3. Even after we have done the best we can our interpretations will still be fallible to some extent. We must walk in the light we have. We must love and respect other believers who have a different understanding (i.e., Rom. 14:1-15:13; I Corinthians 8-10).

4. "Practice makes perfect." This is true in the area of interpretation. Prayer and practice will improve ones ability to interpret.

5. Hermeneutics cannot tell one exactly what every text means, but it can show what it cannot mean!

THE CONTEXTUAL METHOD OF BIBLICAL INTERPRETATION

I. Its History and Development

A. Jewish Interpretation

The most consistent use of the method of Bible study known as the **Historical- Grammatical- Lexical Method** (in this Textbook called the **Contextual/Textual** method) began in Antioch, Syria, in the third century A.D. in reaction to the **Allegorical Method**, which had developed several hundred years earlier in Alexandria, Egypt.

The Alexandrian Method was an adaptation of the method of **Philo**, a Jewish interpreter who lived from 20 B.C. to A.D. 55. Philo also lived in Alexandria. He, being a Jew of the Diaspora, was not very influential among the rabbis, but had a great impact among the Hellenistic intellectuals of Alexandria, which was the seat of learning in that day. Philo agreed with the rabbis that the Old Testament was given by God. He believed God uniquely spoke through the Hebrew Scripture and the Greek philosophers, especially Plato. Therefore, every aspect of the text had meaning—every sentence, clause, word, letter, and even the smallest embellishment or idiosyncrasy of the text.

The rabbis' interpretation is characterized by a focus on "how to," especially in relation to the Law of Moses. Philo, although using some of the same idiosyncrasies of grammar and spelling, found hidden meanings in the text as it related to Platonism. The rabbis were interested in applying the Mosaic Law to daily life, while Philo wanted to reinterpret the history of Israel in light of his Platonic world view. To do this he had to totally remove the Old Testament from its historical context.

> "In his mind many of the insights of Judaism, properly understood, do not differ from
> the highest insights of Greek philosophy. God reveals Himself to the chosen people of
> Israel but He revealed Himself in no radically different way from the way in which He
> reveals Himself to the Greek" (Grant and Tracy 1984, 53-54).

His basic approach was to allegorize the text if:
1. the text spoke of that which seemed to be unworthy of God (physicalness of God)
2. the text contained any perceived inconsistencies
3. the text contained any perceived historical problems
4. the text could be adapted (allegorized) to his philosophical world view (Grant and Tracy 1984, 53)

B. The Alexandrian School

The basics of Philo's approach to interpretation were continued in the **Christian School of Interpretation**, which developed in this same city. One of its first leaders was **Clement of Alexandria** (A.D. 150-215). He believed that the Bible contained different levels of meaning in order to make the Scriptures relevant to different kinds of people, cultures, and periods of time.

These levels were
1. the historical, literal sense
2. the doctrinal sense
3. the prophetic or typological sense
4. the philosophical sense
5. the mystical or allegorical sense (Grant and Tracy 1984, 55-56)

This basic approach was continued by **Origen** (A.D. 185-254), who probably was the greatest mind of the ancient church (Silva 1987, 36-37). He was the first textual critic, apologist, commentator, and systematic theologian. A good example of his approach can be found in his interpretation of Prov. 22:20-21. He combines it with I Thess. 5:23. In this way every passage in the Bible has three levels of interpretation.

1. a "bodily" or literal sense
2. a "soulish" or moral sense
3. a "spiritual or allegorical/mystical" sense (Grant and Tracy 1984, 59)

The hermeneutics of Alexandria held sway over most of the Church in the area of interpretation until the time of the Protestant Reformation. It can be characterized in its developed form by **Augustine** (A.D. 354-430) in his four levels of interpretation.

1. the literal—teaches historical events
2. the allegorical—teaches what you should believe
3. the moral—teaches what you should do
4. the mystical—teaches what you should hope

For the church as a whole, the non-literal (#2,3,4) contained the purist spiritual insight. However, the abuses of the non-historical, non-grammatical method led to the formulation of another school of interpretation.

The **Historical-Grammatical Textual**-focused school of Antioch of Syria (third century) accused the allegorist of

1. importing meaning into the text
2. forcing a hidden meaning into every text
3. putting forth fanciful and far-fetched interpretation
4. not allowing words/ sentences to bear their obvious, normal meaning (Sire 1980, 107)
5. allowing human subjectivity to dominate the plain message of the original author

Allegory, when done by a well-trained, godly interpreter, can have great value. It is obvious that Jesus (Matt. 13:18-23) and Paul (I Cor. 9:9-10; 10:1-4; Gal. 4:21-31) both set a biblical precedent for this approach. However, when used as a tool to prove one's pet theological doctrine or to defend one's inappropriate actions, it becomes a great stumbling block. The major problem is that there is no means to substantiate the meaning from the text itself (Silva 1987, 74).

The sinfulness of mankind has turned this method (and all methods to some extent) into a means to prove almost anything and then to call it biblical.

> "There is always the danger of eisegesis, reading into the Bible the ideas which we have received from elsewhere and then receiving them each with the authority with which we have come to surround the book" (World Council of Churches Symposium on Biblical Authority for Today, Oxford, 1949).
> "Origen, and many others along with him, have seized the occasion of torturing Scripture, in every possible manner, away from the true sense. They concluded that the literal sense is too mean and poor, and that, under the outer back of the letter, there lurks deeper mysteries, which cannot be extracted but by beating out allegories.

And this they had no difficulty in accomplishing; for speculation which appear to be ingenious have always been preferred, and always will be preferred, by the world to solid doctrine. . .with approbation the licentious system gradually attained such a height, that he who handled Scripture for his own amusement not only was suffered to pass unpunished, but even attained the highest applause. For many centuries no man was considered to be ingenious, who had not the skill and daring necessary for changing into a variety of curious shapes the sacred word of God. This was undoubtedly a contrivance of Satan to undermine the authority of Scripture, and to take away from the reading of it the true advantage. God visited this profanation by a just judgment, when he suffered the pure meaning of the Scripture to be buried under false interpretations. Scripture, they say, is fertile, and this produces a variety of meanings. I acknowledge that Scripture is a most rich and inexhaustible fountain of all wisdom; but I deny that its fertility consists in the various

meanings which any man, at his pleasure, may assign. Let us know then, that the true meaning of Scripture is the natural and obvious meaning; and let us embrace and abide by it resolutely. Let us not only neglect as doubtful, but boldly set aside as deadly corruptions, those pretended expositions, which lead us away from the natural meaning" (John Newport dissertation, N.D., 16-17).

C. The Antiochian School

It is obvious that the Alexandrian school was justifiably open to the charge that its interpretations relied more on the cleverness of the interpreter than on the intent of the original inspired author. One could, and can, assert any interpretation and "prove" it from the Bible by using this method. The Antiochian method focuses on the plain, obvious meaning of the text of Scripture (Cole 1964, 87). Its basic focus is understanding the message of the original author. This is why it is call the Historical-Grammatical approach of hermeneutics. Antioch insisted on both a historical context and the normal use of human language. It did not eliminate figures of speech, prophecy, or symbols, but forced them to be linked to the purpose, historical setting, and style of the original author, along with the original author's choice of genre.

> "The school of Antioch insisted on the historical reality of the biblical revelation. They were unwilling to lose it in a world of symbols and shadows. They were more Aristotelian than Platonist" (Grant and Tracy 1984, 66).

Some early leaders of this school of interpretation were: Lucian, Diodorus of Tarsus, Theodore of Mopsuestia, and John Chrysostom. This school became involved in an over- emphasis on the humanity of Jesus. This has been labeled the Nestorian Heresy (Jesus had two natures, one divine and one human)—and it was a heresy (cf. I John 4:1-3). For this reason the school lost its influence and many of its followers. Its headquarters moved from Syria into Persia so as to be beyond the discipline of the Roman Church.

D. The Antiochian School's Basic Tenets

Although the basic tenets of the Antiochian School were continued in isolated places, it burst forth again in full bloom in Martin Luther and John Calvin, as it had been in bud previously in Nicholas of Lyra. It is basically this historically and textually-focused approach to hermeneutics that this Textbook is attempting to introduce. Along with the added emphasis on application, which was one of the strengths of Origen, the Antiochian approach clearly distinguished between exegesis and application (Silva 1987, 101).

Because this Textbook is primarily for non-theologically trained believers, the methodology will focus around the text of Scripture in translation rather than the original languages. Study helps will be introduced and recommended, but the obvious meaning of the original author can, in the vast majority of cases, be ascertained without extensive outside help.

The work of godly, diligent scholars will help us in areas of background material, difficult passages, and seeing the big picture, but first we must struggle with the plain meaning of the Scriptures ourselves. It is our privilege, our responsibility, and our protection.

The Bible, the Spirit, and you are priority! Insight into how to analyze human language on a non- technical level, along with the power of the indwelling Holy Spirit, are the twin pillars of this contextual/textual approach.

Your ability to be somewhat free to interpret the Bible for yourself is the primary goal of this Textbook.

James W. Sire in his book *Scripture Twisting* makes two good points.

> "The illumination comes to the minds of God's people—not just to the spiritually elite. There is no guru class in biblical Christianity, no illuminati, no people through whom all proper interpretation must come. And, so, while the Holy Spirit gives special gifts of wisdom, knowledge, and spiritual discernment, He does not assign these gifted Christians to be the only authoritative
> interpreters of His Word. It is up to each of His people to learn, to judge and to discern by reference to the Bible which stands as the authority over even those to whom God has given special abilities."
> "To summarize, the assumption I am making throughout the entire book is that the Bible is God's true revelation to all humanity, that it is our ultimate authority on all matters about which it speaks, that it is not a total mystery but can be adequately understood by ordinary people in every culture" (pp. 17-18).

We dare not naively trust any other person or denomination with the interpretation of Scripture, which affects not only life, but also the life to come. The secondary goal of this Textbook is gaining the ability to analyze the interpretations of others.

This Textbook desires to provide the individual believer with a method for personal Bible study and a shield against the interpretation of others.

Scholarly helps will be recommended, but must not be accepted without proper analysis and textual documentation.

II. Interpretative Questions

Our discussion of a historically informed and textually-focused methodology will revolve around seven interpretive questions which one must ask in the study of every Scriptural context.

1. **What did the original author say? (textual criticism)**
2. **What did the original author mean? (exegesis)**
3. **What did the original author say elsewhere on the same subject? (parallel passages)**
4. **What do other biblical authors say on the same subject? (parallel passages)**
5. **How did the original hearers understand the message and respond to it? (historical application)**
6. **How does this truth apply to my day? (modern application)**
7. **How does this truth apply to my life? (personal application)**

1. The First Interpretive Question — What did the original author say? (textual criticism)

1. The need to read Hebrew and Greek to interpret Scripture.

The initial step is establishing the original text. Here we come face to face with the subject of the original languages of ancient Hebrew, Aramaic, and Koine Greek. Must one know these languages, and all of their textual variants, before one can adequately interpret Scripture? Let me share my presuppositions about the Bible again.

a. God wants mankind to know Him (the very purpose of creation, Gen. 1:26-27).
b. He has provided us with a written record of His nature, purpose, and acts.
c. He has sent us His supreme revelation, His Son, Jesus of Nazareth. The New Testament contains His life and teachings as well as their interpretations.
d. God speaks to the common person. He wants all humans to be saved (Ezek. 18:23,32; John 3:16; I Tim. 2:4; II Pet. 3:9).
e. The vast majority of the world will never know God's revelation except in a translation (Sterrett 1973, 28).
f. We must not see scholars as infallible interpreters. Even scholars must rely on other scholars. Even scholars within the same field do not always agree (Triana 1985, 9).
g. Scholars can help us. Christian scholars are gifts of God given to the church (I Cor. 12:28; Eph 4:11). Yet, even without their help believers can know the plain, simple truth of the Scriptures. They will not have complete or exhaustive knowledge. They will not see the wealth of detail that a biblical scholar might perceive, but believers can know enough for faith and practice.

2. Use of modern translations

Modern translations are a result of scholarly research. They use differing philosophies in translation. Some are very free in translating concepts (paraphrasing) instead of words (word for word) or clauses (dynamic equivalent).

Because of this wealth of research and effort, believers, by comparing these translations, have a variety of technical information available to them, even if believers do not understand the technical process or theories behind them. By comparing modern translations they are able to more fully understand the message of the original author. This is not meant to imply that there are not dangers.

"The person who reads the Bible only in English is at the mercy of the translator(s), and translators have often had to make choices as to what in fact the original Hebrew or Greek really intended to say" (Fee and Stuart 1982, 29).

"The Bible student can overcome this handicap (not knowing originals and having to use translations) by an educated use of the better commentaries.
Above all, everyone must be aware of the dangers. The student should compare the translations as he studies the passage, and should take none of them for granted" (Osborne and Woodward 1979, 53).

I hope you have been encouraged by the above discussion about the adequacy of English translations. I would suggest that for the purposes of Bible study that you use at least two different translations which vary in translation theory. Primarily you will want to use one that is very literal (i.e., word for word) and compare it with an idiomatic translation (dynamic equivalent). By comparing these two types of translations, most of the problems in word meaning, sentence structure, and textual variants become obvious. When major differences occur, refer to technical commentaries and research tools.

3. **Hebrew and Greek manuscript variants**

Another thorny problem to be dealt with in the area of "what did the original author say?" concerns original manuscripts. We do not have any of the original writings of the biblical authors (autographs). As a matter of fact, we are removed by hundreds of years from those originals (autographs). Until the discovery of the Dead Sea Scrolls in 1947, our oldest Old Testament manuscript was from the ninth century A.D., called the Masoretic Text (MT). The Masoretes were a group of Jewish scholars who placed the vowels (vowel points) into a consonantal, Hebrew text. This project was not completed until the ninth century A.D. The Dead Sea Scrolls allow us to verify this Hebrew text back into the B.C. era. They confirmed the accuracy of our Old Testament based on the MT. This enables scholars to compare Hebrew manuscripts with their Greek translations: the Septuagint, and those of Aquila, Symmachus, and Theodotian. The point of all this is that there are many differences among all of these copies.
The New Testament is also involved in the same difficulty. We do not have the writings of the Apostles, as a matter of fact, our copies are several hundred years removed from them. The oldest manuscripts available of the Greek New Testament are fragments of certain books written on papyri. These date from the second and third centuries A.D. and none have the complete New Testament. The next oldest group of Greek manuscripts comes from the fourth through sixth centuries. They are written in all capital letters with no punctuation marks or paragraph divisions.

After this comes thousands of manuscripts from later centuries, mostly the 12th - 16th (written in small letters). None of these agree completely. However, it needs to be strongly emphasized that none of the variants affect major Christian doctrines (Bruce 1969, 19-20). This is where the science of textual criticism comes onto the scene. Scholars in this area have analyzed and classified these different texts into "families," which are characterized by certain common errors or additions.

If you would like more information on this subject read

    a.   The Books and the Parchments — F. F. Bruce
    b.   "Texts and Manuscripts of the Old Testament," Zondervan's Pictorial Encyclopedia of the Bible, vol. 5, pp. 683ff
    c.   "Texts and Manuscripts of the New Testament," Zondervan's Pictorial Encyclopedia of the Bible, vol. 5, pp. 697ff
    d.   Introduction to New Testament Textual Criticism — J. H. Greenlee

The problem of textual criticism is not solved, but the work thus far has surely helped to clear up much of the confusion in this area.

> "Rarely will one repeat the labors of the textual critics, unless an alternate reading is mentioned as a footnote in the version commonly used" (Liefeld 1984, 41).

I have found that these manuscript problems can be readily found by noticing the marginal notes in our modern English Study Bibles. The Revised Standard Version and The New English Bible provide many interesting alternative translations. All modern translations provide alternate readings to some extent. Another helpful resource at this point is the new *Twenty-Six Translations of the Bible* edited by Curtis Vaughn, published by AMG Publishers. This three volume set provides the King James Version in bold print and three to five alternate translations from a pool of twenty-six translations. This tool quickly shows the textual variations. These variations may then be adequately explored in commentaries and other research tools.

4. The limits of human language

Still another factor involved in the question, "what did the original author say?" involves the ambiguities of human language. When human language, which is basically a set of analogous relationships between words and concepts, is forced to describe God and spiritual things, major problems arise. Our finitude, our sinfulness, our corporality, and our experience of time (past, present, future) all affect our language as we attempt to describe the supernatural. We are forced to express these concepts in human categories (Ferguson 1937, 100).

One type of these metaphorical categories is anthropomorphisms (man-form). These categories were one reason why the rabbis, Philo and Origen (Silva 1987, 61), began to use allegory. In reality, our description and understanding of God and the supernatural is analogous only (i.e., negation, analogy, and metaphor). It can never be complete or exhaustive. It is presuppositional, but by faith Christians believe it is adequate.

This problem of human language is further complicated when put into a written form. So often the inflection of the voice or some bodily gesture helps us understand the subtleties of human communication, but these are not present in a written text. Yet, even with these obvious limits, we are still able, for the most part, to understand each other. Our study of the Bible will be limited by these ambiguities, as well as the additional problem of translating three separate languages (Hebrew, Aramaic, and Koine Greek). We will not be able to know for certain the complete meaning of every passage. A good book in this area is *God's Word in Man's Language* by Eugene Nida. With the help of the Holy Spirit we will be able to understand the plain sense of most Scripture. Maybe the ambiguities are there to humble us and cause us to be dependent on God's mercy.

2. The Second Interpretive Question — What did the original author mean? (exegesis)
  (for a sheet on exegetical procedures, see pp. 96 and 97)

1. Outline the literary units

One way, possibly the best way, to understand a written document is to identify the author's purpose and the major divisions (i.e., literary units) in his presentation. We write with a purpose and goal in mind. So too, did the biblical authors. Our ability to identify this overarching purpose and its major divisions will greatly facilitate our understanding of its smaller parts (paragraphs and words). A key to this deductive approach (Osborne and Woodward 1979, 21) is outlining (Tenney 1950, 52). Before one tries to interpret a paragraph within a biblical book, he needs to know the purpose of the literary unit of which it is a part in light of the surrounding passages and the structure of the whole book. I know that this procedure seems overwhelming at first, as far as putting it into practice, but it is crucial as far as interpretation is concerned.

> "From the standpoint of the Bible or literature, the simplest error of reading is the failure to consider the immediate context of the verse or passage in question" (Sire 1980, 52).

> "The principle of contextual interpretation is, at least in theory, one of the few universally accepted hermeneutical guidelines, even though the consistent application of the principles is a notoriously difficult enterprise" (Silva 1983, 138).

> "The context does not merely help us understand meaning—it virtually makes meaning" (Silva 1983, 139).

> "How the passage fits within that—what it contributes to the entire flow of that book and what the structure of that book contributes to it—constitutes a paramount interest of the literary context step in exegesis" (Stuart 1980, 54).

This task can be accomplished in a very simple way. One can do several steps of interpretation at one time. It is obvious that if one wants to interpret a passage in light of the original author's intent, they need to read and become familiar with the author's whole message (the book). As one reads the biblical book several times in order to gain familiarity with its contents, he should take notes of his observations. On the first reading look for the major purpose of the book and its genre. On the second reading note the large blocks of related material, which we call literary units.

An example from the book of Romans reveals major themes.
  a. Brief introduction and theme (1:1-17)
  b. The lostness of all men (1:18-3:21)
  c. Justification is a gift (4:1-5:21)
  d. Justification affects our lifestyle (6:1-8:39)
  e. The Jews' relationship to justification (9:1-11:36)
  f. Practical section of living out justification on a daily basis (12:1-15:37)
  g. Greetings, farewells, and warnings (16:1-27)

"Try to construct an outline that genuinely represents the major units of information. In other words, the outline should be a natural, not artificial, outgrowth of the passage. Note which components are included within each topic (quantitative) and also the intensity or significance of the components (qualitative). Let the passage speak for itself. When you see a new topic, subject, issue, concept, or the like, you should start a new topic for your outline. After outlining the major divisions work on the more minor divisions such as sentences, clauses and phrases. The outline should be as detailed as you can make it without seeming forced or artificial" (Stuart 1980, 32-33).

Outlining to paragraph level (and beyond) is a key in allowing the original author to speak. It will keep us from majoring on minors or going off on tangents. Your finished outline can then be compared with a Study Bible, such as the NIV Study Bible or NASB Study Bible, a Bible encyclopedia, or a commentary, but only after you have read the book several times and developed your own tentative outline.

"This is the crucial task in exegesis, and fortunately it is something one can do well without necessarily having to consult the 'experts'" (Fee and Stuart 1980, 24).

Once the large literary blocks have been isolated, then the smaller units can be identified and summarized. These smaller units of thought may be several paragraphs or even a chapter or more. In most literary genres the paragraph is a key (Liefeld 1984, 90) to interpretation. One should never attempt to interpret less than a paragraph.

As a sentence forms the context for words, paragraphs form the context for sentences. The basic unit of purposeful writing is the paragraph. In high school we were taught how to isolate the topical sentence of a paragraph.

This same principle will help us tremendously in biblical interpretation. Every paragraph has one major purpose in the author's overall presentation of truth. If we can isolate this purpose and summarize its truth in one simple, declarative sentence, we can complete our outline of the author's structure.

If our interpretation is alien to the purpose or thrust of the original author, we are abusing the Bible and have no biblical authority!

"Do not trust the chapter and verse divisions. They are not original and are often completely wrong" (Stuart 1980, 23).

"Decisions about paragraphing are sometimes subjective, and you will find that the various editors' groupings of contents do not always agree. But if you decide to start your passage where no editor has begun a paragraph or end a paragraph where no editor has ended a paragraph, then it is your responsibility to explain fully for your decision" (Stuart 1980, 45).

2. Note the historical and cultural setting

The previous discussion of literary units is valuable, not only for the first question, "what did the original author say" (textual criticism), but also for the second, "what did the original author mean?" (exegesis). These questions are related, but distinct.

The first focuses on the words of the original author (textual criticism). The second focuses on three very significant aspects of interpretation which are related to meaning.

    a.   the historical background of the author and/or the events of the book
    b.   the type of literary form (genre) in which the message is given
    c.   the basic grammatical and linguistic aspects of the text

One of the characteristics of allegory is that it completely separates the interpretation of a text from its historical setting. It is a major tenet of the contextual/textual or Antiochian Method that one establish the historical context. This principle was reemphasized by Martin Luther. This emphasis on background material in interpretation has come to be called, in a broad sense, "higher criticism"; whereas the information about the original text has come to be called "lower criticism." In higher criticism one tries to ascertain from both internal (the biblical book itself) and external (secular history, archaeology, etc.) the following items.

    a.   information about the author
    b.   information about the date of writing
    c.   information about the recipients of the writing
    d.   information about the occasion of the writing
    e.   information about the writing itself
        (1)   recurrent or unique terms
        (2)   recurrent or unique concepts
        (3)   basic flow of the message
        (4)   the form in which the message appears (genre)

"World view confusion. . .occurs whenever a reader of Scripture fails to interpret the Bible within the intellectual and cultural framework of the Bible itself, but uses instead a foreign frame of reference. The usual way in which it appears is for scriptural statement, stories, commands or symbols which have a particular meaning or set of related meanings within the biblical frame of reference to be lifted out and placed within another frame of reference. The result is that the original intended meaning is lost or distorted, and a new and quite different meaning is substituted" (Sire 1980, 128).

This type of information is often (but not always) helpful in interpreting the writing. This historical aspect of interpretation, like outlining, can be done to some extent without the help of the "experts." As you read the biblical book, write down the historical background information from the Bible itself and it will amaze you the amount of information you have gleaned.

As a matter of fact, most of this information is available only from the biblical book itself (usually the first few verses). There will often be many theories expressed in the commentaries which are actually presuppositions with little biblical or historical evidence. Once you have gathered all the information that is obvious to you from the biblical book, it is time to expand your insight by using one of the following types of research helps:

    a.   introductory books usually divided into separate books on the Old and New Testaments

    b.   articles in Bible encyclopedias, dictionaries, or handbooks, usually under the name of the biblical book

    c.   the introductions found in commentaries

    d.   the introductions found in Study Bibles

These types of research tools are meant to give you the historical setting in a brief amount of study time. Most often these materials will be relatively brief because we simply do not have much information about many aspects of ancient history. Also, this type of material will usually be written in non-technical language. Again, as is obvious to you, my basic approach to interpretation is to see the big picture first and then to analyze the parts in detail.

3. The type of literature (genre)

The next area of interpretation related to the meaning of the original author is related to the literary genre. This is a French term which means a specialized category of literature characterized by style, form, or content. This is significant because the style in which one chooses to write affects how we are to understand it. Often ridiculous interpretations of prophecy or poetry have been propounded on what one calls "the literal" method of interpretation. However, the "literal" method from Antioch means that we interpret human language in its normal meaning. If it is apocalyptic literature, it was not meant to be interpreted literally. This is also true of poetry, idioms, and figures of speech.

The basic unit of thought, which in prose is normally the paragraph, is modified by the genre. Some examples of this significant factor in the identification of capsuled units of thought for the purposes of interpretation follow.

    a.   For poetry the basic unit is the strophe or stanza, which is defined as a series of lines arranged together as a patterned unit (see Appendix Six).

    b.   For a proverb the basic unit is the central or summary theme of the verse in its relation to the same theme located within the same book, another book by the same author, or other wisdom literature. Here, the thematic subject, more than the isolated proverb, is the key to interpretation. Not only synonymous themes (the same), but also antithetical themes (opposites) or synthetical development (additional information) of the same theme are crucial to a proper interpretation of Hebrew wisdom literature (see Appendix Seven).

    c.   For prophecy the basic unit must be the entire oracle. This can vary from a paragraph, a chapter, several chapters, to an entire book. Again, the basic theme and style will isolate the prophetic unit (see Appendices Four and Five).

d. For the <u>Gospel</u> parallels the basic unit will relate to the type of literature involved. Usually the unit will relate to one event, one teaching session, one subject, etc. This could involve an event or a series of events, parable or a series of parables, a prophecy or a series of prophecies, but all focusing on one main theme. It is usually better to look at the literary flow of each Gospel instead of going to the parallel passages in other Gospels.

e. For <u>letters</u> and <u>historical narratives</u> the basic unit is usually the paragraph.

However, several paragraphs usually form larger literary units. These must be identified and characterized as a whole literary unit before the smaller parts can be properly interpreted.
Some examples of these larger literary units follow.

(1) Matthew 5-7 (Sermon on the Mount)
(2) Romans 9-11 (what about unbelieving Israel)
(3) I Corinthians 12-14 (spiritual gifts) [or I Corinthians 11-14 guidelines for public worship]
(4) Revelation 2-3 (letters to churches) or 4-5 (heaven)

Analysis of literary types is crucial to their proper interpretation (Fee and Stuart 1982, 105). As in outlining, and to some extent, the historical background, this can be done by the average reader with the help of a translation which identifies poetry and paragraphs (Fee and Stuart 1982, 24). The reason that classification of literary genre is so important is that besides the general guidelines for interpretation, there are special needs of each literary type. This is only logical. If each type represents a different mode of human communication, then it is obvious that there needs to be special treatment in order to arrive at the author's intent. It is just as condemning to add to the biblical author's intent as it is to detract from it.

4. Special interpretive procedures related to genre

Let me summarize some of the specific guidelines involved in these special genres.

a. Poetry
(1) Structure is important. Ancient Hebrew developed its poetic structure or pattern around thought (expressed in beats per line), not rhyme.
    (a) synonymous (the same thought)
    (b) antithetical (an opposite thought)
    (c) synthetic (the development of thought)

(2) Poetry is usually figurative, not literal. It attempts to speak to our common human desires and experiences. Try to identify figures of speech (Sterrett 1973, 93-100) and understand their function or purpose.

(3) Try to get an overall impression of the literary unit and do not push the details or figures of speech in doctrinal formulations.

b.   Proverbs
(1)   Because they deal with daily life, look for the practical application.
(2)   Parallel passages will be much more helpful here than context or historical setting. Try to compile a list of proverbs with the same practical application, as well as other passages which might modify or develop this same, opposite, or developed truth.
(3)   Try to isolate the figures of speech and identify their purpose in the proverb.
(4)   Be sure that you do not interpret the proverbs in a particularistic manner, but in the sense of a general truth.

c.   Prophecy
(1)   This type of genre must first be seen in light of its own historical setting. It is primarily related to its own day and the immediate history of that day. The historical setting is crucial in this genre.
(2)   One must look for the central truth. To focus on a few details which might fit our day or the last days and ignore the overall message of the oracle is a common mistake.
(3)   Often prophets do speak of future settings, possibly several. Because of the abuse of prophecy I feel it is best to limit the interpretation of Old Testament prophecy to the specific accounts recorded in the New Testament. New Testament prophecy must be interpreted in light of
(a)   its OT usage or allusions
(b)   the teachings of Jesus
(c)   other NT parallel passages
(d)   its own contextual setting
(4)   Remember that most biblical prophecy, especially Old Testament Messianic prophecy, has two focuses: the Incarnation and the Second Coming (Silva 1987, 104-108).

d.   The Four Gospels
(1)   Although we have four Gospels and we are able to compare them, this is not always the best method in trying to find the purpose or meaning of one particular Gospel writer. We must look at the way he uses the material, not how other Gospel writers use it or develop it. Comparison will be helpful, but only after you have determined the meaning of a particular writer.
(2)   The literary or historical context is crucial in interpreting the Gospels. Try to identify the literary limits of the general subject being discussed and not its isolated parts. Try to see this subject in light of first century Palestinian Judaism.
(3)   It is important to remember that the Gospels record the words and acts of Jesus, but it is the Epistles which interpret them into specific church settings. Check the parallels in the Epistles.
(4)   Jesus said some ambiguous and difficult things, some of which we may not fully understand until we see Him. He also said much that is plain and obvious—start there. Act on what you do know and often the rest will be made clear to you. If not, the message is possibly not for us, for our day (Dan. 12:4).

(5) In connection with parables
    (a) Be certain of the context.
Notice
    (1) who Jesus addressed the parable to;
    (2) Jesus' purpose for telling the parable and
    (3) how many parables are told in a series. Read further to see if He interprets it.
    (b) Do not push the details. Major on His major point(s). Usually there is just one central truth per parable or main characters.
    (c) Do not build major doctrines on parables. Doctrine should be grounded on extended clear teaching passages.

e. The Letters and Historical Narratives
    (1) Compared to the other types of literary genres these are the easiest to interpret.
    (2) The contextual setting is the key, both historical and literary.
    (3) The literary unit and the paragraph will be the key literary unit.

These special hermeneutics linked to literary types are discussed in detail in the following excellent books.
1. *How to Read the Bible for All Its Worth* — Gordon Fee and Douglas Stuart
2. *Protestant Biblical Interpretation* — Bernard Ramm
3. *Linguistics and Bible Interpretation* — Peter Cotterell and Max Turner
4. *Literary Approaches to Biblical Interpretation* — Tremper Longman III
5. *Exegetical Fallacies* — D. A. Carson
6. *Plowshares and Pruning Hooks* — D. Brent Sandy
7. *A Basic Guide to Interpreting the Bible* — Robert H. Stein

5. Syntax and grammatical features

Another aspect in obtaining the author's original intent or meaning is called syntax or grammatical structure. This is often difficult because of the idiomatic and structural differences between the biblical languages and our own mother tongue. However, it is a fruitful area in interpretation and needs to be dealt with in some detail. Usually a comparison of modern translations and a basic knowledge of grammar will help tremendously.

> "Grammar may not always show us the actual meaning, but it will show us possible meanings. We cannot accept any meaning that does violence to it. This grammar is important in understanding the Bible. This is not strange. Essentially it means that we understand the Bible according to the normal laws of human language" (Sterrett 1973, 63).

Grammar is something that the common person knows in usage, but not in technical definition. We learn grammar when we learn to speak. Grammar is forming sentences to communicate ideas. We do not need to be experts in grammatical relationships in order to interpret the Bible, however, we do need to try to understand why the original author said it the way he did. Often the structure of a sentence will show us what the author is emphasizing. This can be ascertained in several ways.

a. As you read the passage in several English translations notice the word order. A good example of this is in Heb. 1:1. In the King James Version the subject of the sentence, "God," appears first, but in the Revised Standard Version the descriptive phrase, "in many and various ways," appears first. This is significant because it reflects the true intent of the author. Is the major thrust of this text that God has spoken (revelation) or is it how God has spoken (inspiration)? The latter is true because the Revised Standard Version reflects the Koine Greek word order (use an interlinear). Also, a technical commentary will help on these word order and grammatical issues.

b. As you read the passage in several English translations note the translation of the VERBS. VERBS are very important in interpretation. A good example is I John 3:6,9. When one compares the King James Version with modern translations the difference is obvious. This is a PRESENT TENSE VERB. These verses are not teaching "sinlessness," but "sinning less." At the conclusion of this Textbook a brief definition of Hebrew and Greek grammatical terms is included (see Table of Contents).

c. As you read the passage in several English translations note the thought connectives. Often these help us know the purpose of a clause or how sentences and contexts are related.

Notice the following connectives (Traina 1985, 42-43).

  (1)   temporal or chronological connectives
        (a)   after (Rev. 11:11)
        (b)   as (Acts 16:16)
        (c)   before (John 8:58)
        (d)   now (Luke 16:25)
        (e)   then (I Cor. 15:6)
        (f)   until (Mark 14:25)
        (g)   when (John 11:31)
        (h)   while (Make 14:43)

  (2)   local or geographical connectives (where, Heb. 6:20)

  (3)   logical connectives
        (a)   reason
              because (Rom. 1:25)
              for (Rom. 1:11)
              since (Rom. 1:28)
        (b)   result
              so (Rom. 9:16)
              then (Gal. 2:21)
              therefore (I Cor. 10:12)
              thus (I Cor. 8:12)
        (c)   purpose
              in order that (Rom. 4:16)
              so that (Rom. 5:21)

(d) contrast
     although (Rom. 1:21)
     but (Rom. 2:8)
     much more (Rom. 5:15)
     nevertheless (I Cor. 10:5)
     otherwise (I Cor. 14:16)
     yet (Rom. 5:14)
(e) comparison
     also (II Cor. 1:11)
     as (Rom. 9:25)
     as – so (Rom. 5:18)
     just as – so (Rom. 11:30-31)
     likewise (Rom. 1:27)
     so also (Rom. 4:6)
(f) series of facts
     and (Rom. 2:19)
     first of all (I Tim. 2:1)
     last of all (I Cor. 15:8)
     or (II Cor. 6:15)
(g) condition (e.g., "if," Rom. 2:9)

(4) emphatic connectives
     (a) indeed (Rom. 9:25)
     (b) only (I Cor. 8:9)

These illustrations of thought connectives were taken from *Methodical Bible Study* by Robert A. Traina, pp. 42-43. Although his illustrations are mostly from the writings of Paul and predominately from the book of Romans, they do serve as good examples of how we structure our thoughts with these thought connectives. By comparing modern translations of both the Old and New Testaments these implied and expressed relationships become clear. Traina also has an excellent summary about grammatical structure on pp. 63-68. Be a careful Bible reader!

d. As you read the passage in several English translations, notice the repetition of terms and phrases. This is another way to ascertain the original author's structure for the purpose of communicating his intended meaning.
    Some examples are:
    (1) The repeated phrase in Genesis, "these are the generations of. . .," (2:1; 5:1; 6:9; 10:1; 11:10,27; 25:12,19; 36:1,9; 37:2). This phrase shows us how the author himself divided the book.
    (2) The repeated use of "rest" in Hebrews 3-4. The term is used with three distinct meanings.
         (a) a Sabbath rest as in Genesis 1-2
         (b) the promised land of Exodus through Joshua
         (c) heaven
If one misses this structure then he will probably miss the author's intent and probably think that all the people who died in the wilderness were spiritually lost.

6. Idioms and word studies

Read the passage in several English translations, particularly a word-for-word one, such as the New American Standard Version, with the dynamic equivalent one, such as the New International Version. In this way one is able to identify idioms. Every language has its own quirks or expressions. For one to interpret an idiom literally would be to totally miss the point. A good example is the Hebrew term "hate." If we notice its New Testament usage, particularly Rom. 9:13; Luke 14:26; or John 12:25, one sees that this idiom could be misunderstood. However if its Hebrew background and usage in Gen. 29:31,33 or Deut. 21:15 is identified, then it is obvious that it does not mean "hate" in our English sense of the word, but it is an idiom of comparison.

Technical commentaries will be of real help in these matters. Two good examples of this type of commentary are (1) *The Tyndale Commentary Series* and (2) *The New International Commentary Series.*

The last aspect of this second question, "What did the original author mean?" is word studies. I have chosen to deal with it last because word studies have been so abused! Often etymology has been the only aspect of meaning that one uses to interpret a passage. The writings of James Barr, *The Semantics of Biblical Language*; D. A. Carson, *Exegetical Fallacies*; along with Moises Silva's *Biblical Words and Their Meaning*, have helped modern interpreters to reevaluate their word study techniques. Bible interpreters as a group have been guilty of numerous linguistic fallacies.

> "Perhaps the principal reason why word studies constitute a particularly rich source for exegetical fallacies is that many preachers and Bible teachers know Greek only well enough to use concordances, or perhaps a little more. There is little feel for Greek as a language, and so there is the temptation to display what has been learned in study" (Carson 1984, 66).

It must be stated emphatically that context, not etymology, determines meaning!

> "The root fallacy presupposes that every word has a meaning bound up with its shape or its components. In this view meaning is determined by etymology." (Carson 1984, 26).

> "We must agree the obvious fact that the speakers of a language simply know next to nothing about its development; and this certainly was the case with the writers and immediate readers of Scripture. . .our real interest is the significance of Greek or Hebrew in the consciousness of the biblical writers; to put it boldly, historical considerations are irrelevant to the investigation of the state of Koine, at the time of Christ." (Silva 1983, 38).

> "Since usage is so important, a safe rule for the interpreter is to leave etymology in the hands of the expert and to apply himself diligently to context and usage." (Mickelsen 1963, 121-122).

We must seek out original usage, or to put it another way—the meaning understood and intended by the original author and readily understood by the original hearers. Biblical terms have several different usages (semantical field). D. A. Carson's *Exegetical Fallacies*, pp. 25-66, is very helpful at this point—painful, but helpful. To illustrate, notice how English meanings change over time.

    a. In I Thess. 4:15, the King James Version has "shall not <u>prevent</u> them which are asleep." In the American Standard Version the term is translated "<u>precede</u>." Notice how the meaning of "prevent" has changed.

    b. In Eph. 4:22 the King James version has "put off concerning the former <u>conversation</u> the old man. . ." In the American Standard Version the term is translated "<u>manner of life</u>." Notice how the meaning of "conversation" has changed.

    c. In I Cor. 11:29 the King James has "for he that eateth and drinketh unworthily, eateth and drinketh <u>damnation</u> to himself." In the American Standard version the term "damnation" is translated as "<u>judgment</u>." Notice has the term has changed.

Most of us are prone to define biblical terms in light of our understanding of that term in our denomination or theological system. The problem with this is twofold.

    a. We must be careful that we are using the definition from the original author's intent and not our demoninational or cultural background.

    b. We must be careful not to force a word to mean our technical religious definition in every context where it appears. Often the same author uses the same term in different senses.

    c. Some examples of this follow.

        (1) John's use of "world"

            (a) physical planet (John 3:16; I John 4:1,14)

            (b) human society organized and functioning apart from God (I John 2:15; 3:1; 5:4-5)

        (2) Paul's use of "body"

            (a) physical body (Rom. 1:3)

            (b) sin nature (Rom. 8:3-4)

        (3) Paul's use of "temple"

            (a) the church as a whole (I Cor. 3:16-17)

            (b) the individual believer (I Cor. 6:19)

        (4) James' use of the term "save"

            (a) spiritual salvation (James 1:21; 2:14)

            (b) physical deliverance (James 5:15,20)

The way to proceed in determining the meaning of a word is to check several translations and to note the differences. Look up the term in an exhaustive concordance such as *Analytical Concordance to the Bible* by Robert Young or *The Exhaustive Concordance of the Bible* by James Strong. Look up all other usages in the same biblical book you are studying; look up all of the uses by the same author. Try to sample the other uses in the same Testament.

Walter Henricksen, in *A Layman's Guide to Interpreting the Bible*, 1973, pp. 54-56, gives these steps:

    a. The term's use by the writer.

    b. The term's relation to its immediate context.

    c. The term's ancient use at the time of the writing.

    d. The term's root meaning.

Try to verify the basic meaning from the other Testament (remember that the NT writers were Hebrew thinkers writing Koine Greek). Then it is time to go to a theological word book, Bible encyclopedia, dictionary, or commentary in order to check your definition (see list VII on p. 103). I have written a sample academic guide to NT word studies on p. 98 to illustrate how much effort must be used to ascertain a word's meaning in a specific context.

C.-D. The Third and Fourth Interpretive Questions

The next questions which the interpreter tries to answer is "**what else did the same author say on the same subject?**" It is closely related to the fourth basic question, "**what did other inspired authors say on the same subject?**" These two questions can be combined by the descriptive concept of concentric circles of parallel passages. Basically we are talking about how the word or theological concept is used elsewhere by an inspired author. This principle of interpretation has been called "the analogy of Scripture."

> "The infallible rule of interpretation of Scripture is the Scripture itself; and therefore, when there is a question about the true and full sense of any Scripture (which is not manifold, but one) it may be reached and known by other places that speak more clearly" (Westminister Confession, chap. 9).

It is based on three suppositions.
1. that all Scripture is inspired by God (I Tim. 3:15-17, cf Fee & Stuart 1982, 209)
2. that Scripture does not contradict itself
3. that the best interpreter of Scripture is Scripture (Silva 1987, 68,93,94)

If these are true, then the best way to understand a passage is the contextual concentric circles of inspired writings.
1. the same topic or term in the same immediate context (paragraph or literary unit)
2. the same topic or terms in the same biblical book
3. the same topic or terms by the same author
4. the same topic or terms in the same period, genre, or Testament
5. the same topic or terms in the Bible as a whole

The farther we move from the specific passage that we are attempting to interpret, the more general and, to some extent, tentative the effectiveness of the parallel becomes.

> "Interpret according to the narrow context before the wider. It is commonly agreed that Scripture should interpret Scripture. However, it needs to be understood that a term or passage must be interpreted first in its immediate context before it is studied in light of its broader application to the Bible as a whole" (Osborne and Woodward 1979, 154).

This area of interpretation can be very helpful in seeing how our passage relates to the whole of revelation (McQuilkin 1983, 43; Silva 1987, 83; Sterrett 1973, 86).

Basically we are moving from
1. exegesis (number 1 above) to
2. biblical theology (numbers 2, 3, and 4 above) to
3. systematic doctrine (number 5 above)

We are moving from the magnifying glass to the telescope. We must first be relatively sure of the meaning of our focal passage before we move to systematized doctrine. This is one, though not the only, purpose of systematic theology books "see list IX Theologies p. 105). The move is necessary, but dangerous. Our backgrounds, prejudices, and denominational indoctrinations are always ready and able to intrude. If we use parallel passages (and we must) we must be certain that they are true parallels, not just the same term or phrase.

It is often true that parallel passages bring an overall balance to our interpretation. It has been my experience in interpreting that the Bible is often written in paradoxical or dialectical pairs (eastern mindset). One must recognize the biblical tension between subjects without removing it for the purpose of making simplistic statements, attempting to categorize truth, or protecting cherished theological positions. One inspired text cannot be used to negate or depreciate another inspired text!

Here are some examples of the tension between biblical truths.
1. predestination versus human free will
2. security of the believer versus the need for perseverance
3. original sin versus volitional sin
4. Jesus as God versus Jesus as man
5. Jesus as equal with the Father versus Jesus as subservient to the Father
6. Bible as God's Word versus human authorship
7. sinlessness versus sinning less
8. initial instantaneous justification and sanctification versus progressive sanctification
9. justification by faith (Romans 4) versus justification confirmed by works (cf. James 2:14-26)
10. Christian freedom (cf. Rom. 14:1-23; I Cor. 8:1-13; 10:23-33) versus Christian responsibility (cf. Gal. 5:16-21; Eph. 4:1)
11. God's transcendence versus His immanence
12. God as ultimately unknowable versus knowable in Scripture and Christ
13. Paul's many metaphors for salvation
    a. adoption
    b. sanctification
    c. justification
    d. redemption
    e. glorification
    f. predestination
    g. reconciliation
14. the kingdom of God as present versus a future consummation
15. repentance as a gift of God versus repentance as a mandated response for salvation
16. the OT is permanent versus the OT has passed away and is null and void (cf. Matt. 3:17-19 vs. 5:21-48; Romans 7 vs. Galatians 3)
17. believers are servants/slaves or children/heirs

Moises Silva has been very helpful in listing the tensions which exist in our understanding Scripture.

1. The Bible is divine, yet it has come to us in human form.
2. The commands of God are absolute, yet the historical context of the writings appears to relativize certain elements.
3. The divine message must be clear, yet many passages seem ambiguous.
4. We are dependent only on the Spirit for instruction, yet scholarship is surely necessary.
5. The Scriptures seem to presuppose a literal and historical reading, yet we are also confronted by the figurative and nonhistorical (e.g., the parables).
6. Proper interpretation requires the interpreter's personal freedom, yet some degree of external, corporate authority appears imperative.
7. The objectivity of the biblical message is essential, yet our presuppositions seem to inject a degree of subjectivity into the interpretive process (Silva 1987, 36-38).

Which side of these paradoxes are true?
To all of these I would answer "yes," because they are all true.
Both sides are biblical.
Our task as an interpreter is to see the big picture and integrate all of its parts, not just our favorite, or most familiar, ones.

The answers to interpretation problems are not found in removing the tension so as to affirm only one side of the dialectic (Silva 1987, 38). This balance can be obtained from the proper use of a concordance or from systematic theology books. Be careful not to consult only systematic theologies from the denominational perspective from which you come or with which you agree. Let the Bible challenge you, roar at you—not just whimper. It will unsettle your cherished notions.

It is true that the attempt to systematize doctrine, or relate seemingly contradictory biblical material, is presuppositional and usually conforms to a doctrinal position. This should be less true for biblical theology which is primarily descriptive. This method (biblical theology) of study takes a small slice of the biblical material. It limits itself to an author, a period, or a genre. It tries to draw its theological categories only from a restricted biblical frame of reference. Often, in the act of limiting the biblical material, we are forced to take seriously the difficult statements of Scripture without explaining away their meaning by allusion to other verses. It forces us to take seriously what an author said. It is not looking for a balance, but for the vibrant, clear statement of the biblical author. It is a painful struggle to affirm both poles of biblical paradoxes. We consult all three of these concentric circles of parallel passages.

One hopes to move through each stage in every context.

1. What did the author say and mean? (exegesis)
2. What did he say elsewhere on the same subject? What did others of the same period say? (biblical theology)
3. What does the Bible as a whole say on this and related subjects? (systematic doctrine) Another potential problem in the use of parallel passages is called "the fallacy of collapsing contexts."

> "When two or more unrelated texts are treated as if they belonged together, we have the fallacy of collapsing contexts. This reading error can be especially knotty because it is the corruption of a perfectly good principle of reading: to compare Scripture with Scripture. We are responsible as good readers of the Bible to make use of every text bearing on the subject we wish to understand" (Sire 1980, 140).

> "What gives interpreters the right to link certain verses together and not others? The point is that all such linking eventually produces a grid that effects the interpretation of the other texts" (Carson 1984, 140).

A good example of this problem has already been alluded to in this Textbook—Origen's linking of a passage in Proverbs with an unrelated text in the book of I Thessalonians.

E. How did the original hearers understand the message and respond to it?

This is the **fifth interpretative question**. It relates to only certain kinds of genres (i.e., historical narratives, Gospels, and the book of Acts). It is very helpful if the information is available because this is our goal as an interpreter, "hear as it was heard."

F.-G The Sixth and Seventh Interpretive Questions

1. Application

Up until this point we have been looking at the interpretative questions which relate to the original author's intent. Now we must turn to the equally significant focus concerning its meaning to my day and to my life. No interpretation is complete unless this stage is reached and adequately incorporated. The goal of Bible study is not knowledge alone, but daily Christlikeness. The goal of the Bible is a deeper, closer relationship with the Triune God. Theology must be practical.

> "According to Kierkegaard the grammatical, lexical, and historical study of the Bible was necessary but preliminary to the true reading of the Bible.
> 'To read the Bible as God's word one must read it with his heart in his mouth, on tip-toe, with eager expectancy, in conversation with God. To read the Bible thoughtlessly or carelessly or academically or professionally is not to read the Bible as God's Word. As one reads it as a love letter is read, then one reads it as the Word of God'" (from *Protestant Biblical Interpretation* by Ramm, p. 75).

Application is not an option (Osborne and Woodward 1979, 150). However, application is less structured than interpretation (this is where the creativity and life experiences of the interpreter and proclaimer come into focus). Ideally there is but one original intent in Scripture. This could be expanded to two (multiple prophecy fulfillment or extended parables).

Often the original author's intent was true, but not exhaustive of the Spirit's intent. Application is often determined by one's personal

a. need
b. situation
c. level of maturity
d. desire to know and follow God
e. cultural and denominational traditions
f. current historical situation

It is obvious that the leap from the "then" to the "now" is ambiguous. There are many factors which cannot be identified or controlled. One reason for the development of the allegorical method was the desire to apply the Bible to current needs. Some would say that allegory is necessary for application (Silva 1987, 63,65), but I would deny this. The Spirit is our mandatory guide in application as He is in interpretation. Application must be integrally related to the intended meaning of the original inspired author!

2. Some Helpful Guidelines

a. Be sure to apply the major intent of the biblical author, not just minor details of the passage.
b. Do not look for every aspect of our current situation to be addressed in detail. Often biblical "principles" are our only guide. However, our formulation of these are one more level removed from inspiration. Also, their application is often very presuppositional. Some interpreters find biblical principles in every text. It is safer to limit one's principles to extended teaching passages or else principles can become proof-texts.
c. Not all truth is meant for immediate or personal application. The Bible often records that which it does not advocate. Also, not all biblical truth is applicable to every age, every situation, and every believer.
d. Application should never seem contrary to other clear Bible passages.
e. Application should never seem contrary to Christ-like conduct. Extremes in application are as dangerous as they are in interpretation.
f. Some basic application questions to ask of every biblical passage have been suggested by Richard Mayhue in *How To Interpret the Bible for Yourself*, 1986, p. 64
   (1) Are there examples to follow?
   (2) Are there commands to obey?
   (3) Are there errors to avoid?
   (4) Are there sins to forsake?
   (5) Are there promises to claim?
   (6) Are there new thoughts about God?
   (7) Are there principles by which to live?

H. The Interpreter's Responsibility

At this point it will be helpful to discuss the individual interpreter's responsibility in relation to appropriate application of the Bible's eternal, relevant truths. It has already been stated that this procedure is ambiguous and that the Holy Spirit must be our guide.

For me a key ingredient to this area is our motive and attitude. We must walk in the light we have. I am not responsible for your walk of faith, nor you for mine. We can share our perspective in love and hopefully from our understanding of specific passages of Scripture. We all must be willing to seek new light from the Scripture, but we are only responsible for what we do understand. If we walk in faith in the light that we have, more light will be given (Rom. 1:17).

We must also be aware at this point to remember that our understanding is not always superior to the understanding of others. Romans 14:1-15:13 is so crucial in this area, but I am always surprised that we usually think our group is the stronger brother and everyone who does not agree with us is a member of the weaker group and in need of our help.

We all need help. We all have areas of strengths and areas of weakness in our understanding and application of spiritual truth. I have heard it said that the Bible comforts the uncomfortable and discomforts the comfortable.

We must walk down the tension-filled road of spiritual growth. We are all affected by sin and we will never arrive at complete maturity this side of heaven.

Walk in the light you have—within the light of the Bible.

"Walk in the light as He is in the light" (I John 1:7).

Keep on walking.

Here are some helpful books
1. *Applying the Bible* — Jack Kuhatschek
2. *Understanding and Applying the Bible* — J. Robertson McQuilkin
3. *Living By the Book* — Howard G. Hendricks
4. *Why Christians Fight Over the Bible* — John Newport

SOME POSSIBLE INTERPRETIVE PITFALLS

I. Need for both a Logical Process and a Textual Focus in Interpretation

It is obvious that these principles of interpretation can be abused, for hermeneutics is not a pure science. It is crucial that we state some of the obvious pitfalls involved in the inappropriate use or non-use of the contextually/textually-focused principles previously presented in this Textbook. This Contextual/Textual method is somewhat like the scientific method. Its results are meant to be corroborated and repeated by others. There needs to be a clear trail in our procedural method, points of interpretation and logic. These pieces of evidence will come from several contextual and textually-focused areas.

A. The literary context of the passage
   1. immediate (paragraph)
   2. several related paragraphs
   3. larger literary unit (thought block)
   4. entire biblical book (purpose of the author)
B. The historical context of the passage
   1. background and setting of the author
   2. background and setting of the hearer or reader
   3. background and setting of their culture
   4. background and setting of any problems addressed in the passage
C. The literary genre (type of literature)
D. The grammar/syntax (relationship of the parts of the sentence to each other and surrounding sentences)
E. The original word meanings and connotations (definitions of significant terms)
   1. semantic field
   2. author's usage
   3. other authors of the same period
   4. other biblical authors
F. Appropriate use of parallel passages (concentric circles of significance)
   1. same literary unit
   2. same book
   3. same author
   4. same period
   5. same Testament
   6. the Bible as a whole

One can analyze another's interpretation based on how they utilize these component parts. There will still be disagreement, but at least it will be from the text itself. We hear and read so many different interpretations of God's Word that it becomes crucial that we critically evaluate them, based on the possibility of verification and proper procedures, not just whether we personally agree with them.

As in all human language communication (verbal and written), there is the potential for misunderstanding. Because hermeneutics are the principles for interpreting ancient literature, it is obvious that their abuse is also possible. For every basic principle of interpretation there is the possibility of intentional or unintentional abuse. If we could isolate the potential areas of our own presuppositions, it would help us to be aware of them when we come to our personal interpretations.

II. Examples of Abuses of the First Five Interpretative Questions

A. Our presuppositions

Often our personality, our experience, our denomination, or our culture causes us to interpret the Bible through glasses or filters. We only allow it to say what we want it to say. This existential bias affects all of us, but if we are aware of it we can compensate for it by attempting to allow the Bible and its day to speak before we attempt to apply the message to ourselves and our culture. Some examples of this pitfall can be seen in

1. William Barclay's interpretation of Matt. 15:37-39, where the miraculous multiplication of food by Jesus becomes simply the multitude sharing with one another what they brought. Barclay's philosophical filter of logical positivism radically alters the obvious intent of Matthew. Remember that there were seven baskets full of pieces of bread left over (Matt. 16:37).

2. Accounts of women in ministry can be seen in Exod. 15:20; Jdgs. 4:4ff; II Kgs. 22:14; II Chr. 2:22; Isa. 8:3; Luke 2:36; Acts 21:9; Rom. 16:1; II Cor. 11:5; and I Tim. 3:11. Modern evangelicals who are uneasy about this, either because of preconceived views or the strong statements of I Cor. 14:34 and I Tim. 2:11-15, should not alter the proper and obvious interpretation of these other passages.

3. Roman Catholicism, in the desire to support an episcopal system of polity, uses the text of John 21:15-17. From the text itself it is inappropriate to use the terms "lamb" and "sheep" in relation to bishops and priests and their assigned task of ministry.

B. Our abuse of context

This refers both to the historical context and the literary context of a passage. This may be the most common abuse of Scripture in our day. By removing a passage from the author's day and the author's intended purpose, one can make the Bible say anything. If it were not so common and deadly, the examples of this pitfall would be ludicrous.

1. A preacher of days past preached against the selling of dogs based on Deut. 23:18. The historical and literary settings were ignored. The term "dog" was transferred from male, cultic prostitution (Deuteronomy) to an animal (today).

2. When the modern legalist uses Col. 2:21 to outlaw certain activities without even realizing that this verse is Paul's quote of the false teachers' message, the problem becomes evident.

3. The modern use by soul winners of Rev. 3:20 as the closing appeal of "the plan of salvation," not even realizing that it is in the context of Christian churches (Revelation 2-3). This text is not addressing initial salvation, but the recommitment of a church, beginning with the individuals of that congregation.

4. The modern cult of Mormonism quotes I Cor. 15:29 as a proof for "baptism for the dead." There are no parallel passages for this verse. The immediate context is the validity of the resurrection and this verse is one of several examples used to confirm this truth.

5. C. I. Scofield's quote of II Tim. 2:15, "rightly dividing the Word of truth," is used as Scriptural support for dividing the Bible into seven distinct covenants.

6. Use of John 6:52ff by Roman Catholicism to support the doctrine of transubstantiation (that the elements of the Eucharist actually become the body and blood of Christ) is another example of this pitfall. John does not record the Lord's Supper itself, but only the dialogue of the upper room experience (John 13-17). This passage is in the context of the feeding of the five thousand, not the Eucharist.

7. Preaching on sanctification from Gal. 2:20, not realizing that the focus of the context is on the complete effectiveness of justification.

C. Our abuse of the literary genre

This involves the misunderstanding of the original author's message because of our failure to identify the literary form in which he spoke. Each literary form has some unique elements of interpretation. Some examples of this abuse follow.

1. Some literalists attempt to turn the poetry of Ps. 114:3-6 into historical narrative—often judging others by their literalistic interpretation.

2. Some try to interpret the apocalyptic sections of Revelation 12 and 13 as literal persons and animals.

3. Some try to describe "hell" from the parable of Luke 16:19-31. This is the fifth in a series of five parables, which are related to one central intent of Jesus in addressing the religious leaders (Pharisees) in Luke 15:1-2. Also, the term used is *Hades* and not *Gehenna*.

D. Our abuse of figures of speech or cultural idioms is another pitfall.

We all speak in symbolic language. Yet, because those who hear us live in the same culture, they understand our idiomatic phrases. How unusual our idioms and figures of speech must be to those from other cultures. I recall an Indian pastor who told me that he was so sorry that "I was tickled to death." It is good for us to reflect on our own colorful phrases, such as "that was awfully good"; "I am all ears"; "that just kills me"; or "cross my heart and hope to die."

1. The Bible has idioms also.
   a. The word "hate" in Luke 14:26; John 12:25; Rom. 9:13, and Mal. 1:2-3 is a Hebrew idiom of comparison, as can be seen in Gen. 29:31,33 and Deut. 21:15, but if we do not know this it can cause much misunderstanding.
   b. The phrases, "cut off your limbs" and "pluck out your eyes," in Matt. 5:29-30 are Oriental overstatements, not literal commands.
   c. The Holy Spirit is in the form of a dove in Mark 1:10; however, the Scriptures say, "like a dove" or "as a dove," cf. Luke 3:22.

E. Our abuse by oversimplification.

We say that the gospel is simple and by this we mean that it is easy to understand, however, many simple summaries of the gospel are faulty because they are not complete.

1. God is love, but this omits the concept of God's wrath (Rom. 1:18-2:16).

2. We are saved by grace alone, but this omits the concept that individuals must repent and believe (Mark 1:15; Acts 20:21).

3. Salvation is free (Eph. 2:8-9), but this completely omits the idea that it demands a lifestyle change (Eph. 2:10).
4. Jesus is God, but this omits the concept that He is truly human (I John 4:2).

F. Our abuse by selectivity

This is similar to over simplification and proof-texting. We often select or combine only those Scriptures which support our theology.

1. An example is seen in John 14:13-14; 15:7,16; 16:23, in the phrase "whatever you ask for in prayer, you will receive." For the proper balance one must assert the other biblical criteria concerning this subject.
    (a) "keep on asking, seeking, knocking," Matt. 7:7-8
    (b) "according to God's will," I John 5:14-15, which is really what "in Jesus' name" implies
    (c) "without doubt," James 1:6
    (d) "without selfish goals," James 4:1-3
2. Using the text of I Cor. 11:6 to criticize men who wear long hair without noting Num. 6:5; Lev. 19:27, and the culture of Jesus' day, is inappropriate.
3. Disallowing women to speak or teach in church based on I Cor. 14:34 without consideration of I Cor. 11:5, which is in the same literary unit, is an overstatement.
4. Disallowing or depreciating tongues, often based on I Cor. 13:8 (I Corinthians 13 asserts that everything but love will pass away), without noting the teaching of I Cor. 14:5,18,39, is inappropriate.
5. Emphasizing the food laws of Leviticus 11 without noting Matt. 15:11 and, in an oblique way, Acts 10:10-16, is inappropriate.

G. Our abuse of majoring on minors

Often we miss the original author's intent because we get involved in an interesting, but not central, issue. This can be seen in the following.

1. Whom did Cain marry? Gen. 4:17
2. Many are concerned about the recipients of Jesus preaching while He was in Hades. I Peter 3:19
3. Another question concerns how God is going to destroy the earth. II Peter 3:10

H. Our abuse of the Bible as history — the Bible often records what it does not advocate (Fee and Stuart 1982, 85). We must focus on clear teaching passages, not just historical accounts, for our theology and ethics.

    I. Our abuse of the relationship between the Old and New Testament, Israel and the Church, Law and Grace.

Presuppositionally, Christ is Lord of Scripture (Grant and Tracy 1984, 95). All Scripture must ultimately point to Him. He is the fulfillment of God's plan for humanity (Col. 1:15-23). This means that although the Old Testament must stand on its own feet, it points toward Christ (Sterrett 1973, 157-171). I think we must interpret the OT through the new revelation of the NT. Old Testament emphases have changed and been universalized. The New Covenant has superceded the Mosaic Covenant (cf. the book of Hebrews and Galatians 3)

The examples of each of these pitfalls are legion. However, just because some over- interpret and some under-interpret and some falsely-interpret, does not mean there should be no interpretation. If we stay with the original author's major intent expressed in a context and if we come to the Bible prayerfully and humbly we can avoid the vast majority of these pitfalls.

> "Why is it that people so often find things in the Bible narratives, that are not really there—read into the Bible their own notions rather than read out of the Bible what God wants them to know?
> 1. they are desperate, desperate for information that will apply to their own situation
> 2. they are impatient; they want their answers now, from this book, from this chapter
> 3. they wrongly expect that everything in the Bible applies directly as instruction for their own individual lives" (Fee and Stuart 1980, 84).

Following is a Special Topic from my commentaries on this subject.

SPECIAL TOPIC: WOMEN IN THE BIBLE

I.   The Old Testament
A.   Culturally women were considered property
    1.   included in list of property (Exodus 20:17)
    2.   treatment of slave women (Exodus 21:7-11)
    3.   women's vows annullable by socially responsible male (Numbers 30)
    4.   women as spoils of war (Deut. 20:10-14; 21:10-14)
B.   Practically there was a mutuality
    1.   male and female made in God's image (Gen. 1:26-27)
    2.   honor father and mother (Exod. 20:12 [Deut. 5:16])
    3.   reverence mother and father (Lev. 19:3; 20:9)
    4.   men and women could be Nazarites (Num. 6:1-2)
    5.   daughters have right of inheritance (Num. 27:1-11)
    6.   part of covenant people (Deut. 29:10-12)
    7.   observe teaching of father and mother (Prov. 1:8; 6:20)
    8.   sons and daughters of Heman (Levite family) led music in Temple (I Chronicles 25:5-6)
    9.   son and daughter will prophesy in new age (Joel 2:28-29)
C.   Women were in leadership roles
    1.   Moses' sister, Miriam, called a prophetess (Exod. 15:20-21 also Micah 6:4)
    2.   women gifted by God to weave material for the Tabernacle (Exod. 35:25-26)
    3.   a woman, Deborah, also a prophetess (cf. Jdgs. 4:4), led all the tribes (Jdgs. 4:4-5; 5:7)
    4.   Huldah was a prophetess whom King Josiah asked to read and interpret the newly- found "Book of the Law" (II Kings 22:14; II Chr. 34:22-27)
    5.   Queen Esther, a godly woman, saved Jews in Persia

II. The New Testament

A. Culturally women in both Judaism and the Greco-Roman world were second class citizens with few rights or privileges (the exception was Macedonia)

B. Women in leadership roles

1. Elizabeth and Mary, godly women available to God (Luke 1-2)
2. Anna, godly woman serving at the Temple (Luke 2:36)
3. Lydia, believer and leader of a house church (Acts 16:14,40)
4. Philip's four virgin daughters were prophetesses (Acts 21:8-9)
5. Phoebe, deaconess of church at Cenchrea (Rom. 16:1)
6. Prisca (Priscilla), Paul's fellow-worker and teacher of Apollos (Acts 18:26; Rom. 16:3)
7. Mary, Tryphaena, Tryphosa, Persis, Julia, Nereus' sister, several women co-workers of Paul (Rom. 16:6-16)
8. Junia (KJV), possibly a woman apostle (Rom. 16:7)
9. Euodia and Syntyche, co-workers with Paul (Phil. 4:2-3)

III. How does a modern believer balance the divergent biblical examples?

A. How does one determine historical or cultural truths, which only apply to the original context, from eternal truths valid for all churches, all believers of all ages?

1. We must take the intent of the original inspired author very seriously. The Bible is the Word of God and the only source for faith and practice.
2. We must deal with the obviously historically-conditioned inspired texts.
   a. the cultus (i.e., ritual and liturgy) of Israel (cf. Acts 15; Gal. 3)
   b. first century Judaism
   c. Paul's obviously historically-conditioned statements in I Corinthians
      (1) the legal system of pagan Rome (I Corinthians 6)
      (2) remaining a slave (I Cor. 7:20-24)
      (3) celibacy (I Cor. 7:1-35) (4)   virgins (I Cor. 7:36-38)
      (5) food sacrificed to an idol (I Cor. 8; 10:23-33)
      (6) unworthy actions at Lord's Supper (I Corinthians 11)
3. God fully and clearly revealed Himself to a particular culture, a particular day. We must take seriously the revelation, but not every aspect of its historical accommodation. The Word of God was written in human words, addressed to a particular culture at a particular time.

B. Biblical interpretation must seek the original author's intent.
What was he saying to his day?
This is foundational and crucial for proper interpretation. But then we must apply this to our own day. Now, here is the problem with women in leadership (the real interpretive problem may be defining the term. Were there more ministries than pastors who were seen as leadership? Were deaconesses or prophetesses seen as leaders?) It is quite clear that Paul, in I Cor. 14:34-35 and I Tim. 2:9-15, is asserting that women should not take the lead in public worship! But how do I apply that today? I do not want Paul's culture or my culture to silence God's Word and will. Possibly Paul's day was too limiting, but also my day may be too open.

I feel so uncomfortable saying that Paul's words and teachings are conditional, first century, local situational truths. Who am I that I should let my mind or my culture negate an inspired author?!

However, what do I do when there are biblical examples of women leaders (even in Paul's writings, cf. Romans 16)? A good example of this is Paul's discussion of public worship in I Cor. 11-14. In 11:5 he seems to allow women's preaching and praying in public worship with their heads covered, yet in 14:34-35 he demands they remain silent! There were deaconesses (cf. Rom. 16:1) and prophetesses (cf. Acts 21:9). It is this diversity that allows me freedom to identify Paul's comments (as relates to restrictions on women) as limited to first century Corinth and Ephesus. In both churches there were problems with women exercising their newly-found freedom (cf. Bruce Winter, Corinth After Paul Left), which could have caused difficulty for the church in reaching their society for Christ. Their freedom had to be limited so that the gospel could be more effective.

My day is just the opposite of Paul's. In my day the gospel might be limited if articulate, trained women are not allowed to share the gospel, not allowed to lead! What is the ultimate goal of public worship? Is it not evangelism and discipleship? Can God be honored and pleased with women leaders? The Bible as a whole seems to say "yes"!

I want to yield to Paul; my theology is primarily Pauline. I do not want to be overly influenced or manipulated by modern feminism! However, I feel the church has been slow to respond to obvious biblical truths, like the inappropriateness of slavery, racism, bigotry, and sexism. It has also been slow to respond appropriately to the abuse of women in the modern world. God in Christ set free the slave and the woman. I dare not let a culture- bound text reshackle them.

One more point: as an interpreter I know that Corinth was a very disrupted church. The charismatic gifts were prized and flaunted. Women may have been caught up in this. I also believe that Ephesus was being affected by false teachers who were taking advantage of women and using them as surrogate speakers in the house churches of Ephesus.

C. Suggestions for further reading
    How to Read the Bible For All Its Worth Gordon Fee and Doug Stuart (pp. 61-77)
    Gospel and Spirit: Issues in New Testament Hermeneutics Gordon Fee
    Hard Sayings of the Bible by Walter C. Kaiser, Peter H. Davids, F. F. Bruce & Manfred T. Branch (pp. 613-616; 665-667)

PRACTICAL PROCEDURES FOR INTERPRETATION

I. The Spiritual Aspects

Bible study is a combination of dependence on the Holy Spirit and the sharpening of your God-given abilities of reason and analysis. The spiritual aspect of Bible study is difficult to discuss because of the vast array of differing interpretations affirmed by godly, educated, sincere believers. It is a mystery why there is so much disagreement, even hostility, among believers, all trying to understand and affirm Scripture. The Spirit is crucial, but all believers have the Spirit. The following is simply my attempt to address the needed spiritual attitude of every interpreter.

A. Prayer should be "priority one" in interpretation and application. Prayer is not an automatic link to true interpretation, neither in its quality or quantity, but it is the first indispensable step. To go into Bible study without the Spirit is like going swimming without water. Again, this does not mean to imply that prayer is directly related to the quality of our exegesis—that is determined by additional factors. But one thing is for certain—a person unaided by God cannot know spiritual truth (Calvin). Prayer is not overcoming some reluctance on God's part to open His book to us, but it is a recognition of our dependence on Him. The Spirit was given to help us understand God's Word (John 14:26; 16:13-14; I Cor. 2:10-16).

B. Personal cleansing is also significant. Known, unconfessed sin blocks our relationship with God. He does not require sinlessness in order to understand the Bible, but the Bible is spiritual truth and sin is a barrier to spiritual things. We need to confess known sin (I John 1:9). We need to open ourselves to the Lord for inspection (Ps. 139:1,23-24). Many of His promises are conditional on our faith response, so too, our ability to understand the Bible.

C. We need to develop a desire to know God and His Word (Ps. 9:7-14; 42:1ff; 119:1ff). When we become serious with God, He is able to draw near to us and open His will for our lives (Zech. 1:3-4; James 4:8).

D. We need to immediately apply the truth gleaned from our Bible study (put into practice what we believe to be true) into our lives. Many of us already know much more biblical truth than we are living (I John 1:7). The criteria for more truth is that we walk in the truth we already have. Application is not optional, but it is daily. Walk in the light you have and more light will be given (Rom. 1:17).

"It perceives that no merely intellectual understanding of the Bible, however complete, can possess all its treasures. It does not despise such understanding, for it is essential to a complete understanding. But it must lead to a spiritual understanding of the spiritual treasures of this book if it is to be complete. And for that spiritual understanding something more than intellectual alertness is necessary. Spiritual things are spiritually discerned, and the Bible student needs an attitude of spiritual receptivity, an eagerness to find God that he may yield himself to Him, if he is to pass beyond his scientific study into the richer inheritance of this greatest of all books" *The Relevance of the Bible*, H. H. Rowley (p. 19).

II. The Logical Process

Read the Bible! One cannot know what it means if he does not know what it says. Analytical reading and outlining are the keys to understanding. In this step several cycles (four) of reading the entire biblical book in one setting are involved.

A. Read in several translations. It is hoped that you will read translations that utilize different theories of translation.
   1. formal correspondence (word-for-word) such as
      a. the King James Version
      b. the American Standard Version
      c. the New American Standard Bible
      d. the Revised Standard Version
   2. dynamic equivalence translations such as
      a. the New International Version
      b. the New American Bible
      c. Good News for Modern Man (Today's English Version)
      d. the Jerusalem Bible
      e. the New English Bible
      f. Williams translation
   3. concept for concept translations such as
      a. the Amplified Bible
      b. Phillips translation
      c. the Living Bible

Your personal study Bible should be from category (1) or (2). Also, a parallel Bible which utilizes several translations on the same page is very helpful.

B. Read the entire book or literary unit in one sitting
   1. When you read, allow yourself a prolonged period of study time, a scheduled or regular time and find a quiet place. Reading is an attempt to understand another person's thoughts. You would not think of reading a personal letter in sections. Try to read complete books of the Bible in one sitting.
   2. One key to this non-technical, textually-focused methodology is reading and re-reading. It will amaze you how understanding is related to familiarity. This Textbook's practical method is focused around these procedures.
      a. seven interpretive questions
      b. four stages of reading with assignments
      c. use of research tools at appropriate places

C. Write down your textual observations (i.e., good note taking)
   Take notes of what you read. There are several steps in this section. They are not meant to be burdensome, but we must control our desire for instant Bible knowledge by depending too heavily on the interpretations of others. Personal Bible study takes prayer, time, training, and persistence.

It is not an easy road, but the benefits are outstanding.

1. Read the book that you want to study one time through. I recommend that you choose a shorter New Testament book first. The study of an entire book is best. It is better stewardship of your time and it is easier to retain background information and context between study times. Book studies, over a period of time, will give you a biblical balance. It will force you to deal with difficult, unfamiliar, and paradoxical truths.

   Try to put into your own words, in one concise, precise sentence, what the author's overarching purpose was for writing the book. Also, try to isolate this central theme in a key verse, paragraph, or chapter. Remember that the purpose is often expressed by the type of literary genre that is used. If books are made up of other genres than historical narrative, consult the special hermeneutical procedural section concerning literary genre (See *How to Read The Bible For All Its Worth* by Fee and Stuart).

2. Read it again in the same translation. This time notice the major divisions (literary units) of the author's thoughts. These are identified by changes in subject, time, topic, tone, place, style, etc. At this point do not try to outline the structure of the book, only its obvious subject changes. Do not base your divisions on the chapter and verse of your English Bible. These are not original and are often misleading and incorrect. Summarize each of your divisions by using short, descriptive sentences which characterize the subject or topic of the section. Once you have isolated sections, see if you can link them together into related topics, contrasts, comparisons, persons, events, etc. This step is an attempt to isolate and relate the large blocks of seemingly unrelated material, which in reality, are the literary units of the author's overarching structure. These literary units show us the flow of the thoughts of the original author and point us toward his original intent.

D. At this point it is helpful to check your outline and overarching purpose with other believers.

"When your private interpretation leads you to a conclusion different from the historical meaning men of God have given to the passage, an amber light of caution should flash in your mind" (Henricksen 1973, 38).

"In order for the exegesis to be your work and not merely a mechanical compendium of other's views, it is wise to do your own thinking and to arrive at your own conclusions as much as possible prior to this step" (Stuart 1980, 39).

"Constantly cross checking our grasp of Scripture with:
1. our pastor
2. our fellow Christians
3. the historic understanding of Scripture by orthodox Christians" (Sire 1980, 15)

Often your Study Bible will have an outline at the beginning of each book. If not, most have the subject of each chapter at the top of the page or somehow positioned in the text. Never look at theirs until you have written your own. You may have to modify yours, but shortcuts at this step will cripple your ability to analyze the literary units for yourself.

Not only do Study Bibles contain outlines of biblical books, but also
1.   commentaries
2.   books of introduction to the Old or New Testament
3.   Bible encyclopedias or dictionaries under the name of the biblical book

E. Re-read the entire biblical book and
1.   on a separate sheet of paper, write down the paragraph divisions of your Bible under the literary units (different topics) that you have isolated and outlined. An outline is nothing more than recognizing the original author's thoughts and their relationship to each other. Paragraphs will form the next logical division under literary units. As you identify the paragraph under each literary unit, characterize the context in one sentence as you did earlier to the larger division of the book. This simple outlining procedure will help keep you from majoring on minors.
      Up until this point you have worked from only one translation. Now, compare your divisions with other translations.
      a.   the larger units
      b.   the paragraph divisions
Make a notation at the places of divergence.
      a.   subject divisions
      b.   paragraph divisions c.   word choice
      d.   sentence structure
      e.   marginal notes (This usually involves manuscript variations. For this technical information consult commentaries)
2.   At this point look for verses in the biblical text to answer these questions (the historical setting).
      a.   who wrote the passage
      b.   to whom was the passage addressed
      c.   why was the passage written to them
      d.   when was the passage written
      e.   what historical circumstances were involved

This type of material can be gleaned from the book itself. Often all we know about the historical setting of biblical books is found within the book itself (internal evidence) or within parallel biblical passages. Certainly it is quicker to consult a "professional" commentator at this point, but resist doing it. You can do this for yourself. It will give you joy, increase your confidence, and help you remain independent of the "experts" (Osborne and Woodward 1979, 139; Jensen 1963, 20). Write down the questions you think might be helpful such as: Are there repeated words or phrases? Is there a noticeable structure? Is there a series of parallel passages from one other specific biblical book? With your questions before you, re-read the entire book. When you find an item in the text that relates to any of these questions, write it down under that section. With practice and careful reading it will amaze you how much you can learn from the text itself.

F. Check your observations

Now it is time to check your observations of the biblical book with those of God's gifted men and women of the past and present.

"Interpretation is a social process. The best results can be achieved only by the cooperation of many minds. The results of scholars in one age are the natural and rightful heritage of those who labor in the same field in succeeding ages, and should be used by them. No interpreter of the New Testament can wisely ignore the results wrought by past generations and strike out for totally independent and original conclusions on all points. He should become familiar as far as possible with what has previously been accomplished. . .The commentaries which have been produced by the scholarship of the past form a very essential part of the materials for interpretation" (Dana 1946, 237).

"Charles H. Spurgeon. . .'It seems odd that certain men who talk so much of what the Holy Spirit reveals to them should think so little of what He revealed to others'" (Henricksen 1973, 41).

"This stress on the primacy of firsthand study does not imply that an examination of commentaries is not recommended. On the contrary, when done in the proper place, it is recognized as an indispensable step in a methodical approach. Spurgeon rightly indicates that 'two opposite errors beset the student of the Scripture: the tendency to take everything second hand from others, and the refusal to take anything from others'" (Traina 1985, 9).

For those who do not have commentaries or research tools available in their language, it is possible to fulfill this step by studying the same biblical book with other mature Christians in your area and comparing notes. Be sure to study with people from different perspectives.

Be careful to notice the commentator's theories about historical setting versus their documentation of historical circumstances, either from the Bible itself or historical sources. If one is not careful one's presuppositions about the author's purpose and setting can affect his/her interpretation. A good example of this would be the supposed background of the book of Hebrews. Chapters six and ten are very difficult. Often, an interpretation is proposed based solely on supposed historical circumstances or denominational traditions.

G. Check the Significant Parallel Passages

Notice the concentric circles (parallel passages) of interpretive significance. One of the great dangers in interpretation is allowing other parts of the Bible to determine what a particular text means, but also, at the same time, it is one of our greatest helps. It is a matter of timing. At what point do you look to the wider scope of biblical truth? There is disagreement at this point (Ferguson 1937, 101), but for me the point of focus must first be the original author and the contextual book you are studying. God inspired the biblical authors to say something to their day.

We must first understand this message fully before we relate it to other Bible passages we know. If not, we begin reading our favorite, familiar and denominational views into every passage. We allow our personal systematic theology or denomination biases to crush and replace inspired texts! Texts have priority!

These concentric circles, as I call them, move from a specific passage to the entire Bible, but only in graded, marked steps.

1. Carefully observe the logical and literary position of your passage within the biblical book. Studying an entire biblical book is crucial. We must see the whole before the significance of the parts is obvious. We must let the author speak in his setting and for his purpose. Never go beyond the particular passage and its immediate context until you have allowed it to speak with its own force. So often we want to solve all of the problems before we take seriously what is being said by a particular inspired biblical author. We often try to protect our theological bias!

2. Once we feel that we have wrestled with the text sufficiently enough to understand the basic message, then we move to the next logical step, which is the same author in his other writings. This is very helpful in twin writings, such as Ezra and Nehemiah; Mark and I and II Peter; Luke and Acts; John and I John; Colossians and Ephesians; Galatians and Romans.

3. The next concentric circle concerns different writers, but those who wrote in the same historical setting, such as Amos and Hosea or Isaiah and Micah, or Haggai and Zechariah. This concentric circle could also relate to the same type of literary genre on the same subject. An example is linking Matthew 24, Mark 13, and Luke 21 with Daniel, Zechariah, and the book of Revelation. All of these, though written by different authors, relate to the end-time and are written in an apocalyptic genre. This circle is often identified as "biblical theology." It is an attempt to allow specific sections of Scripture to relate to one another on a controlled basis. If exegesis is a bite of the pie, biblical theology is a slice. If exegesis is a solo, then biblical theology is an ensemble. We are looking for trends, themes, motifs, characteristic words, phrases, or structures of a given period, literary genre, subject, or author.

4. Since all of the Bible is inspired (II Tim. 3:16) and since our basic presupposition is that it does not contradict itself (analogy of Scripture), then we must allow the Bible to fully explain itself on a given subject. If exegesis is a bite and biblical theology is a slice, then systematic doctrine is the whole pie. If exegesis is a solo and biblical theology is an ensemble, then systematic doctrine is the full choir. Be careful, try never to say, "the Bible says. . ." until you have carefully advanced through each concentric circle of interpretation.

H. Eastern people present truth in tension-filled pairs

The Bible often presents truth in dialectical pairs. If we miss the balancing truth (paradox) we have perverted the overarching biblical message. Unbalanced presentation of truth is what characterizes modern denominations. We must allow the biblical authors to speak, but also the Bible as a whole (other inspired authors). At this stage of interpretation a relevant parallel passage, either confirming, modifying, or seemingly contradicting, is extremely helpful.

It must be emphatically stated that it is as damaging to add to the Bible's message as it is to take away from it. Bible truth is presented in clear, simple statements, but the relationship between these clear statements is often quite involved. The crowning glory of interpretation is the big picture, the balanced truth.

I.   Systematic Theology
     How does one present a doctrine systematically? It is similar to biblical theology in that we allow concepts, themes, and words to guide us to
     1.   other related passages (pro and con)
     2.   the definitive teaching passage on that subject
     3.   other elements of the same truth
     4.   the interchange of the two Testaments
     The Bible speaks truly, but not always fully in a given context on a given subject. We must find the clearest biblical presentation of a given truth. This is done by using certain research tools. Again, you should try to work with the least interpretive helps first. An exhaustive concordance of the Bible can be very helpful. It will help you to find word parallels. Often this is all we need to discover the thought or concept parallels. The concordance will show us the different biblical terms which are translated into English. Concordances are now available for the King James Version, the New American Standard Bible, and the New International Version. We need to be sure that we are not confusing English words with Hebrew or Greek synonyms. A good concordance will list the different original words and the places of their occurrence. The concentric circles (parallel passages) come into relevance again here. The order of priority will be
     1.   the immediate context of the literary unit
     2.   the larger context of the whole book
     3.   the same author
     4.   the same period, literary genre, or Testament
     5.   the entire Bible
     Systematic theology books attempt to divide Christian truth into categories and then find all the references on that subject. Often they link these together in very denominational ways. Systematic theologies are the most biased of all reference books. Never consult just one. Always use those from other theological perspectives to force yourself to rethink what you believe, why you believe it, and where you can substantiate it from Scripture.

J.   Use of Parallel Passages
     If there are only a few references for the word you are studying, read all of them and also the entire paragraph in which they occur. If there are too many references, refer to the concentric circles again by reading the references that occur in the immediate context of the literary unit and the larger context of the entire book and select several to read in the other biblical books by the same author, or the same period, literary genre, Testament, or the entire Bible. Be careful because often the same word is used in a different senses in different contexts. Be sure to keep the biblical texts separate.
     Never allow a mixture of texts from all genres in the Bible without carefully checking the context of each one! Rather try to find parallel truths (pro and con). Some examples of this follow.

1. The use of the term "heavenlies" within the book of Ephesians. At first it seems to mean "heaven when we die," but when all five uses are compared, it means "the spiritual realm coexisting with us now" (Eph. 1:3,20; 2:6; 3:10; 6:12).

2. The phrase "filling with the Spirit" is used in Eph. 5:18. This has been the focus of great controversy. The book of Colossians helps us with an exact parallel. The Colossian parallel has "let the mind of Christ richly dwell in you" (Col. 3:16).

The next source of help on locating these types of meaningful parallels is a good reference Study Bible. Like all good things, practice makes perfect. As you practice these procedures they will become easier. This is also true of research tools.

At this stage I would like to share with you a practical way to use a type of research tool that most believers do not ever use—systematic theology books. These books are usually extensively indexed by both text and topic. Check the index for your text. Write down the page numbers. Notice what "theological category" they are in. Look at the page and find your text. Read the paragraph; if it is helpful and thought provoking read the page (the whole section).

Check the index for your text. Write down the page numbers. Notice what "theological category" they are in. Look at the page and find your text. Read the paragraph if it is helpful and thought-provoking, read the page (the whole section). Find out how your context fits into the whole of Christian theology. It may be the only text on this topic or one of several. It may be the dialectical paradox to another doctrine. These books can be a great help in seeing the big picture if they are used critically and in concert with several authors, denominations, systematic theologies! A complete listing of the better ones is found at the conclusion of this Textbook (IX p. 105). These books are not for light, devotional reading, but they are so helpful in checking your formulation of the big picture.

A note of caution should be given here.

These books are very interpretive. Whenever we put our theology into a structure it becomes biased and presuppositional. This is unavoidable. Therefore, do not consult only one author, but several (this is also true of commentaries). Read systematic theologies from authors with whom you disagree or who are from other denominational backgrounds. Look at their evidence and ponder their logic. Growth comes with struggle. Force them to show you from the Bible what they are saying:

1. context (immediate and larger)
2. syntax (grammatical structure)
3. etymology and current usage (word study)
4. parallel passages (concentric circles)
5. history and culture of the original setting

God has spoken through Israel, Jesus, and the Apostles, and in a lesser way, He continues to illumine the church to understand the Scriptures (Silva 1987, 21). The believing community is a guard against wild, radical interpretations. Read the gifted men and women of the past and present. Do not believe all they write, but listen to them through your own Spirit-led filter. We are all historically conditioned.

III. Proposed Order for the Use of Research Tools

Throughout this Textbook you have been encouraged to do your own analysis, but there comes a point beyond which none of us can go personally. We cannot be scholarly specialists in all areas. We must find capable, godly, gifted researchers to help us. This does not mean to imply that we do not critique them and their findings. There are so many research tools available today in the English language that the wealth of these tools can be overwhelming. Here is a proposed order. After you have done all of the preliminary observations of the passage yourself then supplement your information with the following (use different colored ink for your notes and for those from the helps in each area).

A. Start with the historical background
    1. Bible introductions
    2. articles in Bible encyclopedias, handbooks, or dictionaries
    3. opening chapters of commentaries
B. Use several types of commentaries
    1. short commentaries
    2. technical commentaries
    3. devotional commentaries
C. Use supplementary specialized reference materials
    1. word study books
    2. cultural background books
    3. geographically-oriented books
    4. archaeology books
    5. apologetics books
D. Finally, try to get the big picture

Remember that we receive truth in increments; do not take shortcuts in your study—do not expect instantaneous results—stay with the program. Expect tension and disagreement in interpretation. Remember that interpretation is a Spirit-led task as well as a logical process.

Read the Bible analytically and research tools critically. Practice makes perfect.

Start now. Make a commitment of at least thirty minutes a day, find a quiet place and set aside a time, choose a small New Testament book first, assemble several Bible translations and Study Bibles, get paper and pencil, pray, start.

SAMPLE CATEGORIES FOR NOTE TAKING

The first suggestion is the use of a written work sheet or form. This will help you to record certain types of information as you read through the biblical book. If you take your personal observation notes

in one color of ink, then use other colors for insight from different research tools. The following worksheet is tentative, but it is one which is helpful to me. You may want to develop your own order and headings. The following worksheet is merely a listing of categories of information which may be helpful in interpretation. You will need to leave more space between items on your worksheet. The enclosed sample form is primarily for topics and their relation to the four cycles of readings. Included at the end of this Textbook is a sample of the book of Romans., chapters 1-3 (literary unit) and the book of Titus (book summary).

NOTE TAKING

I. Reading Cycles

A. First reading

1. The overarching theme or purpose of the whole book is: (brief description)

2. This theme is exemplified in (choose one)
   a. Verse

   b. Paragraph

   c. Chapter

3. The type of literary genre is

B. Second reading

1. The major literary units or content divisions are
   a.

   b.

   c.

   Etc.

2. Summarize the subject (in a declarative sentence) of each major division and note their relationship to each other (chronological, logical, theological, etc.)

3. List the places you checked your outline

C. Third reading

1. Internal information concerning the historical setting (give chapter and verse)
    a. Author of the book
        (1)
        (2)
        (3)
    b. Date of its writing or date of event
        (1)
        (2)
        (3)
    c. Recipients of the book
        (1)
        (2)
        (3)
    d. Occasion of the writing

2. Fill in your working content outline by adding the paragraph divisions. Compare translations from the different translation theory groups, especially from the literal and idiomatic (dynamic equivalent). Then write out your own outline.

3. Summarize each paragraph in a declarative sentence.

4. List possible application points with each major division and/or paragraphs.

D. Fourth reading

1. Make note of significant parallel passages (both positive and negative). Observe these concentric circles of significance.
    a. Same book or literary units
    b. Same author
    c. Same period, subject or literary genre
    d. Same Testament
    e. Entire Bible

2. Check systematic theology books.

3. Develop specialized lists in order to discern structure.
   a. List the major and minor characters.

   b. List key terms (theological, recurrent or unusual terms)

   c. List major events

   d. List geographical movements

4. Make note of difficult passages.
   a. Textual problems
      (1) from margin of your English Bible

      (2) from comparing English translations

   b. Historical problems and uniqueness

   c. Theological problems of uniqueness

   d. Those verses that cause you confusion

E. **Application truths**

   1. Write your detailed outline on the left side of a sheet.

   2. On the right side write down (in pencil) possible application truths for the major literary units and/or the paragraphs.

F. **Use of Research Tools**

   1. Read research tools in appropriate order. Take notes on a "work sheet."

      Look for
      a. points of agreement
      b. points of disagreement
      c. new thoughts or applications
      d. record possible interpretations on difficult passages

   2. Analyze insights from research tools and develop a final detailed outline with application points. This master outline should help you to discern the original author's structure and purpose.

       a.   Do not major on minors.

       b.   Do not forget the context.

       c.   Do not read into the text more than, or less than, the original author intended.

       d.   Application points should be done on three levels:
           (1)   theme of the whole book—first reading
           (2)   major literary units—second reading
           (3)   paragraphs—third reading

       e.   Allow parallel passages to confirm and clarify your interpretation as the final step. This allows the Bible to interpret itself. However, doing it last safeguards us from allowing our overall systematic theological understanding of the Bible from silencing, ignoring, or skewing difficult passages.

II. Exegetical Procedures

  A. The Text (minimum one paragraph in English)

      1.   Establish the original text (note any manuscript variants)

      2.   Translation options
          a.   Word for word (KJV, ASV, NASB, RSV, NRSV)
          b.   Dynamic equivalent (NIV, NEB, Jerusalem Bible, Williams, TEV)
          c.   Other ancient translations (LXX, Vulgate, Peshitta, etc.)
          d.   No paraphrase translations (i.e., commentaries) at this stage

      3.   Check any significant variables in the translations and why
          a.   Greek manuscript problem(s)
          b.   Difficult word(s)
          c.   Unique construction(s)
          d.   Theological truth(s)

  B. Exegetical items to be checked
      1.   Note immediate contextual unit (how is your paragraph related to the literary unit and how is it related to the surrounding paragraphs)

      2.   Note possible structural elements
          a.   Parallel structures
          b.   Quotes/Allusions
          c.   Figures of speech
          d.   Illustrations
          e.   Poem/Hymn/Song

3. Note grammatical elements (syntax)
    a. VERBS or VERBALS (TENSE, VOICE, MOOD, NUMBER, GENDER)
    b. Special construction (CONDITIONAL SENTENCES, prohibitions, etc.)
        c. Word or clause order

4. Note key words
    a. Give full semantical field
    b. Which meaning(s) fit the context best
    c. Be careful of set theological definitions

5. Note significant biblical parallels of words, topics or quotes
    a. Same context
    b. Same book
    c. Same author
    d. Same genre
    e. Same period
    f. Entire Bible

C. Historical Summary
    1. How the specific occasion of the writing effects the truth statements.

    2. How the cultural milieu effects the truth statements.

    3. How recipients effect the truth statements.

D. Theological Summary
    1. Theological truths
        a. State clearly the author's theological assertion:
            (1) Special terminology
            (2) Significant clause or phrase
            (3) Central truth of sentence(s) or paragraph(s)
        b. How does this relate to the subject or truth of the literary unit?
        c. How does this relate to the subject or truth of the entire book?
        d. How does this relate to the subject or truth as revealed in Scripture?

    2. Special points of interest
    3. Personal insights
    4. Insights from commentaries

E. Application Truths
    1. Application truth of literary unit
    2. Application truth(s) of paragraph(s) level
    3. Application truth of theological elements within the text

III. Basic Procedures for an Academic NT Word Study

A. Establish the basic meaning and semantic field
Use *A Greek-English Lexicon* by Bauer, Arndt, Gingrich, Danker

B. Establish the contemporary usage (Koine Greek)
1. *Use The Vocabulary of the Greek Testament* Moulton, Milligan for Egyptian papyri
2. Use the Septuagint and Redpath's *Concordance of the LXX for Palestinian Judaism*

C. Establish the semantic domain
Use *Greek-English Lexicon of the New Testament* by Louw, Nida or *Expository Dictionary of New Testament Words* by Vine

D. Establish the Hebrew background
Use *Strong's Concordance* with its numbers linked to the Hebrew and English Lexicon of the Old Testament by Brown, Driver, Briggs; *New International Dictionary of Old Testament Theology and Exegesis*, edited by Van Gemneren (5 vols.) or *Synonyms of the Old Testament* by Girdlestone

E. Establish the grammatical form of the word in context
Use an interlinear Greek-English New Testament and an analytical lexicon or *Analytical Greek New Testament* by Timothy and Barbara Friberg

F. Check the frequency of usage by genre, authors, subject, etc.
Use a concordance.

G. Check your study with
– a Bible encyclopedia
– use Zondervan's *Pictorial Bible Encyclopedia* (5 vols) or
– *The International Bible Encyclopedia* (5 vols)

– a Bible Dictionary
– use *Anchor Bible Dictionary* or *Interpreter's Bible Dictionary*

– a theological word book
– use *The New International Dictionary of New Testament Theology* (3 vols) edited by
    Colin Brown, or
– *Theological Dictionary of the New Testament* (abridged) by Bromiley

– a systematic theological book
– use *Systematic Theology* by Berkhof;
– *A Theology of the New Testament* by Ladd; *New Testament Theology* by Stagg;

H. Write out summary of significant interpretive findings

IV. A Brief Summary of Hermeneutical Principles

A. Always pray first. The Spirit is essential. God wants you to understand.

B. Establish the Original Text
1. Check the notes in the margin of your Study Bible for Greek manuscript variants.
2. Do not build a doctrine on a disputed text, look for a clear parallel passage.

C. Understanding the Text
1. Read the entire context (literary context is crucial). Check the outline in a Study Bible or commentary to determine the literary unit.
2. Never try to interpret less than a paragraph. Try to outline the main truths of the paragraphs in the literary unit. This way we can follow the original author's thoughts and their development.
3. Red the paragraph in several translations which use different translation theories.
4. Consult good commentaries and other Bible study aids only after you have studied the text first (remember the Bible, the Spirit, and you are priority in biblical interpretation).

D. Understanding the Words
1. The NT writers were Hebrew thinkers, writing in Koine (street) Greek.
2. We must find the contemporary meaning and connotations, not modern English definitions (see the Septuagint and Egyptian papyri).
3. Words have meaning only in sentences. Sentences have meaning only in paragraphs. Paragraphs have meaning only in literary units. Check the semantic field (i.e., various meanings of words).

E. Use Parallel Passages
1. The Bible is the best interpreter of the Bible. It has only one author, the Holy Spirit.
2. Look for the clearest teaching text on the truth of your paragraph (reference Bible or concordance).
3. Look for the paradoxical truths (tension-filled pairs of eastern literature).

F. Application
1. You cannot apply the Bible to your day until you understand what the inspired author was saying to his/her day (historical context is crucial).
2. Be careful of personal biases, theological systems, or agendas. Let the Bible speak for itself!
3. Be careful of principlizing every verse. Not all texts have universal relevance. Not all texts apply to modern individuals.
4. Respond immediately to new truth or insight. Bible knowledge is meant to produce daily Christlikeness and kingdom service.

A SELECTED LIST OF RECOMMENDED RESEARCH TOOLS
BY CATEGORY

I. The Bible

    A. Understanding the process of translating.
1. *Translating the Word of God* J. Beekman and J. Callow,
2. *God's Word in Man's Language* Eugene Nida, (William Carey, N.D.)
3. *So Many Versions* Sakae Kubo and Walter Specht, (Zondervan, 1983)
4. *The Book and the Parchments* F. F. Bruce, (Revell, 1963)

    B. History of the English Bible
1. *The English Bible: A History of Translations From the Earliest Versions to the New English* Bible F. F. Bruce, (Oxford, 1970)
2. *The Ancestry of Our English Bible* Ira Maurice Price, (Harper, 1956)

II. How to do Research

    A. How To Use New Testament Greek Study Aids Walter J. Clark, (Loizeaux Brothers, 1983)

    B. Multipurpose Tools for Bible Study F.W. Danker, (Concordia, 1970)

    C. A Bibliographic Guide to New Testament Research R.T. France, (JSOT Press, 1979)

    D. A Basic Bibliographic Guide for New Testament Exegesis W. Scholer, (Eerdmans, 1973)

III. Hermeneutics

    A. *How to Study the Bible* James Braga, (Multnomah, 1982)

    B. *How to Read the Bible for All Its Worth* Gordon Fee, Douglas Stuart, (Zondervan, 1982)

    C. *How to Interpret the Bible for Yourself* Richard Mayhue, (Moody, 1986)

    D. *Understanding and Applying the Bible* J. Robertson McQuilkin, (Moody, 1983)

    E. *Interpreting the Bible* A. Berkeley Mickelsen, (Eerdmans, 1963

    F. *Rediscovering Expository Preaching* John MacArthur, Jr., (Word, 1992)

    G. *Biblical Hermeneutics* Bruce Corley, Steve Lemke, and Grant Lovejoy, (Broadman & Holman, 1996)

    H. *A Basic Guide to Interpreting the Bible* Robert Stein,

IV. Basic Introductions to Biblical Books

A. Old Testament
1. *Introduction to the Old Testament* R. K. Harrison, (Eerdmans, 1969)
2. *Old Testament Survey* William Sanford LaSor, David Allen Hubbard and Frederic Wm. Bush, (Eerdmans, 1982)
3. *An Introduction to the Old Testament* Edward J. Young, (Eerdmans, 1949)
4. *Encountering the Old Testament* T. Arnold and Bryan E. Beyer, (Baker, 1998)
5. *The Old Testament: Its Background, Growth and Context* Peter C. Craigie, (Abingdon,1990)

B. New Testament
1. *New Testament Introduction* Donald Guthrie, (IVP, 1970)
2. *The New Testament: Its Background, Growth and* Content Bruce M. Metzger, (Abingdon, 1965)
3. *An Introduction to the New Testament* D. A. Carson, Douglas J. Moo, and Leon Morris, (Zondervan 1992)
4. *Encountering the New Testament* Walter A. Elwell and Robert W. Yarbrough, (Baker 1998)
5. *A Survey of the New Testament* Robert H. Gundry, (Zondervan, 1994)

V. Bible Encyclopedias and Dictionaries (multi-volume)

A. *The Zondervan Pictorial Bible Encyclopedia* 5 vols. Ed. M. Tenney, (Zondervan, 1976)

B. *The Interpreter's Dictionary of the Bible and Supplement* ed. G. A. Buttrick, 5 vols. (Abingdon, 1962-1977)

C. *The International Standard Bible Encyclopedia* ed. Geoffrey W. Bromiley, 5 vols., rev. ed. (Eerdmans, 1979-1987)

D. *Dictionary of Jesus and the Gospels* ed. Joel B. Green, Scot McKnight and J. Howard Marshall, (IVP, 1992)

E. *Dictionary of Paul and His Letters* Gerald F. Hawthorne, Ralph P. Martin and Daniel G. Reid editors, (IVP, 1993)

F. *The Anchor Bible Dictionary* ed. David Noel Freedman, 6 vols. (Doubleday, 1992)

VI. Commentary Sets

A. Old Testament
1. *The Tyndale Old Testament Commentaries* ed. D. J. Wiseman, (InterVarsity, 1970)
2. *A Study Guide Commentary Series* (Zondervan, 1977)
3. *The New International Commentary* ed. R. K. Harrison, (Eerdmans, 1976)
4. *The Expositor's Bible Commentary* ed. Frank E. Gaebelein, (Zondervan, 1958)
5. *www.freebiblecommentary.org* Bob Utley

B. New Testament
1. *The Tyndale New Testament Commentaries* ed. R. V. G. Tasker, (Eerdmans, 1959)
2. *A Study Guide Commentary Series* (Zondervan, 1977)
3. *The Expositor's Bible Commentary* Frank E. Gaebelein, (Zondervan, 1958)
4. *The New International Commentary* (Eerdmans, 1976)
5. *www.freebiblecommentary.org* Bob Utley

VII. Word Studies

A. Old Testament
1. *Synonyms of the Old Testament* Robert B. Girdlestone, (Eerdmans, 1897)
2. *Dictionary of Old Testament Words* Aaron Pick, (Kregel, 1977)
3. *Theological Wordbook of the Old Testament* R. Laird Harris, Gleason L. Archer, Jr. and Bruce K. Waltke, (Moody, 1980)
4. *Dictionary of Old Testament Theology and Exegesis* William A. Van Gemeren, ed., 5 vols. (Zondervan, 1997)

B. New Testament
1. *Word Pictures in the New Testament* A. T. Robertson, (Broadman, 1930)
2. *Word Studies in the New Testament* M. R. Vincent, (MacDonald, 1888)
3. *Vine's Expository Dictionary of New Testament Words* W. E. Vine, (Revell, 1968)
4. *A New Testament Wordbook* William Barclay, (SCM, 1955)
5. *More New Testament Words* William Barclay, (Harper, 1958)
6. *The New Dictionary of New Testament Theology* C. Brown, et. al., 5 vols. (Zondervan, 1975-1979)

C. Theological
1. *A Theological Word Book of the Bible* ed. Alan Richardson, (MacMillan, 1950)
2. *Baker's Dictionary of Theology* ed. Everett F. Harrison, (Baker, 1975)

VIII. Cultural setting

A. Customs
1. *Light From the Ancient East* Adolf Deissman, (Baker, 1978)
2. *Ancient Israel* Roland de Vaux, 2 vols. (McGraw-Hill, 1961)
3. *Manners and Customs of the Bible* James M. Freeman, (Logos, 1972)
4. *Manners and Customs of Bible Lands* Fred H. Wright, (Moody, 1953)
5. *Light From the Ancient Past* Jack Finegan, 2 vols. (Princeton University Press, 1974)
6. *Manners and Customs in the Bible* Victor H. Matthews, (Hendrickson, 1988)

B. Histories
1. *A History of Israel* John Bright, (Westminster, 1981)
2. *Peoples of Old Testament Times* ed. D. J. Wiseman, (Oxford, 1973)
3. *The Cambridge History of the Bible* ed. P. R. Ackroyd and C. F. Evans, vol. 1 (Cambridge, 1970)

C. New Testament
1. *Light From the Ancient East* Adolf Deissmann, (Baker, 1978)
2. *New Testament History* F. F. Bruce, (Doubleday, 1969)
3. *Harper's World of the New Testament* Edwin M. Yamauchi, (Harper and Row, 1981)
4. *The Life and Times of Jesus the Messiah* Alfred Edersheim, (Eerdmans, 1971)
5. *Roman Society and Roman Law in the New Testament* A. N. Sherwin-White, (Oxford, 1963)
6. *The Christ of the Gospels* J. W. Shepard, (Eerdmans, 1939)

D. Archaeology
1. *Light From the Ancient Past* Jack Finegan, 2 vols. (Princeton University Press, 1946)
2. *Archaeology of Bible Lands* H. T. Vos, (Moody, 1977)
3. *The Stones and the Scriptures* Edwin M. Yamauchi, (Holman, 1972)
4. *Ancient Orient and the Old Testament* K. A. Kitchen, (InterVarsity Press, 1966)
5. *Ancient Israelite Literature in Its Cultural Context* John H. Walton, (Zondervan, 1989)

E. Geography
1. *The Wycliffe Historical Geography of Bible Lands* C. F. Pfeiffer and H. F. Vos, (Moody, 1967)
2. *The Moody Atlas of Bible Lands* Barry J. Beitzel, (Moody, 1985)
3. *Holman Bible Atlas* ed. Thomas V. Brisco (Broadman and Holman, 1998)

IX. Theologies

A. Old Testament
1. *The Theology of the Old Testament* A. B. Davidson, (Clark, 1904)
2. *Theology of the Old Testament* Edmond Jacob, (Harper & Row, 1958)
3. *Toward an Old Testament Theology* Walter C. Kaiser, (Zondervan, 1978)
4. *Old Testament Theology* Paul R. House, (IVP, 1998)

B. New Testament
1. *New Testament Theology* Donald Guthrie, (InterVarsity, 1981)
2. *A Theology of the New Testament* George Eldon Ladd, (Eerdmans, 1974)
3. *New Testament Theology* Frank Stagg, (Broadman, 1962)
4. *Essentials of Evangelical Theology* Donald G. Bloesch, vol. 2 (Harper & Row, 1978)

C. Entire Bible
1. *Biblical Theology* Geerhardus Vos, (Eerdmans, 1948)
2. *Systematic Theology* L. Berkhof, (Eerdmans, 1939)
3. *Christian Theology* H. Orton Wiley, (Beacon Hill Press, 1940)
4. *Christian Theology* Millard J. Erickson, 2nd ed. (Baker, 1998)

D. Doctrine—historically developed
1. *The History of Christian Doctrines* L. Berkhof, (Baker, 1975)
2. *A History of Christian Thought* Justo L. Gonzales, vol. 1 (Abingdon, 1970)

X. Apologetics

A. *Christian Apologetics* Norman Geisler, (Baker, 1976)

B. *Varieties of Christian Apologetics* Bernard Ramm, (Baker, 1962)

C. *Your God Is Too Small* J. B. Phillips, (MacMillan, 1953)

D. *Mere Christianity* C. S. Lewis, (MacMillan, 1978)

E. *History, Criticism and Faith* ed. Colin Brown, (InterVarsity, 1976)

F. *Answers to Questions* F. F. Bruce, (Zondervan, 1972)

G. *Hard Sayings of the Bible* Walter C. Kaiser Jr., Peter H. Davids, F. F. Bruce and Manfred T. Brauch, (IVP, 1996)

XI. Bible difficulties

A. *Questions and Answers* F. F. Bruce,

B. *Encyclopedia of Bible Difficulties* Gleason L. Archer, (Zondervan, 1982)

C. *When Critics Ask* Norman Geisler and Thomas Howe, (Victor, 1992)

D. *Hard Sayings of the Bible* (IVP, 1996) and More Hard Sayings of the Bible Walter C., Kaiser, Jr., Peter H. Davids, F. F. Bruce and Manfred F. Baruch,

XII. Textual Criticism

A. *The Text of the New Testament, Its Transmission, Corruption and Restoration*   Bruce M. Metzger, (Oxford, 1964)

B. *Introduction to New Testament Textual Criticism*   J. Harold Greenlee, (Eerdmans, 1964)

C. *A Textual Commentary on the Greek New Testament*   Bruce M. Metzger, (United Bible Societies.)

XIII. Lexicons

A. Old Testament (Hebrew)
   1.   *Hebrew and English Lexicon*   Francis Brown, S. R. Driver, and Charles A. Briggs, (Clarendon Press, 1951)
   2.   *Index to Brown, Driver and Briggs Hebrew Lexicon*   Bruce Einspahr,
   3.   *Analytical Hebrew and Chaldee Lexicon*   Benjamin Davidson, (MacDonald)
   4.   *The Hebrew and Aramaic Lexicon of the Old Testament*   Ludwig Koehler and Walter Baumgartner, 2 vols.

B. New Testament (Greek)
   1.   *A Greek-English Lexicon*   Walter Bauer, William F. Arndt, F. Wilbur Gingrich and Frederick W. Danker (University of Chicago Press, 1979
   2.   *Greek-English Lexicon*   Johannes P. Louw and Eugene A. Nida, eds., 2 vols. (United Bible Societies, 1989)
   3.   *The Vocabulary of the Greek Testament*   James Hope Moulton and George Milligan, (Eerdmans, 1974)
   4.   *The Analytical Lexicon to the Greek New Testament*   William D. Mounce, (Zondervan, 1993)

XIV. Available web sites to buy out of print, used, and discounted books

A. www.Christianbooks.com
B. www.Half.com
C. www.Overstock.com
D. www.Alibris.com
E. www.Amazon.com
F. www.BakerBooksRetain.com
G. www.ChristianUsedBooks.net

A GUIDE TO GOOD BIBLE READING:
A PERSONAL SEARCH FOR VERIFIABLE TRUTH

Can we know truth? Where is it found? Can we logically verify it? Is there an ultimate authority? Are there absolutes which can guide our lives, our world? Is there meaning to life? Why are we here? Where are we going? These questions—questions that all rational people contemplate—have haunted the human intellect since the beginning of time (Eccl. 1:13-18; 3:9-11). I can remember my personal search for an integrating center for my life. I became a believer in Christ at a young age, based primarily on the witness of significant others in my family. As I grew to adulthood, questions about myself and my world also grew. Simple cultural and religious clichés did not bring meaning to the experiences I read about or encountered. It was a time of confusion, searching, longing, and often a feeling of hopelessness in the face of the insensitive, hard world in which I lived.

Many claimed to have answers to these ultimate questions, but after research and reflection I found that their answers were based upon (1) personal philosophies, (2) ancient myths, (3) personal experiences, or (4) psychological projections. I needed some degree of verification, some evidence, some rationality on which to base my world-view, my integrating center, my reason to live.

I found these in my study of the Bible. I began to search for evidence of its trustworthiness, which I found in (1) the historical reliability of the Bible as confirmed by archaeology, (2) the accuracy of the prophecies of the Old Testament, (3) the unity of the Bible message over the sixteen hundred years of its production, and (4) the personal testimonies of people whose lives had been permanently changed by contact with the Bible. Christianity, as a unified system of faith and belief, has the ability to deal with complex questions of human life. Not only did this provide a rational framework, but the experiential aspect of biblical faith brought me emotional joy and stability.

I thought that I had found the integrating center for my life—Christ, as understood through the Scriptures. It was a heady experience, an emotional release. However, I can still remember the shock and pain when it began to dawn on me how many different interpretations of this book were advocated, sometimes even within the same churches and schools of thought. Affirming the inspiration and trustworthiness of the Bible was not the end, but only the beginning. How do I verify or reject the varied and conflicting interpretations of the many difficult passages in Scripture by those who were claiming its authority and trustworthiness?

This task became my life's goal and pilgrimage of faith. I knew that my faith in Christ had (1) brought me great peace and joy. My mind longed for some absolutes in the midst of the relativity of my culture (post-modernity); (2) the dogmatism of conflicting religious systems (world religions); and (3) denominational arrogance. In my search for valid approaches to the interpretation of ancient literature, I was surprised to discover my own historical, cultural, denominational and experiential biases. I had often read the Bible simply to reinforce my own views. I used it as a source of dogma to attack others while reaffirming my own insecurities and inadequacies. How painful this realization was to me!

Although I can never be totally objective, I can become a better reader of the Bible. I can limit my biases by identifying them and acknowledging their presence. I am not yet free of them, but I have confronted my own weaknesses. The interpreter is often the worst enemy of good Bible reading!

Let me list some of the presuppositions I bring to my study of the Bible so that you, the reader, may examine them along with me:

I. Presuppositions

A. I believe the Bible is the sole inspired self-revelation of the one true God. Therefore, it must be interpreted in light of the intent of the original divine author (the Spirit) through a human writer in a specific historical setting.

B. I believe the Bible was written for the common person—for all people! God accommodated Himself to speak to us clearly within a historical and cultural context. God does not hide truth—He wants us to understand! Therefore, it must be interpreted in light of its day, not ours. The Bible should not mean to us what it never meant to those who first read or heard it. It is understandable by the average human mind and uses normal human communication forms and techniques.

C. I believe the Bible has a unified message and purpose. It does not contradict itself, though it does contain difficult and paradoxical passages. Thus, the best interpreter of the Bible is the Bible itself.

D. I believe that every passage (excluding prophesies) has one and only one meaning based on the intent of the original, inspired author. Although we can never be absolutely certain we know the original author's intent, many indicators point in its direction:
    1. the genre (literary type) chosen to express the message
    2. the historical setting and/or specific occasion that elicited the writing
    3. the literary context of the entire book as well as each literary unit
    4. the textual design (outline) of the literary units as they relate to the whole message
    5. the specific grammatical features employed to communicate the message
    6. the words chosen to present the message
    7. parallel passages

The study of each of these areas becomes the object of our study of a passage. Before I explain my methodology for good Bible reading, let me delineate some of the inappropriate methods being used today that have caused so much diversity of interpretation, and that consequently should be avoided:

II. Inappropriate Methods

A. Ignoring the literary context of the books of the Bible and using every sentence, clause, or even individual words as statements of truth unrelated to the author's intent or the larger context. This is often called "proof-texting."

B. Ignoring the historical setting of the books by substituting a supposed historical setting that has little or no support from the text itself.

C. Ignoring the historical setting of the books and reading it as the morning hometown newspaper written primarily to modern individual Christians.

D. Ignoring the historical setting of the books by allegorizing the text into a philosophical/theological message totally unrelated to the first hearers and the original author's intent.

E. Ignoring the original message by substituting one's own system of theology, pet doctrine, or contemporary issue unrelated to the original author's purpose and stated message. This phenomenon often follows the initial reading of the Bible as a means of establishing a speaker's authority. This is often referred to as "reader response" ("what-the-text-means-to-me" interpretation).

At least three related components may be found in all written human communication:

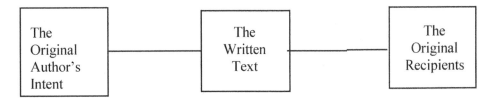

In the past, different reading techniques have focused on one of the three components. But to truly affirm the unique inspiration of the Bible, a modified diagram is more appropriate:

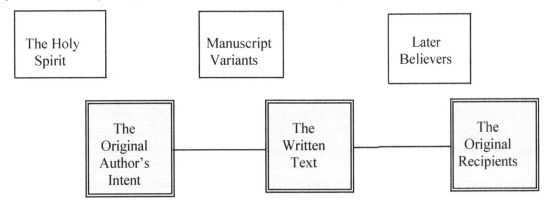

In truth all three components must be included in the interpretive process. For the purpose of verification, my interpretation focuses on the first two components: the original author and the text. I am probably reacting to the abuses I have observed (1) allegorizing or spiritualizing texts and (2) "reader response" interpretation (what-it-means-to-me). Abuse may occur at each stage. We must always check our motives, biases, techniques, and applications. But how do we check them if there are no boundaries to interpretations, no limits, no criteria? This is where authorial intent and textual structure provide me with some criteria for limiting the scope of possible valid interpretations.

In light of these inappropriate reading techniques, what are some possible approaches to good Bible reading and interpretation which offer a degree of verification and consistency?

III. Possible Approaches to Good Bible Reading

At this point I am not discussing the unique techniques of interpreting specific genres but general hermeneutical principles valid for all types of biblical texts. A good book for genre-specific approaches is *How To Read The Bible For All Its Worth*, by Gordon Fee and Douglas Stuart, published by Zondervan.

My methodology focuses initially on the reader allowing the Holy Spirit to illumine the Bible through four personal reading cycles. This makes the Spirit, the text and the reader primary, not secondary. This also protects the reader from being unduly influenced by commentators. I have heard it said: "The Bible throws a lot of light on commentaries." This is not meant to be a depreciating comment about study aids, but rather a plea for an appropriate timing for their use.

We must be able to support our interpretations from the text itself. Three areas provide at least limited verification:
1. the original author's
    a.   historical setting
    b.   literary context
2. the original author's choice of
    a.   grammatical structures (syntax)
    b.   contemporary work usage
    c.   genre
3. our understanding of appropriate
    a.   relevant parallel passages
    b.   relationship between doctrines (paradox)

We need to be able to provide the reasons and logic behind our interpretations. The Bible is our only source for faith and practice. Sadly, Christians often disagree about what it teaches or affirms. It is self-defeating to claim inspiration for the Bible and then for believers not to be able to agree on what it teaches and requires!

The four reading cycles are designed to provide the following interpretive insights:

A. The first reading cycle
1.   Read the book in a single sitting. Read it again in a different translation, hopefully from different translation theory
    a.   word-for-word (NKJV, NASB, NRSV)
    b.   dynamic equivalent (TEV, JB)
    c.   paraphrase (Living Bible, Amplified Bible)
2.   Look for the central purpose of the entire writing. Identify its theme.
3.   Isolate (if possible) a literary unit, a chapter, a paragraph or a sentence which clearly expresses this central purpose or theme.

4. Identify the predominant literary genre
   a. Old Testament
      (1) Hebrew narrative
      (2) Hebrew poetry (wisdom literature, psalm)
      (3) prophecy (prose, poetry)
      (4) codes

   b. New Testament
      (1) Narratives (Gospels, Acts)
      (2) Parables (Gospels)
      (3) Letters/epistles
      (4) Apocalyptic literature

B. The second reading cycle
1. Read the entire book again, seeking to identify major topics or subjects.
2. Outline the major topics and briefly state their contents in a simple statement.
3. Check your purpose statement and broad outline with study aids.

C. The third reading cycle
1. Read the entire book again, seeking to identify the historical setting and specific occasion for the writing from the Bible book itself.
2. List the historical items that are mentioned in the Bible book
   a. the author
   b. the date
   c. the recipients
   d. the specific reason for writing
   e. aspects of the cultural setting that relate to the purpose of the writing
   f. references to historical people and events
3. Expand your outline to paragraph level for that part of the biblical book you are interpreting. Always identify and outline the literary unit. This may be several chapters or paragraphs. This enables you to follow the original author's logic and textual design.
4. Check your historical setting by using study aids.

D. The fourth reading cycle
1. Read the specific literary unit again in several translations
   a. word-for-word (NKJV, NASB, NRSV)
   b. dynamic equivalent (TEV, JB)
   c paraphrase (Living Bible, Amplified Bible)
2. Look for literary or grammatical structures
   a. repeated phrases, Eph. 1:6,12,13
   b. repeated grammatical structures, Rom. 8:31
   c. contrasting concepts

3. List the following items
    a. significant terms
    b. unusual terms
    c. important grammatical structures
    d. particularly difficult words, clauses, and sentences
4. Look for relevant parallel passages
    a. look for the clearest teaching passage on your subject using
        (1) "systematic theology" books
        (2) reference Bibles
        (3) concordances
    b. Look for a possible paradoxical pair within your subject. Many biblical truths are presented in dialectical pairs; many denominational conflicts come from proof-texting half of a biblical tension. All of the Bible is inspired, and we must seek out its complete message in order to provide a Scriptural balance to our interpretation.
    c. Look for parallels within the same book, same author or same genre; the Bible is its own best interpreter because it has one author, the Spirit.
5. Use study aids to check your observations of historical setting and occasion
    a. study Bibles
    b. Bible encyclopedias, handbooks and dictionaries
    c. Bible introductions
    d. Bible commentaries (at this point in your study, allow the believing community, past and present, to aid and correct your personal study.)

IV. Application of Bible interpretation

At this point we turn to application. You have taken the time to understand the text in its original setting; now you must apply it to your life, your culture. I define biblical authority as "understanding what the original biblical author was saying to his day and applying that truth to our day."

Application must follow interpretation of the original author's intent both in time and logic. We cannot apply a Bible passage to our own day until we know what it was saying to its day! A Bible passage should not mean what it never meant!

Your detailed outline, to paragraph level (reading cycle #3), will be your guide. Application should be made at paragraph level, not word level. Words have meaning only in context; clauses have meaning only in context; sentences have meaning only in context. The only inspired person involved in the interpretive process is the original author. We only follow his lead by the illumination of the Holy Spirit. But illumination is not inspiration. To say "thus saith the Lord," we must abide by the original author's intent. Application must relate specifically to the general intent of the whole writing, the specific literary unit and paragraph level thought development.

Do not let the issues of our day interpret the Bible; let the Bible speak! This may require us to draw principles from the text. This is valid if the text supports a principle. Unfortunately, many times our principles are just that, "our" principles—not the text's principles.

In applying the Bible, it is important to remember that (except in prophecy) one and only one meaning is valid for a particular Bible text. That meaning is related to the intent of the original author as he addressed a crisis or need in his day. Many possible applications may be derived from this one meaning. The application will be based on the recipients' needs but must be related to the original author's meaning.

V. The Spiritual Aspect of Interpretation

So far I have discussed the logical and textual process involved in interpretation and application. Now let me discuss briefly the spiritual aspect of interpretation. The following checklist has been helpful for me:

A. Pray for the Spirit's help (cf. I Cor. 1:26-2:16).
B. Pray for personal forgiveness and cleansing from known sin (cf. I John 1:9).
C. Pray for a greater desire to know God (cf. Ps. 19:7-14; 42:1ff.; 119:1ff).
D. Apply any new insight immediately to your own life.
E. Remain humble and teachable.

It is so hard to keep the balance between the logical process and the spiritual leadership of the Holy Spirit. The following quotes have helped me balance the two:

A. from James W. Sire, *Scripture Twisting*, pp. 17-18:
"The illumination comes to the minds of God's people—not just to the spiritual elite. There is no guru class in biblical Christianity, no illuminati, no people through whom all proper interpretation must come. And so, while the Holy Spirit gives special gifts of wisdom, knowledge and spiritual discernment, He does not assign these gifted Christians to be the only authoritative interpreters of His Word. It is up to each of His people to learn, to judge and to discern by reference to the Bible which stands as the authority even to those to whom God has given special abilities. To summarize, the assumption I am making throughout the entire book is that the Bible is God's true revelation to all humanity, that it is our ultimate authority on all matters about which it speaks, that it is not a total mystery but can be adequately understood by ordinary people in every culture."

B. on Kierkegaard, found in Bernard Ramm, *Protestant Biblical Interpretation*, p. 75:
According to Kierkegaard the grammatical, lexical, and historical study of the Bible was necessary but preliminary to the true reading of the Bible. "To read the Bible as God's word one must read it with his heart in his mouth, on tip-toe, with eager expectancy, in conversation with God. To read the Bible thoughtlessly or carelessly or academically or professionally is not to read the Bible as God's Word. As one reads it as a love letter is read, then one reads it as the Word of God."

C. H. H. Rowley in *The Relevance of the Bible*, p. 19:
"No merely intellectual understanding of the Bible, however complete, can possess all its treasures. It does not despise such understanding, for it is essential to a complete understanding. But it must lead to a spiritual understanding of the spiritual treasures of this book if it is to be complete. And for that spiritual understanding something more than intellectual alertness is necessary. Spiritual things are spiritually discerned, and the Bible student needs an attitude of spiritual receptivity, an eagerness to find God that he may yield himself to Him, if he is to pass beyond his scientific study unto the richer inheritance of this greatest of all books."

VI. This Commentary's Method

The *Study Guide Commentary* is designed to aid your interpretive procedures in the following ways:

A. A brief historical outline introduces each book. After you have done "reading cycle #3" check this information.

B. Contextual insights are found at the beginning of each chapter. This will help you see how the literary unit is structured.

C. At the beginning of each chapter or major literary unit the paragraph divisions and their descriptive captions are provided from several modern translations:
1. *The United Bible Society Greek Text*, fourth edition revised(UBS[4])
2. *The New American Standard Bible*, 1995 Update (NASB)
3. *The New King James Version* (NKJV)
4. *The New Revised Standard Version* (NRSV)
5. *Today's English Version* (TEV)
6. *The Jerusalem Bible* (JB)

Paragraph divisions are not inspired. They must be ascertained from the context. By comparing several modern translations from differing translation theories and theological perspectives, we are able to analyze the supposed structure of the original author's thought. Each paragraph has one major truth. This has been called "the topic sentence" or "the central idea of the text." This unifying thought is the key to proper historical, grammatical interpretation. One should never interpret, preach or teach on less than a paragraph! Also remember that each paragraph is related to its surrounding paragraphs. This is why a paragraph level outline of the entire book is so important. We must be able to follow the logical flow of the subject being addressed by the original inspired author.

D. Bob's notes follow a verse-by-verse approach to interpretation. This forces us to follow the original author's thought. The notes provide information from several areas:
1.   literary context
2.   historical, cultural insights
3.   grammatical information
4.   word studies
5.   relevant parallel passages

E. At certain points in the commentary, the printed text of the New American Standard Version (1995 update) will be supplemented by the translations of several other modern versions:

1.   *The New King James Version* (NKJV), which follows the textual manuscripts of the "Textus Receptus."
2.   *The New Revised Standard Version* (NRSV), which is a word-for-word revision from the National Council of Churches of the Revised Standard Version.
3.   *The Today's English Version* (TEV), which is a dynamic equivalent translation from the American Bible Society.
4.   *The Jerusalem Bible* (JB), which is an English translation based on a French Catholic dynamic equivalent translation.

F. For those who do not read Greek, comparing English translations can help in identifying problems in the text:
1.   manuscript variations
2.   alternate word meanings
3.   grammatically difficult texts and structure
4.   ambiguous texts

Although the English translations cannot solve these problems, they do target them as places for deeper and more thorough study.

G. At the close of each chapter relevant discussion questions are provided which attempt to target the major interpretive issues of that chapter.

BRIEF DEFINITIONS OF HEBREW VERBAL FORMS WHICH IMPACT EXEGESIS

I. Brief Historical Development of Hebrew

Hebrew is part of the Shemitic (Semitic) family of southwest Asian language. The name (given by modern scholars) comes from Noah's son, Shem (cf. Gen. 5:32; 6:10). Shem's descendants are listed in Gen. 10:21-31 as Arabs, Hebrews, Syrians, Arameans, and Assyrians. In reality some Semitic languages are used by nations listed in Ham's line (cf. Gen. 10:6-14), Canaan, Phoenicia, and Ethiopia.

Hebrew is part of the northwest group of these Semitic languages. Modern scholars have samples of this ancient language group from:
A. Amorite (*Mari Tablets* from 18th century B.C. in Akkadian)
B. Canaanite (*Ras Shamra Tablets* from 15th century in Ugaritic)
C. Canaanite (*Amarna Letters* from 14th century in Canaanite Akkadian) D. Phoenician (Hebrew uses Phoenician alphabet)
E. Moabite (Mesha stone, 840 B.C.)
F. Aramaic (official language of the Persian Empire used in Gen. 31:47 [2 words]; Jer. 10:11; Dan. 2:4-6; 7:28; Ezra 4:8-6:18; 7:12-26 and spoken by Jews in the first century in Palestine)

The Hebrew language is called "the lip of Canaan" in Isa. 19:18. It was first called "Hebrew" in the prologue of Ecclesiasticus (Wisdom of Ben Sirah) about 180 B.C. (and some other early places, cf. *Anchor Bible Dictionary*, vol. 4, pp. 205ff). It is most closely related to Moabite and the language used at Ugarit.

Examples of ancient Hebrew found outside the Bible are:
1. the Gezer calendar, 925 B.C. (a school boy's writing)
2. the Siloam Inscription, 705 B.C. (tunnel writings)
3. Samaritan Ostraca, 770 B.C. (tax records on broken pottery)
4. Lachish letters, 587 B.C. (war communications)
5. Maccabean coins and seals
6. some Dead Sea Scroll texts
7. numerous inscriptions (cf. "Languages [Hebrew]," ABD 4:203ff)

It, like all Semitic languages, is characterized by words made up of three consonants (tri-consonantal root). It is an inflexed language. The three-root consonants carry the basic word meaning, while prefixed, suffixed, or internal additions show the syntactical function (later vowels, cf. Sue Green, *Linguistic Analysis of Biblical Hebrew*, pp. 46-49).

Hebrew vocabulary demonstrates a difference between prose and poetry. Word meanings are connected to folk etymologies (not linguistic origins). Word plays and sound plays are very common (*paronomasia*).

II. Aspects of Predication

A. VERBS

The normal expected word order is VERB, PRONOUN, SUBJECT (with modifiers), OBJECT (with modifiers). The basic non-flagged VERB is the Qal, PERFECT, MASCULINE, SINGULAR form. It is how Hebrew and Aramaic lexicons are arranged.

VERBS are inflected to show
1. number—SINGULAR, PLURAL, DUAL
2. gender—MASCULINE and FEMININE (no neuter)
3. MOOD—INDICATIVE, SUBJUNCTIVE, IMPERATIVE (relation of the action to reality)
4. TENSE (aspect)
   a. PERFECT, which denotes completion, in the sense of the beginning, continuing, and concluding of an action. Usually this form was used of past action, the thing has occurred.

   J. Wash Watts, A Survey of Syntax in the Hebrew Old Testament, says:
   "The single whole described by a perfect is also considered as certain. An imperfect may picture a state as possible or desired or expected, but a perfect sees it as actual, real, and sure" (p. 36).

   S. R. Driver, A Treatise on the Use of the Tenses in Hebrew, describes it as, "The PERFECT is employed to indicate actions the accom-plishment of which lies indeed in the future, but is regarded as dependant upon such an unalterable determination of the will that it may be spoken of as having actually taken place: thus a resolution, promise, or decree, especially of Divine one, is frequently announced in the perfect tense" (p. 17, e.g., the prophetic perfect).

   Robert B. Chisholm, Jr. From Exegesis to Exposition, defines this VERBAL form as "views a situation from the outside, as a whole. As such it expresses a simple fact, whether it be an action or state (including state of being or mind). When used of actions, it often views the action as complete from the rhetorical standpoint of the speaker or narrator (whether it is or is not complete in fact or reality is not the point). The perfect can pertain to an action/state in the past, present or future. As noted above, time frame, which influences how one translates the perfect into a tense-oriented language like English, must be determined from the context" (p. 86).

   b. IMPERFECT, which denotes an action in progress (incomplete, repetitive, continual, or contingent), often movement toward a goal. Usually this form was used of Present and Future action.

J. Wash Watts, A Survey of Syntax in the Hebrew Old Testament, says:
> "All IMPERFECTS represent incomplete states. They are either repeated or developing or contingent. In other words, or partially developed, or partially assured. In all cases they are partial in some sense, i.e., incomplete" (p. 55).

Robert B. Chisholm, Jr. *From Exegesis to Exposition*, says:
> "It is difficult to reduce the essence of the imperfect to a single concept, for it encompasses both aspect and mood. Sometimes the imperfect is used in an indicative manner and makes an objective statement. At other times it views an action more subjectively, as hypothetical, contingent, possible, and so on" (p. 89).

    c.   The added *waw*, which links the VERB to the action of the previous VERB(s).

    d.   IMPERATIVE, which is based on the volition of the speaker and potential action by the hearer.

    e.   In ancient Hebrew only the larger context can determine the authorial-intended time orientations.

B.   The seven major inflected forms (STEMS) and their basic meaning. In reality these forms work in conjunction with each other in a context and must not be isolated.

    1.   *Qal* (*Kal*), the most common and basic of all the forms. It denotes simple action or a state of being. There is no causation or specification implied.

    2.   *Niphal*, the second most common form. It is usually PASSIVE, but this form also functions as reciprocal and reflexive. It also has no causation or specification implied.

    3.   *Piel*, this form is active and expresses the bringing about of an action into a state of being. The basic meaning of the *Qal* stem is developed or extended into a state of being.

    4.   *Pual*, this is the PASSIVE counterpart to the *Piel*. It is often expressed by a PARTICIPLE.

    5.   *Hithpael*, which is the reflexive or reciprocal stem. It expresses iterative or durative action to the *Piel* stem. The rare PASSIVE form is called *Hothpael*.

    6.   *Hiphil*, the active form of the causative stem in contrast to *Piel*. It can have a permissive aspect, but usually refers to the cause of an event. Ernst Jenni, a German Hebrew grammarian, believed that the *Piel* denoted something coming into a state of being, while *Hiphil* showed how it happened.

    7.   *Hophal*, the PASSIVE counterpart to the *Hiphil*. These last two stems are the least used of the seven stems.

Much of this information comes from *An Introduction to Biblical Hebrew Syntax*, by Bruce K. Walke and M. O'Connor, pp. 343-452.

Agency and causation chart. One key in understanding the Hebrew VERB system is to see it as a pattern of VOICE relationships. Some stems are in contrast to other stems (i.e., *Qal - Niphal; Piel - Hiphil*)

The chart below tries to visualize the basic function of the VERB stems as to causation.

Voice or Subject Agency	No Secondary Agency	An Active Secondary Agency	A Passive Secondary Agency
ACTIVE	*Qal*	*Hiphil*	*Piel*
MIDDLE PASSIVE	*Niphal*	*Hophal*	*Pual*
REFLEXIVE// RECIPROCAL	*Niphal*	*Hiphil*	*Hithpael*

This chart is taken from the excellent discussion of the VERBAL system in light of new Akkadian research (cf. Bruce K. Waltke, M. O'Conner, *An Introduction to Biblical Hebrew Syntax*, pp.354-359.

R. H. Kennett, *A Short Account of the Hebrew Tenses*, has provided a needed warning:
"I have commonly found in teaching, that a student's chief difficulty in the Hebrew verbs is to grasp the meaning which they conveyed to the minds of the Hebrews themselves; that is to say, there is a tendency to assign as equivalents to each of the Hebrew Tenses a certain number of Latin or English forms by which that particular Tense may commonly be translated. The result is a failure to perceive many of these fine shades of meaning, which give such life and vigor to the language of the Old Testament.

"The difficulty in the use of the Hebrew verbs lies solely in the point of view, so absolutely different from our own, from which the Hebrews regarded an action; the *time*, which with us is the first consideration, as the very word, 'tense' shows, being to them a matter of secondary importance. It is, therefore, essential that a student should clearly grasp, not so much the Latin or English forms which may be used in translating each of the Hebrew Tenses, but rather the aspect of each action, as it presented itself to a Hebrew's mind.

"The name 'tenses' as applied to Hebrew verbs is misleading. The so-called Hebrew 'tenses' do not express the *time* but merely the *state* of an action. Indeed were it not for the confusion that would arise through the application of the term 'state' to both nouns and verbs, 'states' would be a far better designation than 'tenses.' It must always be borne in mind that it is impossible to translate a Hebrew verb into English without employing a limitation, which is entirely absent in the Hebrew. The ancient Hebrews never thought of an action as past, present, or future, but simply as *perfect*, i.e., complete, or *imperfect*, i.e., as in course of development. When we say that a certain Hebrew tense corresponds to a Perfect, Pluperfect, or Future in English, we do not mean that the Hebrews thought of it as Perfect, Pluperfect, or Future, but merely that it must be so translated in English. The *time* of an action the Hebrews did not attempt to express by any verbal form" (preface and p. 1).

For a second good warning, Sue Groom, *Linguistic Analysis of Biblical Hebrew*, reminds us, "There is no way of knowing whether modern scholars' reconstruction of semantic fields and sense relations in an ancient dead language are merely a reflection of their own intuition, or their own native language, or whether those fields existed in Classical Hebrew" (p. 128).

C. MOODS (MODES)
1. It happened, is happening (INDICATIVE), usually uses PERFECT tense or PARTICIPLES (all PARTICIPLES are INDICATIVE).
2. It will happen, could happen (SUBJUNCTIVE)
    a. uses a marked IMPERFECT tense
        (1) COHORTATIVE (added h), FIRST PERSON IMPERFECT form which normally expresses a wish, a request, or self-encouragement (i.e., actions willed by the speaker)
        (2) JUSSIVE (internal changes), THIRD PERSON IMPERFECT (can be second person in negated sentences) which normally expresses a request, a permission, an admonition, or advice
    b. uses a PERFECT tense with *lu* or *lule*
    These constructions are similar to SECOND CLASS CONDITIONAL sentences in Koine Greek. A false statement (*protasis*) results in a false conclusion (*apodosis*).
    c. uses an IMPERFECT tense and *lu*
    Context and *lu*, as well as a future orientation, mark this SUBJUNCTIVE usage. Some examples from J. Wash Watts, *A Survey of Syntax in the Hebrew Old Testament* are Gen. 13:16; Deut. 1:12; I Kgs. 13:8; Ps. 24:3; Isa. 1:18 (cf. Pp. 76-77).

D. *Waw* - Conversive/consecutive/relative. This uniquely Hebrew (Canaanite) syntactical feature has caused great confusion through the years. It is used in a variety of ways often based on genre. The reason for the confusion is that early scholars were European and tried to interpret in light of their own native languages. When this proved difficult they blamed the problem on Hebrew being a "supposed" ancient, archaic language. European languages are TENSE (time) based VERBS. Some of the variety and grammatical implications were specified by the letter *waw* being added to the PERFECT or IMPERFECT VERB stems. This altered the way the action was viewed.
1. In historical narrative the VERBS are linked together in a chain with a standard pattern.
2. The *waw* prefix showed a specific relationship with the previous VERB(s).
3. The larger context is always the key to understanding the VERB chain. Semitic VERBS cannot be analyzed in isolation.

J. Wash Watts, *A Survey of Syntax in the Hebrew Old Testament*, notes the distinctive of Hebrew in its use of the *waw* before PERFECTS and IMPERFECTS (pp. 52-53).
As the basic idea of the PERFECT is past, the addition of *waw* often projects it into a future time aspect. This is also true of the IMPERFECT whose basic idea is present or future; the addition of *waw* places it into the past. It is this unusual time shift which explains the *waw's* addition, not a change in the basic meaning of the tense itself. The *waw* PERFECTS work well with prophecy, while the *waw* IMPERFECTS work well with narratives (pp. 54, 68).

Watts continues his definition

> "As a fundamental distinction between *waw* conjunctive and *waw* consecutive, the following interpretations are offered:
> 1. *Waw* conjunctive appears always to indicate a parallel.
> 2. *Waw* consecutive appears always to indicate a sequence. It is the only form of *waw* used with consecutive imperfects. The relation between the imperfects linked by it may be temporal sequence, logical consequence, logical cause, or logical contrast. In all cases there is a sequence" (p. 103).

E. INFINITIVES - There are two kinds of INFINITIVES
1. INFINITIVE ABSOLUTES, which are "strong, independent, striking expressions used for dramatic effect. . .as a subject, it often has no written verb, the verb 'to be' being understood, of course, but the word standing dramatically alone" J. Wash Watts, *A Survey of Syntax in the Hebrew Old Testament*" (p. 92).
2. INFINITIVE CONSTRUCT, which are "related grammatically to the sentence by prepositions, possessive pronouns, and the construct relationship" (p. 91).

J. Weingreen, *A Practical Grammar for Classical Hebrew*, describes the construct state as: "When two (or more) words are so closely united that together they constitute one compound idea, the dependent word (or words) is (are) said to be in the construct state" (p. 44).

F. INTERROGATIVES
1. They always appear first in the sentence.
2. Interpretive significance
   a. *ha* - does not expect a response
   b. *halo'* - the author expects a "yes" answer

G. NEGATIVES
1. They always appear before the words they negate.
2. Most common negation is *lo'*.
3. The term *'al* has a contingent connotation and is used with COHORTATIVES and JUSSIVES.
4. The term *lebhilit*, meaning "in order that. . .not," is used with INFINITIVES.
5. The term *'en* is used with PARTICIPLES.

H. CONDITIONAL SENTENCES
1. There are four kinds of CONDITIONAL SENTENCES which basically are paralleled in Koine Greek.
   a. something assumed to be happening or thought of as fulfilled (FIRST CLASS in Greek)
   b. something contrary to fact whose fulfillment is impossible (SECOND CLASS)
   c. something which is possible or ever probable (THIRD CLASS)
   d. something which is less probable, therefore, the fulfillment is dubious (FOURTH CLASS)

2. GRAMMATICAL MARKERS
   a. the assumed-to-be-true or real condition always uses an INDICATIVE PERFECT or PARTICIPLE and usually the *protasis* is introduced by:
      (1) *'im*
      (2) *ki* (or *'asher*)
      (3) *hin* or *hinneh*
   b. the contrary to fact condition always uses a PERFECT aspect VERB or a PARTICIPLE with the introductory PARTICIPLE *lu* or *lule*
   c. the more probable condition always used IMPERFECT VERB or PARTICIPLES in the *protasis*, usually *'im* or *ki* are used as introductory PARTICLES
   d. the less probable condition uses IMPERFECT SUBJUNCTIVES in the *protasis* and always uses *'im* as an introductory PARTICLE

DEFINITIONS OF GREEK GRAMMATICAL FORMS
WHICH IMPACT INTERPRETATION

Koine Greek, often called Hellenistic Greek, was the common language of the Mediterranean world beginning with Alexander the Great's (336-323 B.C.) conquest and lasting about eight hundred years (300 B.C.- A.D. 500). It was not just a simplified, classical Greek, but in many ways a newer form of Greek that became the second language of the Ancient Near East and Mediterranean world.

The Greek of the New Testament was unique in some ways because its users, except Luke and the author of Hebrews, probably used Aramaic as their primary language. Therefore, their writing was influenced by the idioms and structural forms of Aramaic. Also, they read and quoted the Septuagint (Greek translation of the OT) which was also written in Koine Greek. But the Septuagint was also written by Jewish scholars whose mother tongue was not Greek.

This serves as a reminder that we cannot push the New Testament into a tight grammatical structure. It is unique and yet has much in common with (1) the Septuagint; (2) Jewish writings such as those of Josephus; and (3) the papyri found in Egypt. How then do we approach a grammatical analysis of the New Testament?

The grammatical features of Koine Greek and New Testament Koine Greek are fluid. In many ways it was a time of simplification of grammar. Context will be our major guide. Words only have meaning in a larger context, therefore, grammatical structure can only be understood in light of (1) a particular author's style; and (2) a particular context. No conclusive definitions of Greek forms and structures are possible.

Koine Greek was primarily a VERBAL language. Often the key to interpretation is the type and form of the VERBALS. In most main clauses the VERB will occur first, showing its preeminence. In analyzing the Greek VERB three pieces of information must be noted: (1) the basic emphasis of the TENSE, VOICE and MOOD (accidence or morphology); (2) the basic meaning of the particular VERB (lexicography); and (3) the flow of the context (syntax).

I. TENSE

A. TENSE or aspect involves the relationship of the VERBS to completed action or incomplete action. This is often called "perfective" and "imperfective."
    1. Perfective TENSES focus on the occurrence of an action. No further information is given except that something happened! Its start, continuation or culmination is not addressed.
    2. Imperfective TENSES focus on the continuing process of an action. It can be described in terms of linear action, durative action, progressive action, etc.
B. TENSES can be categorized by how the author sees the action as progressing
    1. It occurred = AORIST
    2. It occurred and the results abide = PERFECT
    3. It was occurring in the past and the results were abiding, but not now = PLUPERFECT
    4. It is occurring = PRESENT
    5. It was occurring = IMPERFECT
    6. It will occur = FUTURE

A concrete example of how these tenses help in interpretation would be the term "save." It was used in several different tenses to show both its process and culmination:

1. AORIST - "saved" (cf. Rom. 8:24)
2. PERFECT - "have been saved and the result continues" (cf. Eph. 2:5,8)
3. PRESENT - "being saved" (cf. I Cor. 1:18; 15:2)
4. FUTURE - "shall be saved" (cf. Rom. 5:9, 10; 10:9)

C. In focusing on VERB TENSES, interpreters look for the reason the original author chose to express himself in a certain tense. The standard "no frills" tense was the AORIST. It was the regular "unspecific," "unmarked," or "unflagged" VERB form. It can be used in a wide variety of ways which the context must specify. It simply was stating that something occurred. The past time aspect is only intended in the INDICATIVE MOOD. If any other TENSE was used, something more specific was being emphasized. But what?

1. PERFECT TENSE. This speaks of a completed action with abiding results. In some ways it was a combination of the AORIST and PRESENT TENSES. Usually the focus is on the abiding results or the completion of an act. Example: Eph. 2:5 & 8, "you have been and continue to be saved."

2. PLUPERFECT TENSE. This was like the PERFECT except the abiding results have ceased.
    Example: "Peter was standing at the door outside" (John 18:16).

3. PRESENT TENSE. This speaks of an incomplete or imperfect action. The focus is usually on the continuation of the event. Example: "Everyone abiding in Him does not continue sinning," "everyone having been begotten of God does not continue to commit sin" (I John 3:6, 9).

4. IMPERFECT TENSE. In this TENSE the relationship to the PRESENT TENSE is analogous to the relationship between the PERFECT and the PLUPERFECT. The IMPERFECT speaks of incomplete action that was occurring, but has now ceased or the beginning of an action in the past. Example: "Then all Jerusalem were continuing to go out to him" or "then all Jerusalem began to go out to him" (Matt. 3:5).

5. FUTURE TENSE. This speaks of an action that was usually projected into a future time frame. It focused on the potential for an occurrence rather than an actual occurrence. It often speaks of the certainty of the event. Example: "Blessed are. . .they will. . ." (Matt. 5:4-9).

II. VOICE

A. VOICE describes the relationship between the action of the VERB and its SUBJECT.

B. ACTIVE VOICE was the normal, expected, unemphasized way to assert that the SUBJECT was performing the action of the VERB.

C. The PASSIVE VOICE means that the SUBJECT was receiving the action of the VERB produced by an outside agent. The outside agent producing the action was indicated in the Greek NT by the following PREPOSITIONS and CASES:

1. a personal direct agent by *hupo* with the ABLATIVE CASE (cf. Matt.1:22; Acts 22:30).
2. a personal intermediate agent by *dia* with the ABLATIVE CASE (cf. Matt. 1:22).
3. an impersonal agent usually by *en* with the INSTRUMENTAL CASE.
4. sometimes either a personal or impersonal agent by the INSTRUMENTAL CASE alone.

D. The MIDDLE VOICE means that the SUBJECT produces the action of the VERB and is also directly involved in the action of the VERB. It is often called the voice of heightened personal interest. This construction emphasized the subject of the clause or sentence in some way. This construction is not found in English. It has a wide possibility of meanings and translations in Greek.

Some examples of the form are:
1. REFLEXIVE - the direct action of the SUBJECT on itself. Example: "Hanged himself" (Matt. 27:5).
2. INTENSIVE - the SUBJECT produces the action for itself. Example: "Satan himself masquerades as an angel of light" (II Cor. 11:14).
3. RECIPROCAL - the interplay of two SUBJECTS. Example: "They counseled with one another" (Matt. 26:4).

III. MOOD (or "MODE")

A. There are four MOODS in Koine Greek. They indicate the relation of the VERB to reality, at least within the author's own mind. The MOODS are divided into two broad categories: that which indicated reality (INDICATIVE) and that which indicated potentiality (SUBJUNCTIVE, IMPERATIVE AND OPTATIVE).

B. The INDICATIVE MOOD was the normal mood for expressing action that had occurred or was occurring, at least in the author's mind. It was the only Greek mood that expressed a definite time, and even here this aspect was secondary.

C. The SUBJUNCTIVE MOOD expressed probable future action. Something had not yet happened, but the chances were likely that it would. It had much in common with the FUTURE INDICATIVE. The difference was that the SUBJUNCTIVE expresses some degree of doubt. In English this is often expressed by the terms "could," "would," "may," or "might."

D. The OPTATIVE MOOD expressed a wish which was theoretically possible. It was considered one step further from reality than the SUBJUNCTIVE. The OPTATIVE expressed possibility under certain conditions. The OPTATIVE was rare in the New Testament. Its most frequent usage is Paul's famous phrase, "May it never be" (KJV, "God forbid"), used fifteen times (cf. Rom. 3:4, 6, 31; 6:2, 15; 7:7, 13; 9:14; 11:1, 11; I Cor. 6:15; Gal. 2:17; 3:21; 6:14). Other examples are found in Luke 1:38, 20:16, Acts 8:20, and I Thess. 3:11.

E. The IMPERATIVE MOOD emphasized a command which was possible, but the emphasis was on the intent of the speaker. It asserted only volitional possibility and was conditioned on the choices of another. There was a special use of the IMPERATIVE in prayers and 3rd person requests. These commands were found only in the PRESENT and AORIST TENSES in the NT

F. Some grammars categorize PARTICIPLES as another type of MOOD. They are very common in the Greek NT, usually defined as a VERBAL ADJECTIVE. They are translated in conjunction with the main VERB to which they relate. A wide variety was possible in translating PARTICIPLES. It is best to consult several English translations. *The Bible in Twenty Six Translations* published by Baker is a great help here.

G. The AORIST ACTIVE INDICATIVE was the normal or "unmarked" way to record an occurrence.

Any other TENSE, VOICE, or MOOD had some specific interpretive significance that the original author wanted to communicate.

IV. GREEK RESOURCE TOOLS

(for the person not familiar with Greek, the following study aids will provide the needed information)

A. Friberg, Barbara and Timothy. *Analytical Greek New Testament*. Grand Rapids: Baker, 1988.
B. Marshall, Alfred. *Interlinear Greek-English New Testament*. Grand Rapids: Zondervan, 1976.
C. Mounce, William D. *The Analytical Lexicon to the Greek New Testament*. Grand Rapids: Zondervan, 1993.
D. Summers, Ray. *Essentials of New Testament Greek*. Nashville: Broadman, 1950.
E. Academically accredited Koine Greek correspondence courses are available through MoodyBible Institute in Chicago, IL.

V. NOUNS

Syntactically, nouns are classified by CASE. CASE was that inflected form of a NOUN that showed its relationship to the VERB and other parts of the sentence. In Koine Greek many of the CASE functions were indicated by PREPOSITIONS. Since the CASE form was able to identify several different relationships, the PREPOSITIONS developed to give clearer separation to these possible functions.

B. Greek CASES are categorized in the following eight ways:
1. The NOMINATIVE CASE was used for naming and it usually was the SUBJECT of the sentence or clause. It was also used for PREDICATE NOUNS and ADJECTIVES with the linking VERBS "to be" or "become."
2. The GENITIVE CASE was used for description and usually assigned an attribute or quality to the word to which it was related. It answered the question, "What kind?" It was often expressed by the use of the English preposition "of."
3. The ABLATIVE CASE used the same inflected form as the GENITIVE, but it was used to describe separation. It usually denoted separation from a point in time, space, source, origin, or degree. It was often expressed by the use of the English PREPOSITION "from."
4. The DATIVE CASE was used to describe personal interest. This could denote a positive or negative aspect. Often this was the INDIRECT OBJECT. It was often expressed by the English PREPOSITION "to."
5. The LOCATIVE CASE was the same inflected form as the DATIVE, but it described position or location in space, time or logical limits. It was often expressed by the English PREPOSITIONS "in, on, at, among, during, by, upon, and beside."
6. The INSTRUMENTAL CASE was the same inflected form as the DATIVE and LOCATIVE cases. It expressed means or association. It was often expressed by the English PREPOSITIONS, "by" or "with."
7. The ACCUSATIVE CASE was used to describe the conclusion of an action. It expressed limitation. Its main use was the DIRECT OBJECT. It answered the question, "How far?" or "To what extent?"
8. The VOCATIVE CASE was used for direct address.

VI. CONJUNCTIONS AND CONNECTORS

A. Greek is a very precise language because it has so many connectives. They connect thoughts (clauses, sentences, and paragraphs). They are so common that their absence (asyndeton) is often exegetically significant. As a matter of fact, these conjunctions and connectors show the direction of the author's thought. They often are crucial in determining what exactly he is trying to communicate.

B. Here is a list of some of the conjunctions and connectors and their meanings (this information has been gleaned mostly from H. E. Dana and Julius K. Mantey's *A Manual Grammar of the Greek New Testament*).
1. Time connectors
   a. *epei, epeid ē, hopōte, hōs, hote, hotan* (SUBJ.) - "when"
   b. *heōs* - "while"
   c. *hotan, epan* (SUBJ.) - "whenever"
   d. *heōs, achri, mechri* (SUBJ.) - "until"
   c. *priv* (INFIN.) - "before"
   d. *hōs* - "since," "when," "as"

2. Logical connectors
   a. Purpose
      (1) *hina* (SUBJ.), *hopōs* (SUBJ.), *hōs* - "in order that," "that"
      (2) *hōste* (ARTICULAR ACCUSATIVE INFINITIVE) - "that"
      (3) *pros* (ARTICULAR ACCUSATIVE INFINITIVE) or *eis* (ARTICULAR
          ACCUSATIVE INFINITIVE) - "that"
   b. Result (there is a close association between the grammatical forms of purpose
      and result)
      (1) *hōste* (INFINITIVE, this is the most common) - "in order that," "thus"
      (2) *hiva* (SUBJ.) - "so that"
      (3) *ara* - "so"
   c. Causal or reason
      (1) *gar* (cause/effect or reason/conclusion) - "for," "because"
      (2) *dioti, hotiy* - "because"
      (3) *epei, epeidē*, *hōs* - "since"
      (4) *dia* (with ACCUSATIVE) and (with ARTICULAR INFINITIVE.) - "because"
   d. Inferential
      (1) *ara, poinun, hōste* - "therefore"
      (2) *dio* (strongest INFERENTIAL CONJUNCTION) - "on which account,"
          "wherefore," "therefore"
      (3) *oun* - "therefore," "so," "then," "consequently"
      (4) *toinoun* - "accordingly"
   e. Adversative or contrast
      (1) *alla* (strong ADVERSATIVE) - "but," "except"
      (2) *de* - "but," "however," "yet," "on the other hand"
      (3) *kai* - "but"
      (4) *mentoi, oun* - "however"
      (5) *plēn* - "never-the-less" (mostly in Luke) (6) *oun* - "however"
   f. Comparison
      (1) *hōs, kathōs* (introduce comparative clauses)
      (2) *kata* (in compounds, *katho, kathoti, kathōsper, kathaper*)
      (3) *hosos* (in Hebrews)
      (4) *ē* - "than"
   g. Continuative or series
      (1) *de* - "and," "now"
      (2) *kai* - "and"
      (3) *tei* - "and"
      (4) *hina, oun* - "that"
      (5) *oun* - "then" (in John)

3. Emphatic usages
   a. *alla* - "certainty," "yea," "in fact"
   b. *ara* - "indeed," "certainly," "really"
   c. *gar* - "but really," "certainly," "indeed"
   d. *de* - "indeed"
   e. *ean* - "even"

f. *kai* - "even," "indeed," "really"

g. *mentoi* - "indeed"

h. *oun* - "really," "by all means"

VII. CONDITIONAL SENTENCES

A. A CONDITIONAL SENTENCE is one that contains one or more CONDITIONAL CLAUSES. This grammatical structure aids interpretation because it provides the conditions, reasons or causes why the action of the main VERB does or does not occur. There were four types of CONDITIONAL SENTENCES. They move from that which was assumed to be true from the author's perspective or for his purpose to that which was only a wish.

B. The FIRST CLASS CONDITIONAL SENTENCE expressed action or being which was assumed to be true from the writer's perspective or for his purposes even though it was expressed with an "if." In several contexts it could be translated "since" (cf. Matt. 4:3; Rom. 8:31). However, this does not mean to imply that all FIRST CLASSES are true to reality. Often they were used to make a point in an argument or to highlight a fallacy (cf. Matt. 12:27).

C. The SECOND CLASS CONDITIONAL SENTENCE is often called "contrary to fact." It states something that was untrue to reality to make a point. Examples:
    1. "If He were really a prophet, which He is not, He would know who and of what character the woman is who is clinging to Him, but He does not" (Luke 7:39).
    2. "If you really believed Moses, which you do not, you would believe me, which you do not" (John 5:46). Also see John 4:10; 8:19,39,42; 9:33,41; 11:21,32; 14:2,11,28; 15:19; 19:11.
    3. "If I were still trying to be pleasing to men, which I am not, I would not be a slave of Christ at all, which I am" (Gal. 1:10).

D. The THIRD CLASS speaks of possible future action. It often assumes the probability of that action. It usually implies a contingency. The action of the main VERB is contingent on the action in the "it" clause. Examples from I John: 1:6-10; 2:4,6,9,15,20,21,24,29; 3:21; 4:20; 5:14,16.

E. The FOURTH CLASS is the farthest removed from possibility. It is rare in the NT. As a matter of fact, there is no complete FOURTH CLASS CONDITIONAL SENTENCE in which both parts of the condition fit the definition. An example of a partial FOURTH CLASS is the opening clause in I Peter 3:14. An example of a partial FOURTH CLASS in the concluding clause is Acts 8:31.

VIII. PROHIBITIONS

A. The PRESENT IMPERATIVE with M [PARTICLE often (but not exclusively) has the emphasis of stopping an act already in process. Some examples: "stop storing up your riches on earth. . ." (Matt. 6:19); "stop worrying about your life. . ." (Matt. 6:25); "stop offering to sin the parts of your bodies as instruments of wrongdoing. . ." (Rom. 6:13); "you must stop offending the Holy Spirit of God. . ." (Eph. 4:30); and "stop getting drunk on wine. . ." (5:18).

B. The AORIST SUBJUNCTIVE with M [PARTICLE has the emphasis of "do not even begin or start an act." Some examples: "Do not even begin to suppose that. . ." (Matt. 5:17); "never start to worry. . ." (Matt. 6:31); "you must never be ashamed. . ." (II Tim. 1:8).

C. The DOUBLE NEGATIVE with the SUBJUNCTIVE MOOD is a very emphatic negation. "Never, no never" or "not under any circumstance." Some examples: "he will never, no never experience death" (John 8:51); "I will never, no, never. . ." (I Cor. 8:13).

IX. THE ARTICLE

A. In Koine Greek the DEFINITE ARTICLE "the" had a use similar to English. Its basic function was that of "a pointer," a way to draw attention to a word, name or phrase. The use varies from author to author in the New Testament. The DEFINITE ARTICLE could also function
   1. as a contrasting device like a DEMONSTRATIVE PRONOUN
   2. as a sign to refer to a previously introduced SUBJECT or person
   3. as a way to identify the SUBJECT in a sentence with a LINKING VERB. Examples: "God is Spirit" John 4:24; "God is light" I John 1:5; "God is love" 4:8,16

B. Koine Greek did not have an INDEFINITE ARTICLE like the English "a" or "an." The absence of the DEFINITE ARTICLE could mean
   1. a focus on the characteristics or quality of something
   2. a focus on the category of something

C. The NT authors varied widely as to how the ARTICLE was employed.

X. WAYS OF SHOWING EMPHASIS IN THE GREEK NEW TESTAMENT

A. The techniques for showing emphasis vary from author to author in the New Testament. The most consistent and formal writers were Luke and the author of Hebrews.

B. We have stated earlier that the AORIST ACTIVE INDICATIVE was standard and unmarked for emphasis, but any other TENSE, VOICE, or MOOD had interpretive significance. This is not to imply that the AORIST ACTIVE INDICATIVE was not often used in a significant grammatical sense. Example: Rom. 6:10 (twice).

C. Word order in Koine Greek
  1. Koine Greek was an inflected language which was not dependent, like English, on word order. Therefore, the author could vary the normal expected order to show
     a. what the author wanted to emphasize to the reader
     b. what the author thought would be surprising to the reader
     c. what the author felt deeply about
  2. The normal word order in Greek is still an unsettled issue. However, the supposed normal order is:
     a. for LINKING VERBS
        (1) VERB
        (2) SUBJECT
        (3) COMPLEMENT
     b. for TRANSITIVE VERBS
        (1) VERB
        (2) SUBJECT
        (3) OBJECT
        (4) INDIRECT OBJECT
        (5) PREPOSITIONAL PHRASE
     c. for NOUN PHRASES
        (1) NOUN
        (2) MODIFIER
        (3) PREPOSITIONAL PHRASE
  3. Word order can be an extremely important exegetical point. Examples:
     a. "right hand they gave to me and Barnabas of fellowship" (Gal. 2:9). The phrase "right hand of fellowship" is split and fronted to show its significance.
     b. "with Christ" (Gal. 2:20), was placed first. His death was central.
     c. "It was bit by bit and in many different ways" (Heb. 1:1), was placed first. It was how God revealed Himself that was being contrasted, not the fact of revelation.

D. Usually some degree of emphasis was shown by
  1. The repetition of the PRONOUN which was already present in the VERB's inflected form.
  Example: "I, myself, will surely be with you. . ." (Matt. 28:20).

2. The absence of an expected CONJUNCTION, or other connecting device between words, phrases, clauses, or sentences. This is called an asyndeton ("not bound"). The connecting device was expected, so its absence would draw attention. Examples:
    a. The Beatitudes, Matt. 5:3ff (emphasized the list)
    b. John 14:1 (new topic)
    c. Romans 9:1 (new section)
    d. II Cor. 12:20 (emphasize the list)
3. The repetition of words or phrases present in a given context. Examples: "to the praise of His glory" (Eph. 1:6, 12 & 14). This phrase was used to show the work of each person of the Trinity.
4. The use of an idiom or word (sound) play between terms
    a. euphemisms - substitute words for taboo subjects like "sleep" for death (John 11:11-14) or "feet" for male genitalia (Ruth 3:7-8; I Sam. 24:3).
    b. circumlocutions - substitute words for God's name, like "Kingdom of heaven" (Matt. 3:21) or "a voice from heaven" (Matt. 3:17).
    c. FIGURES OF SPEECH
        (1) impossible exaggerations (Matt. 3:9; 5:29-30; 19:24).
        (2) mild over-statements (Matt. 3:5; Acts 2:36).
        (3) personifications (I Cor. 15:55).
        (4) irony (Gal. 5:12)
        (5) poetic passages (Phil. 2:6-11).
        (6) sound plays between words
            (a) "church"
                i. "church" (Eph. 3:21)
                ii. "calling" (Eph. 4:1,4)
                iii. "called" (Eph. 4:1,4)
            (b) "free"
                i. "free woman" (Gal. 4:31)
                ii. "freedom" (Gal. 5:1)
                iii. "free" (Gal. 5:1)
    d. idiomatic language - language which is usually cultural and language specific:
        (1) This was the figurative use of "food" (John 4:31-34).
        (2) This was the figurative use of "Temple" (John 2:19; Matt. 26:61).
        (3) This was a Hebrew idiom of compassion, "hate" (Gen. 29:31; Deut. 21:15; Luke 14:36; John 12:25; Rom. 9:13).
        (4) "All" versus "many." Compare Isa. 53:6 ("all") with 53:11 & 12 ("many"). The terms are synonymous as Rom. 5:18 and 19 show.
5. The use of a full linguistic phrase instead of a single word. Example: "The Lord Jesus Christ."

6. The special use of *autos*
    a. when with the ARTICLE (attributive position) it was translated "same."
    b. when without the ARTICLE (predicate position) it was translated as an INTENSIVE REFLEXIVE PRONOUN—"himself," "herself," or "itself.

E. The non-Greek reading Bible student can identify emphasis in several ways:
   1. The use of an analytical lexicon and interlinear Greek/English text.
   2. The comparison of English translations, particularly from the differing theories of translations. Example: comparing a "word-for-word" translation (KJV, NKJV, ASV, NASB, RSV, NRSV) with a "dynamic equivalent" (Williams, NIV, NEB, REB, JB, NJB, TEV). A good help here would be *The Bible in Twenty-Six Translations* published by Baker.
   3. The use of *The Emphasized Bible* by Joseph Bryant Rotherham (Kregel, 1994).
   4. The use of a very literal translation
      a. *The American Standard Version* of 1901
      b. *Young's Literal Translation of the Bible* by Robert Young (Guardian Press, 1976).

The study of grammar is tedious but necessary for proper interpretation. These brief definitions, comments, and examples are meant to encourage and equip non-Greek reading persons to use the grammatical notes provided in this volume. Surely these definitions are oversimplified. They should not be used in a dogmatic, inflexible manner, but as stepping stones toward a greater understanding of New Testament syntax. Hopefully these definitions will also enable readers to understand the comments of other study aids such as technical commentaries on the New Testament.

We must be able to verify our interpretation based on items of information found in the texts of the Bible. Grammar is one of the most helpful of these items; other items would include historical setting, literary context, contemporary word usage, and parallel passages.

SAMPLE WORK SHEET ON ROMANS 1-3

I. First Reading

    A.   The overarching purpose: How is man right with God, both initially and ongoing?
    B.   The key theme: 1:16-17
    C.   The literary genre: letter

II. Second Reading

    A.   The major literary units
        1.   1:1-17
        2.   1:18-3:21
        3.   4:1-5:21
        4.   6:1-8:39
        5.   9:1-11:36
        6.   12:1-15:37
        7.   16:1-27

    B.   Summary of the major literary units
        1.   Introduction and theme, 1:1-17
        2.   The lostness of all men, 1:18-3:21
        3.   Justification is a gift, 4:1-5:21
        4.   Justification is a lifestyle, 6:1-8:39
        5.   The Jews' relationship to justification, 9:1-11:36
        6.   How to live out justification in daily life, 12:1-15:37
        7.   Closing greetings and warnings, 16:1-27

III. Third Reading

    A.   Internal information concerning the historical setting
        1.   Author
            a.   Paul, 1:1
            b.   Bond servant of Christ Jesus, 1:1
            c.   An Apostle, 1:1, 5
            d.   To Gentiles, 1:5, 14
        2.   Date
            a.   After Paul's conversion and call, 1:1.
            b.   After time of the start of the church in Rome and its influence to grow, 1:8.
        3.   Recipients
            a.   Saints, 1:7
            b.   At Rome, 1:7

4. Occasion
   a. Their faith is well known, 1:8.
   b. Paul prays often for them, 1:9-10.
   c. Paul wants to personally meet them, 1:11.
   d. Paul wants to impart spiritual gift to them, 1:11, 15.
   e. Their meeting would encourage both of them, 1:12
   f. Paul prevented from coming, 1:13.
5. Historical Setting
   a. Written to the church in the capital of the Roman Empire.
   b. Apparently Paul had never been there, 1:1-13.
   c. Apparently the Roman Empire, and particularly Rome itself, was very immoral and idolatrous, 1:11ff.
      (1) Idols, 1:21-23
      (2) Homosexuality, 1:26-27
      (3) Depraved mind, 1:28-31
   d. Apparently there was a large Jewish population in Rome, 2:17-2:31; 9-11 (possibly a growing tension between believing Jews and believing Gentiles.)

B. Various Paragraph Divisions

ASV (literal)	Jerusalem Bible (idiomatic)	Williams (idiomatic)
1st unit, 1:1-17	**1st unit, 1:1-17**	**1st unit, 1:1-17**
1:1-7	1:1-2	1:1-7
1:8-15	1:3-7	1:8-15
1:16-17	1:8-15	
2nd unit, 1:18-3:31	**2nd unit, 1:16-3:31**	**2nd unit**
1:18-23	1:16-17	1:16-23
	1:18-25	
1:24-25		**3rd unit**
1:26-27	1:26-27	1:24-32
1:28-32	1:28-32	
2:1-16	2:1-11	**4th unit**
2:17-29	2:12-16	2:1-11
3:1-8	2:17-24	2:12-26
3:9-18	2:25-29	
3:19-20	3:1-8	**5th unit**
3:21-30	3:9-18	2:26-29
3:31	3:19-20	
	3:21-26	**6th unit**
	3:27-31	3:1-8
		3:9-18
		7th unit
		3:19-20
		3:21-26
		3:27-31

C.   Content Outline with Summaries
      1.   Introduction and theme, 1:1-17
            a.   Introduction of author, 1:1-2
            b.   Introduction of recipients, 1:3-7
            c.   Introductory prayer, 1:8-15
            d.   The theme, 1:16-17
      2.   Th e lostness of all men, 1:18-3:21
            a.   Lostness of pagans seen in their acts, 1:18-32
            b.   Lostness of Jews seen in their acts, 2:1-11
            c.   Their national hope, 2:12-3:8
                  (1) Their Law will not deliver them, 2:12-24
                  (2) Their circumcision will not deliver them, 2:25-29
                  (3) Their heritage will not deliver them, 3:1-8
            d.   The lostness of all men, 3:9-20
            e.   The hope of all men, 3:21-

IV. Fourth Reading (sample, 1:1-3:21, focal text only)

A.   Specialized list
      1.   (Although this sample is limited to 1:1-3:21 a good example of specialized lists
            is found in the term "therefore," 2:1; 5:1; 8:1; 12:1, which is used as a way of
            summarizing the flow of Paul's thought.)
      2.   Use of "gospel"
            a.   1:1, set apart for the gospel of God b. 2:9, the gospel of His Son
            c.   1:15, to preach the gospel
            d.   1:16, I am not ashamed of the gospel e. 2:16, according to my gospel
            [From this list and context much about the gospel itself can be ascertained.]
      3.   References to God's wrath and judgment
            a.   1:18, wrath of God
            b.   1:24, 26, 28, God gave them over
            c   2:1, the judgment of God falls upon those who practice such things d. 2:3,
                  the judgment of God
            e.   2:5-6, (both verses)
            f.   2:12, will perish
            g.   2:16, the day. . .God will judge the secrets of men h. 3:6, God judges the
                  world

B.   Key Words or Phrases
      1.   1:1, apostle
      2.   1:1, gospel of God
      3.   1:4, Son of God
      4.   1:5, grace. . .faith
      5.   1:6, the called
      6.   1:7, saints
      7.   1:11, spiritual gift. . .some fruit (v. 13

8. 1:16, salvation
9. 1:17, righteousness
10. 1:18, wrath of God. . .judgment of God (2:2)
11. 2:4, repentance
12. 2:7, immortality, eternal life
13. 2:12, the Law
14. 2:15, conscience
15. 3:4, justified
16. 3:24, redemption
17. 3:25, propitiation

C. Difficult Passages
   1. Textual or translational
      - 1:4, "<u>S</u>pirit of holiness" or "<u>s</u>pirit of holiness"
   2. Is the proper translation of Hab. 2:4 found in Rom. 1:1-7?
   3. Historical
      - 2:21-23, "you who preach that . . ." (when, how and where did the Jews do these things?)
   4. Theological
      a. 1:4, ". . . who was <u>declared</u> with power to be the Son of God. . ." (or was Jesus born divine?)
      b. 2:14-15 (2:27), "Gentiles who do not have the law do instinctively the things of the law, are a law to themselves. . ." (What about those who never heard the law but perform some of it?)
      c. 3:1, "What advantage has the Jew?"

D. Significant Parallels
   1. Same book
      - 1:18-3:21 is one literary unit
   2. Same author
      - The book of Galatians expounds the same doctrinal truths.
   3. Same period - no direct parallels.
   4. Same Testament - no direct parallels.
   5. Entire Bible - Paul uses Hab. 1:4. (He will major on Old Testament characters in chapter 4.)

E. Theological Uniqueness
   1. Natural revelation
      a. In creation, 1:18-23
      b. In inner moral consciousness, 2:14-16
   2. All humankind is lost

V. Application (sample 1:1-3:21)

Detailed Content Outline	**Application Points**
A. Introduction and theme (1:1-17)	A. God's free grace through Christ is the calling both Paul and the Romans have believed and received. This offer is open to all.
1. Introduction of author, 1:1-2	
2. Introduction of recipients, 1:3-7	
3. Introductory prayer, 1:8-15	
4. The theme, 1:16-17	
B. The lostness of all men, 1:18-3:21	B. All men regardless of their outward religious life, or lack of it, to be saved by trust in Christ's finished work, not their
1. lostness of pagans seen in their acts, 1:18-3:21	
2. lostness of Jews seen in their own acts, 2:1-11	The key summary passage of 1:18-3:31 is 3:21-30.
3. Their national hope, 2:12-3:8	
a. their Law will not deliver them, 2:12-24	
b. their circumcision will not deliver them, 2:25-29	
c. their heritage will not deliver them, 3:1-8	
4. the lostness of all men, 3:9-20	
5. the hope of all men, 3:21-31	

SAMPLE WORK SHEET ON TITUS (a whole book)

I. First Reading

A. The overarching purpose of this biblical book is:
While in the process of establishing local churches with their elders, the continuing need for orthodoxy and orthopraxy is emphasized.

B. The key theme
1. Establishing local churches and elders, 1:5.
2. Emphasizing the need for:
   a. orthodoxy - 1:9-11, 14; 2:1
   b. orthopraxy - 1:16; 3:8

C. The literary genre: letter
1. Opening 1:1-4
2. Closing 3:12-15

II. Second Reading

A. The major literary units or content divisions:

1. 1:14   2. 1:5-9   3. 1:10-16
4. 2:1-10a   5. 2:10b-15   6. 3:1-11
7. 3:12-15

B. Summary of the themes of the major literary units or content divisions.
1. Traditional Christian introduction to the letter, 1:1-4
2. Guidelines for elders, 1:5-9.
3. Guidelines for determining false teachings, 1:10-16
4. Guidelines for believers in general, 2:1-10a.
5. Theological basis for the guidelines, 2:10b-15
6. Guidelines for those who could cause problems, 3:1-11
7. Traditional Christian close to the letter, 3:12-15

III. Third Reading

A. Internal information concerning the historical setting of the book
1. Author
   a. Paul, 1:1   b. Bond-servant of God, 1:1c. Apostle of Jesus Christ, 1:1
2. Date
   a. Written to Titus, 1:4
      (1) He is not mentioned in Acts at all
      (2) He was apparently converted and recruited on one of Paul's missionary journeys, Gal. 2:1.
      (3) He was an uncircumcised Gentile, Gal. 2:3.

(4) He became Paul's trouble shooter, II Cor. 2:13; II Tim. 4:10; Titus 1:4.
- b. Paul left him in Crete, 1:5
  (1) Because the travel itinerary of the Pastoral Epistles does not fit into the chronology of Acts, this is probably Paul's fourth missionary journey.
  (2) It is assumed that Paul was released from prison after the close of the book of Acts. However, he was rearrested and killed under Nero who died in A.D. 68.
- 3. Recipient: Paul's faithful co-worker, Titus, but also to be read to the local congregations.
- 4. Occasion: Continuing the ministry of establishing local churches on the Island of Crete.
  - a. Appointing elders, 1:5
  - b. Refuting false teachers, 1:9-11, 14-16; 3:9-11
  - c. Encouraging the faithful

B. Various paragraph divisions
  1. Paragraph divisions

Literal		Dynamic Equivalent		
NASB	**NRSV**	**Jerusalem Bible***	**NIV***	**Williams***
1st Unit	1st Unit	1st Unit	1st Unit	1st Unit
1:1-4	1:1-3	1:1-4	1:1-4	1:1-4
	1:4		1:5-9	
			1:10-16	
2nd Unit	2nd Unit	2nd Unit	2nd Unit	
1:5-9	1:5-9	1:5-9	1:5-9	
1:10-16	1:10-16		1:10-16	
		3rd Unit		
		1:10-14		
		1:15-16		
3rd Unit	3rd Unit	4th Unit	3rd Unit	2nd Unit
2:1-14	2:1-2	2:1-10	2:1-2	2:1-10
2:15	2:3-5		2:3-5	2:11-14
	2:6-8		2:6-8	2:15
	2:9-10	5th Unit	2:9-10	
	2:11-14	2:11-14	2:11-14	
	2:15	2:15	2:15	
4th Unit	4th Unit	6th Unit	4th Unit	3rd Unit
3:1-11	3:1-11	3:1-3	3:1-2	3:1-2
		3:4-8a	3:3-8	3:3-7
		7th Unit	3:9-11	3:8-11
		3:8b-11	5th Unit	3:12
			3:12-14	3:13-14
		8th Unit	3:15	3:15
		3:12-14	3:12-14	3:12-14
		3:15	3:15	3:15

2. Various translations content summaries.
    a. Jerusalem Bible
        (1) 1st Unit, "address," 1:1-4
        (2) 2nd Unit, "the appointment of elders," 1:5-9
        (3) 3rd Unit, "opposing false teachers," 1:10-14, 15, 16
        (4) 4th Unit, "some specific moral instructions," 2:1-10
        (5) 5th Unit, "the basis of the Christian moral life," 2:11-14
        (6) 6th Unit, "general instructions for believers," 3:1-3, 4-8a
        (7) 7th Unit, "personal advise to Titus," 3:8b-11
        (8) 8th Unit, "practical recommendations, farewells, good wishes," 3:12-14, 15
    b. New International Version
        (1) 1st Unit, salutation, 1:1-4
        (2) 2nd Unit, "Titus' task on Crete," 1:5-9, 10-16
        (3) 3rd Unit, "what must be taught to various groups," 2:1-2, 3-5, 6-8, 91-0, 11-14, 15
        (4) 4th Unit, "doing what is good," 3:1-2, 3-8, 9-11
        (5) 5th Unit, "final remarks," 3:12-14, 15
    c. Williams Translation
        (1) 1st Unit, "God's people distinguished by actions," 1:1-4, 5-9, 10-16
        (2) 2nd Unit, "God's people called to righteousness," 2:1-10, 11-14, 15
        (3) 3rd Unit, "believers are to do good," 3:1-2, 3-7, 8-11, 12, 13-14, 15

C. Summaries of paragraph divisions
    1. Traditional Christian introduction to the letter, 1:1-4
        a. From whom, 1:1a
            (1) Paul
            (2) A slave of God
            (3) An apostle of Jesus Christ
        b. Why, 1:1b-3
            (1) To stimulate faith
            (2) To lead them to full knowledge
                (a) In hope of eternal life which God promised
                (b) At the proper time God made known
                (c) By the message entrusted to Paul by God's command
        c. To whom, 1:4a
            (1) To Titus
            (2) My genuine child in the common faith
        d. Prayer, 1:4b
            (1) Spiritual blessing
            (2) Peace
            (3) From
                (a) God our Father
                (b) Christ Jesus our Savior

2. Guide for elders, 1:5-9
   a. Above reproach, 1:6, 7 b. One wife
   c. Believing children
   d. Not accused of reckless living e. Not accused of disobedience
   f. Not stubborn
   g. Not quick-tempered
   h. Not addicted to strong drink i. Not pugnacious
   j. Not addicted to dishonest gain k. Hospitable
   l. Lover of goodness m. Sensible
   n. Upright o. Pure life
   p. Self-controlled
   q. Continue to cling to the trustworthy message
   r. Competent to encourage others with wholesome teaching
   s. Convict those who oppose him (2:15)

3. Guidelines for determining false teaching, 1:10-16
   a. Insubordinate
   b. Mere talkers with nothing to say c. Deceivers of their own minds
   d. Jewish elements
      (1) Circumcision, 1:10
      (2) Jewish myths, 1:14
      (3) Pedigrees, 3:9
      (4) Wrangles about the law, 3:9
   e. Upset whole families' teaching what they ought not
   f. For the sake of dishonest gain
   g. Their minds and consciences are impure
   h. Their actions disowns Him
   i. Detestable
   j. Disobedient
   k. Useless for anything good

4. Guidelines for believers, 2:1-10a, 12
   a. For older men, 2:2
      (1) Temperate
      (2) Serious
      (3) Sensible
      (4) Healthy in faith
      (5) Healthy in love
      (6) Steadfast
   b. For older women, 2:3
      (1) Reverent in deportment
      (2) Not slanderers
      (3) Not slaves to heavy drinking
      (4) Teachers of what is right
      (5) Trainers of younger women

      c.   For younger women, 2:4-5
          (1) Be affectionate wives
          (2) Be affectionate mothers
          (3) Serious
          (4) Pure
          (5) Homekeepers
          (6) Kind
          (7) Subordinate to their husbands
      d.   For younger men, 2:6-8
          (1) Sensible
          (2) Set a worthy example of doing good
          (3) Sincere
          (4) Serious in your teaching
          (5) Wholesome message
          (6) Unobjectionable
      e.   Believing slaves, 2:9-10
          (1) Practice perfect submission to their masters
          (2) Stop resisting them
          (3) Stop stealing from them

5.   Theological basis for the guidelines, 2:10b-15; 3:4-7
      a.   To adorn, in everything they do, the teaching of God our Savior, 2:10b.
      b.   The grace of God has appeared to all mankind, 2:11.
      c.   Waiting for the blessed hope (the second coming), 2:13
      d.   Jesus purchased a people to reveal God, 2:14
      e.   Goodness and loving-kindness of God has been revealed, 3:4
      f.   God saved us not based on our deeds, 3:5.
      g.   God saved us based on His mercy, 3:5.
          (1) Through a bath of regeneration
          (2) Renewal of the Holy Spirit
          (3) Both given through Christ
          (4) We have right standing with God
          (5) We are heirs of eternal life

6.   Guidelines for those who could cause problems, 3:1-11
      a.   Be subject to those in authority, 3:1-2.
          (1) Ready for any good enterprise
          (2) Stop abusing anyone
          (3) Be peaceable
          (4) Showing perfect gentleness to everyone
      b.   Be gentle toward all mankind because, 3:3-8
          (1) Believers were once:
          (a) Without understanding
          (b) Disobedient
          (c) Misled
          (d) Habitual slaves to all sorts of passion

     (e) Spending our lives in malice
     (f) Spending our lives in envy
   c. Beware of, 3:9-11
     (1) Foolish controversies
     (2) Pedigrees
     (3) Strife
     (4) Wrangles about the law
     (5) A man who is factious
      (a) crooked
      (b) sinful
      (c) self-condemned

  7. Traditional Christian closing to the letter, 3:12-15
   a. Titus' replacement is coming, 3:12
     (1) Artemas (or)
     (2) Tychicus
   b. Titus come and meet me at Nicopolis, 3:12
   c. Encourage the believers to help, 3:13-14
     (1) Zenos (and)
     (2) Apollos
   d. Final greetings and close, 3:15

  D. List applicable application points: With this detailed outline on the far left of a page(s) write in possible application truths for every major literary unit and every paragraph division. State the application truth in one short declarative sentence. This outline will become the points of your sermon.

IV. Fourth Reading

A. Significant parallels (other Pastoral Epistles)
  1. I Timothy (esp. chapter 3:1-13)
  2. II Timothy

B. Specialized lists
  1. Use of the title "Savior"
   a. God our Savior, 1:3; 2:10; 3:4
   b. Christ our Savior, 1:4; 2:13; 3:6
  2. Doctrinal truths of the Gospel used as basis for our Christ-like lifestyle: (cf. III., c.5.)
   a. 2:10b-14
   b. 3:4-7
  3. List of qualifications for elders, 1:7-9 (cf. III., c.2. compare I Timothy 3:1ff)
  4. List of characteristics of false teachers: (cf. IV., c.3.)
   a. 1:10-16
   b. 3:9-11

C. Difficult passages
   1. Textual - Does the phrase in 1:6b refer to the elder or his children?
      a. Elder - NASB and NRSV
      b. Children of elder - NIV and Williams
   2. Historical - Is there any biblical or historical evidence for a fourth missionary journey?
      a. Biblical
         (1) Paul wanted to go to Spain, Rom. 15:24, 28
         (2) Paul's travel itinerary in the Pastoral Epistles does not fit his travel itinerary of the book of Acts.
      b. Historical
         (1) Eusebius in his book, Ecclesiastical History, 2:22:2-3 implies that Paul was released from prison after the close of Acts.
         (2) Other early church traditions that Paul took the Gospel to the far west of the Mediterranean Sea
            (a) Clement of Rome
            (b) Muratorian Fragment
   3. Theological - is the doctrine of baptismal regeneration supported from 3:5?
   4. Verses that cause confusion - elders not total abstainers, but "not addicted to much wine," 1:7. The same thing expressed for older women, 2:3.

EPHESIANS 2

PARAGRAPH DIVISIONS OF MODERN TRANSLATIONS

UBS4	NKJV	NRSV	TEV	NJB
From Death to Life	By Grace Through Faith	Christ's Benefits	From Death to Life	Salvation in Christ
2:1-10	2:1-10	2:1-10	2:1-3	2:1-6
			2:4-10	
				2:7-10
One in Christ	Brought Near by His Blood		One in Christ	Reconciliation of the Jews and the Pagans with Others and with God
2:11-13	2:11-13	2:11-22	2:11-12	2:11-18
	Christ Our Peace		2:13-18	
2:14-22	2:14-22			
			2:19-22	2:19-22

READING CYCLE THREE

This is a study guide commentary, which means that you are responsible for your own interpretation of the Bible. Each of us must walk in the light we have. You, the Bible, and the Holy Spirit are priority in interpretation. You must not relinquish this to a commentator.

Read the chapter in one sitting. Identify the subjects. Compare your subject divisions with the five translations above. Paragraphing is not inspired, but it is the key to following the original author's intent, which is the heart of interpretation. Every paragraph has one and only one subject.

1. First paragraph
2. Second paragraph
3. Third paragraph
4. Etc.

CONTEXTUAL INSIGHTS TO 2:1-22

A. The Gnostic and Jewish emphasis on human works-oriented salvation is depreciated by Paul's emphasis on (1) God's election in chapter 1; (2) God's initiating grace in 2:1-10; and (3) the mystery of God's redemptive plan hidden from the ages (i.e., Jew and Gentile now are one in Christ) in 2:11-3:13. Paul emphasizes the three things in which humans have no part! Salvation is all of God (cf. 1:3-14; 2:4-7), but individuals must personally respond (cf. 2:8-9) and live in light of the New Covenant (2:10).

B. There are three enemies of fallen humanity delineated in vv. 2-3 (cf. James 4:1,4,7): (1) the fallen world system, v. 2; (2) the angelic adversary, Satan, v. 2; and (3) mankind's fallen nature (Adamic nature), v. 3. Verses 1-3 show the hopelessness and helplessness of fallen mankind apart from and in rebellion to God (cf. Rom. 1:18-2:16).

C. As verses 1-3 describe the pitiable state of humanity, verses 4-6 contrast the riches of God's love and mercy for fallen mankind. Human sin is bad, but God's love and mercy are greater (cf. Rom. 5:20)! What God did for Christ (cf. 1:20), Christ has now done for believers (cf. 2:5-6).

D. There is real tension in the New Testament between the free grace of God and human effort.

This tension can be expressed in paradoxical pairs: indicative (a statement) and imperative (a command); grace/faith objective (the content of the gospel) and subjective (one's experience of the gospel); won the race (in Christ) and run the race (for Christ). This tension is clearly seen in 2:8-9, which emphasizes grace, while 2:10 emphasizes good works. It is not an either/or but a both/and theological proposition. However, grace always comes first and is the foundation of a Christlike lifestyle. Verses 8-10 are a classical summary of the paradox of the Christian gospel—free, but it costs everything! Faith <u>and</u> works (cf. James 2:14-26)!

E. A new topic is introduced in 2:11-3:13. It is the mystery, hidden from the beginning, that God desires the redemption of all mankind, Jew (cf. Ezek. 18:23,32) and Gentile (cf. I Tim. 2:4; II Pet. 3:9), through personal faith in the substitutionary atonement of the Messiah. This universal offer of salvation was predicted in Gen. 3:15 and 12:3. This radically free forgiveness (cf. Rom. 5:12-21) shocked the Jews and all religious elitists (gnostic false teachers, Judaizers) and all modern "works-righteousness" proponents.

WORD AND PHRASE STUDY

NASB (UPDATED) TEXT: 2:1-10

¹And you were dead in your trespasses and sins, ²in which you formerly walked according to the course of this world, according to the prince of the power of the air, of the spirit that is now working in the sons of disobedience. ³Among them we too all formerly lived in the lusts of our flesh, indulging the desires of the flesh and of the mind, and were by nature children of wrath, even as the rest. ⁴But God, being rich in mercy, because of His great love with which He loved us,

⁵even when we were dead in our transgressions, made us alive together with Christ (by grace you have been saved), ⁶and raised us up with Him, and seated us with Him in the heavenly *places* in Christ Jesus, ⁷so that in the ages to come He might show the surpassing riches of His grace in kindness toward us in Christ Jesus. ⁸For by grace you have been saved through faith; and that not of yourselves, *it is* the gift of God; ⁹not as a result of works, so that no one may boast. ¹⁰For we are His workmanship, created in Christ Jesus for good works, which God prepared beforehand so that we would walk in them.

2:1 Either verses 1-7 or 1-10 form one sentence in Greek, with the main verb in v. 5. It is one sustained argument. Paul's presentation includes
(1) the hopelessness, helplessness, and spiritual lostness of all mankind, vv. 1-3;
(2) the unmerited grace of God, vv. 4-7; and
(3) the necessary human response, faith and life, vv. 8-10.

} **"you"** In Colossians and Ephesians this PLURAL PRONOUN always refers to believing Gentiles (cf. 1:13; 2:12).

} **"were dead"** This is a PRESENT ACTIVE PARTICIPLE meaning "being dead." This refers to spiritual death (cf. v. 5; Rom. 5:12-21; Col. 2:13). The Bible speaks of three stages of death: (1) spiritual death (cf. Gen. 2:17; 3; Isa. 59:2; Rom. 7:10-11; James 1:15); (2) physical death (cf. Gen. 5); and (3) eternal death, called "the second death" (cf. Rev. 2:11; 20:6,14; 21:8).

} **"trespasses"** This Greek term (*paraptÇma*) means "falling to one side" (cf. 1:7). All Greek words for "sins" are related to the Hebrew concept of deviation from the standard of God's righteousness. The term "right," "just," and their derivatives in Hebrew are from a construction metaphor for a measuring reed. God is the standard. All humans deviate from that standard (cf. Ps. 14:1-3; 5:9; 10:7; 36:1; 53:1-4; 140:3; Isa. 53:6; 59:7-8; Rom. 3:9-23; I Pet. 2:25).

} **"sins"** This Greek term (*hamartia*) means "missing the mark" (cf. 4:26). The two terms for sin in verse 1 are used as synonyms to illustrate mankind's fallen, estranged condition (cf. Rom. 3:9,19,23; 11:32; Gal. 3:22).

} **2:2 "in which you formerly walked"** "Walk" is a biblical metaphor for lifestyle (cf. 2:1,10; 4:1,17; 5:2,8,15).

} NASB, NKJV   **"according to the course of this world"**
   NRSV   **"following the course of this world"**
   TEV   **"followed the world's evil way"**
   NJB   **"living by the principles of this world"**
This current fallen world system (i.e., age) is personified as an enemy (cf. Gal. 1:4). It is fallen mankind attempting to meet all needs apart from God. In John's writing it is called "the world" (cf. I John 2:2,15-17; 3:1,13,17; 4:1-17; 5:4,5,19) or "Babylon" (cf. Rev. 14:8; 16:19; 17:5; 18:2,10,21). In our modern terminology it is called "atheistic humanism." See Special Topic: Paul's Use of *Kosmos* at Col. 1:6.

} NASB, NKJV   **"according to the prince of the power of the air"**
   NRSV   **"following the rules of the power of the air"**
   TEV   **"you obeyed the ruler of the spiritual powers in space"**
   NJB   **"obeying the ruler who governs the air"**
This is the second enemy of fallen mankind, Satan, the accuser. Mankind is subjected to a personal angelic tempter (cf. Gen. 3, Job. 1-2, Zech. 3). He is called the ruler or god of this world (cf. John 12:31; 14:30; 16:11; II Cor. 4:4; I John 5:19).

In the NT the air is the realm of the demonic. The lower air (*a'r*) was seen by the Greeks to be impure and therefore the domain of evil spirits. Some see this use of "air" as referring to the immaterial nature of the spiritual realm. The concept of "the rapture of the church" comes from the Latin translation of I Thess. 4:17, "caught up." Christians are going to meet the Lord in the midst of Satan's kingdom, "the air," to show its overthrow! See Special Topic below.

SPECIAL TOPIC: PERSONAL EVIL

This is a very difficult subject for several reasons
1. The OT does not reveal an archenemy to good, but a servant of YHWH who offers mankind an alternative and accuses mankind of unrighteousness.
2. The concept of a personal archenemy of God developed in the inter-biblical (non-canonical) literature under the influence of Persian religion (*Zoroastrianism*). This, in turn, greatly influenced rabbinical Judaism.
3. The NT develops the OT themes in surprisingly stark, but selective, categories.

If one approaches the study of evil from the perspective of biblical theology (each book or author or genre studied and outlined separately), then very different views of evil are revealed.

If, however, one approaches the study of evil from a non-biblical or extra-biblical approach of world religions or eastern religions, then much of the NT development is foreshadowed in Persian dualism and Greco-Roman spiritism.

If one is presuppositionally committed to the divine authority of Scripture, then the NT development must be seen as progressive revelation. Christians must guard against allowing Jewish folk lore or western literature (i.e., Dante, Milton) to define the biblical concept. There is certainly mystery and ambiguity in this area of revelation. God has chosen not to reveal all aspects of evil, its origin, its purpose, but He has revealed its defeat!

In the OT the term Satan or accuser seems to relate to three separate groups
1. human accusers (I Sam. 29:4; II Sam. 19:22; I Kgs. 11:14,23,25; Ps. 109:6)
2. angelic accusers (Num. 22:22-23; Zech. 3:1)
3. demonic accusers (I Chr. 21:1; I Kgs. 22:21; Zech. 13:2)

Only later in the intertestamental period is the serpent of Gen. 3 identified with Satan (cf. Book of Wisdom 2:23-24; II Enoch 31:3), and not until even later does this become a rabbinical option (cf. *Sot* 9b and *Sanh.* 29a). The "sons of God" of Genesis 6 become angels in I Enoch 54:6. I mention this, not to assert its theological accuracy, but to show its development. In the NT these OT activities are attributed to angelic, personified evil (i.e., Satan) in II Cor. 11:3; Rev. 12:9.

The origin of personified evil is difficult or impossible (depending on your point of view) to determine from the OT. One reason for this is Israel's strong monotheism (cf. I Kgs. 22:20-22; Eccl. 7:14; Isa. 45:7; Amos 3:6). All causality was attributed to YHWH to demonstrate His uniqueness and primacy (cf. Isa. 43:11; 44:6,8,24; 45:5-6,14,18,21,22).

Sources of possible information focus on (1) Job 1-2 where Satan is one of the "sons of God" (i.e., angels) or (2) Isa. 14; Ezek. 28 where prideful near eastern kings (Babylon and Tyre) are used to illustrate the pride of Satan (cf. I Tim. 3:6). I have mixed emotions about this approach. Ezekiel uses Garden of Eden metaphors not only for the king of Tyre as Satan (cf. Ezek. 28:12-16), but also for the king of Egypt as the Tree of the Knowledge of Good and Evil (Ezek. 31). However, Isa. 14, particularly vv. 12-14, seems to describe an angelic revolt through pride. If God wanted to reveal to us the specific nature and origin of Satan this is a very oblique way and place to do it. We must guard against the trend of systematic theology of taking small, ambiguous parts of different testaments, authors, books, and genres and combining them as pieces of one divine puzzle.

Alfred Edersheim (*The Life and Times of Jesus the Messiah*, vol. 2, appendices XIII [pp. 748-763] and XVI [pp. 770-776]) says that Rabbinical Judaism has been overly influenced by Persian dualism and demonic speculation. The rabbis are not a good source for truth in this area. Jesus radically diverges from the teachings of the Synagogue. I think that the rabbinical concept of angelic mediation and opposition in the giving of the law to Moses on Mt. Sinai opened the door to the concept of an arch- angelic enemy of YHWH as well as mankind. There are two high gods of Iranian (Zoroastrian) dualism, *Ahkiman* and *Ormaza*, good and evil. This dualism developed into a Judaic limited dualism of YHWH and Satan.

There is surely progressive revelation in the NT as to the development of evil, but not as elaborate as the rabbis proclaim. A good example of this difference is the "war in heaven." The fall of Satan is a logical necessity, but the specifics are not given. Even what is given is veiled in apocalyptic genre (cf. Rev. 12:4,7,12-13). Although Satan is defeated and exiled to earth, he still functions as a servant of YHWH (cf. Matt. 4:1; Luke 22:31-32; I Cor. 5:5; I Tim. 1:20).

We must curb our curiosity in this area. There is a personal force of temptation and evil, but there is still only one God and mankind is still responsible for his/her choices. There is a spiritual battle, both before and after salvation. Victory can only come and remain in and through the Triune God. Evil has been defeated and will be removed!

} NASB, NKJV	"in the sons of disobedience"
NRSV	"among those who are disobedient"
TEV	"the people who disobey God"
NJB	"in the rebellious"

This was a Hebrew idiom for rebellion and settled character (cf. 5:6).

2:3 "we too all formerly lived" In Ephesians "we" refers to the Jewish believers, in this case, Paul and his ministry team. The ending phrase "even as the rest," makes it possible that this phrase refers to all of the OT chosen people, the Jews. This VERB is an AORIST PASSIVE INDICATIVE. The PASSIVE VOICE would emphasize that fallen mankind was being manipulated by outside evil spiritual forces, like Satan or the demonic, mentioned in v. 2 and 3:10; 6:12.

} NASB, NKJV	"in the lusts of our flesh"
NRSV	"in the passions of our flesh"
TEV	"according to our natural desires"
NJB	"sensual lives"

This is the third enemy of fallen man. Although it is not listed in a grammatically parallel structure ("according to...") with the two enemies in v. 2, it is a theological parallel. Mankind's fallen, egocentric self (cf. Gen. 3) is its worst enemy (cf. Gal. 5:19-21). It twists and manipulates everything and everyone to one's own self interest (cf. Rom. 7:14-25).

Paul uses the term "flesh" in two distinct ways. Only context can determine the distinction. In 2:11,14; 5:29,31; 6:5 and 12 it means "the human person," not "the fallen sin nature" as here.

} NASB	"indulging the desires of the flesh and of the mind"
NKJV	"fulfilling the desires of the flesh and of the mind"
NRSV	"following the desires of the flesh and senses"
TEV	"and did whatever suited the wishes of our own bodies and minds"
NJB	"ruled entirely by our own physical desires and our own ideas"

This is a PRESENT ACTIVE PARTICIPLE which emphasizes continual, on-going, habitual action. The human body and the mind are not evil in and of themselves, but they are the battleground of temptation and sin (cf. 4:17-19; Romans 6 & 7).

} **"by nature"** This refers to mankind's fallen, Adamic propensities (cf. Gen. 3; Ps. 51:5; Job 14:4; Rom. 5:12-21; 7:14-25). It is surprising that the rabbis in general do not emphasize the fall of humanity in Gen. 3. They instead assert that mankind has two intents (*yetzers*), one good, one bad. Humans are dominated by their choices. There is a famous rabbinical proverb: "Every man has a black and a white dog in his heart. The one he feeds the most is the one that becomes the biggest." However, the NT presents several theological reasons for mankind's sin (1) the fall of Adam, (2) willful ignorance and (3) sinful choices.

} **"children of wrath"** "Children of. . .", like "sons of. . .", is an Hebraic idiomatic phrase for a person's character. God is opposed to sin and rebellion in His creation. The wrath of God is both temporal (in time) and eschatological (at the end of time).

} NASB	"even as the rest"
NKJV	"made us sit together"
NRSV, TEV	"like everyone else"
NJB	"as the rest of the world"

This refers to the lostness of all humans, both Jew and Gentile (cf. Rom. 1:18-3:21). Paul often uses the term "rest" to refer to the lost (cf. I Thess. 4:13; 5:6).

2:4 "But God, being rich in mercy, because of His great love with which He loved us" There is such a dramatic switch between the hopelessness and helplessness of vv. 1-3 and the marvelous grace and mercy of God in vv. 4-7.

What a great truth! God's mercy and love are the keys to salvation (cf. v. 7). It is His merciful character (cf. 1:7,18; 2:7; 3:8,16), not mankind's performance, that offers a way of righteousness. See note on "riches" at 1:7.

It is significant that this verse on God's grace contains a PRESENT PARTICIPLE and an AORIST ACTIVE INDICATIVE. God has loved us in the past and continues to love us (cf. I John 4:10)!

2:5 "even when we were dead in our transgressions," This phrase is parallel to v. 1a. Paul returns to his original thought after his parenthetical thought (cf. vv. 1-3) about the lostness of mankind. In the midst of our need, God acted in love (cf. Rom. 5:6,8).

} **"made us alive together with Christ"** This English phrase reflects one Greek word (*suzōpoieō*). This is the main verb of the sentence (AORIST ACTIVE INDICATIVE) which begins in v. 1. This is the first of three compound VERBS with the Greek PREPOSITION, *syn*, which meant "joint participation with." Jesus was raised from the dead in 1:20 and believers have been quickened to spiritual life through Him (cf. Col. 2:13). Believers are now truly alive with Christ.

} **2:5,8 "by grace you have been saved"** This is a PERFECT PASSIVE PERIPHRASTIC PARTICIPLE, repeated in v. 8 for emphasis. This meant that believers have been saved in the past, by an outside agent, with abiding results; "they have been and continue to be saved by God." This same construction is repeated in v. 8 for emphasis. See Special Topic at Eph. 1:7.

This is one of the biblical passages which forms the basis for the doctrine of the security of the believer (cf. John 6:37, 39; 10:28; 17:2, 24; 18:9; Rom. 8:31-39). Like all biblical doctrines, it must be balanced (held in tension) with other truths and texts.

2:6 "raised us with Him" This is the second of the AORIST compounds with *syn*. Believers have already been raised with Christ. Believers were buried with Him in baptism (cf. Col. 2:12; Rom. 6:3-11) and raised with Him by the Father (cf. Col. 2:13; Rom. 6:4-5) who raised Jesus (raised by the Spirit in Rom. 8:11). These are special redemptive analogies. Believers spiritually participate in the major events of Jesus' experience: crucifixion, death, burial, resurrection, and enthronement! Believers share His life and suffering; they will also share His glory (cf. Rom. 8:17)!

} NASB, NRSV	"seated us with Him"
NKJV	"made us sit together"
TEV	"to rule with him"
NJB	"gave us a place with him"

This is the third of the AORIST compounds with *syn*. Our position in Him is one of present, as well as future, victory (cf. Rom. 8:37)! The concept of sitting down with Him meant reigning with Him. Jesus is the King of Kings sitting on the throne of God the Father and believers are even now co-reigning with Him (cf. Matt. 19:28; Rom. 5:17; Col. 3:1; II Tim. 2:12; Rev. 22:5). See Special Topic below.

SPECIAL TOPIC: REIGNING IN THE KINGDOM OF GOD

The concept of reigning with Christ is part of the larger theological category called "the Kingdom of God." This is a carry-over from the OT concept of God as the true king of Israel (cf. I Sam. 8:7). He symbolically reigned (I Sam. 8:7; 10:17-19) through a descendant from the tribe of Judah (cf. Gen. 49:10) and the family of Jesse (cf. II Sam. 7).

Jesus is the promised fulfillment of OT prophecy concerning the Messiah. He inaugurated the Kingdom of God with His incarnation at Bethlehem. The Kingdom of God became the central pillar of Jesus' preaching. The Kingdom had fully come in Him (cf. Matt: 10:7; 11:12; 12:28; Mark 1:15; Luke 10:9,11; 11:20; 16:16; 17:20-21).

However, the Kingdom was also future (eschatological). It was present but not consummated (cf. Matt. 6:10; 8:11; 16:28; 22:1-14; 26:29; Luke 9:27; 11:2; 13:29; 14:10-24; 22:16,18). Jesus came the first time as a suffering servant (cf. Isa. 52:13-53:12); as humble (cf. Zech. 9:9) but He will return as King of Kings (cf. Matt. 2:2; 21:5; 27:11-14). The concept of "reigning" is surely a part of this "kingdom" theology. God has given the kingdom to Jesus' followers (see Luke 12:32).

The concept of reigning with Christ has several aspects and questions:

1. Do the passages which assert that God has given believers "the kingdom" through Christ refer to "reigning" (cf. Matt. 5:3,10; Luke 12:32)?

2. Do Jesus' words to the original disciples in the first century Jewish context refer to all believers (cf. Matt. 19:28; Luke 22:28-30)?

3. Does Paul's emphasis on reigning in this life now contrast or complement the above texts (cf. Rom. 5:17; I Cor. 4:8)?

4. How are suffering and reigning related (cf. Rom. 8:17; II Tim. 2:11-12; I Pet. 4:13; Rev. 1:9)?

5. The recurrent theme of Revelation is sharing the glorified Christ's reign, but is it
   a. earthly, 5:10
   b. millennial, 20:5,6
   c. eternal, 2:26; 3:21; 22:5 and Dan. 7:14,18,27?

} NASB, NKJV,
  NRSV   "in the heavenly *places*"
  TEV   "in the heavenly world"
  NJB   "in heaven"

This LOCATIVE (of sphere) NEUTER PLURAL ADJECTIVE, "in the heavenly places," is used only in Ephesians (cf. 1:20; 2:6; 3:10; 6:12). From the context of all of its usages, it must mean the spiritual realm in which believers live here and now, not heaven.

2:7 "in the ages to come" The Jews believed in two ages, the current evil age (Gal. 1:4) and the coming righteous age (see Special Topic at 1:21). This New Age of righteousness would be inaugurated by the coming of the Messiah in the power of the Spirit. In 1:20 "age" is SINGULAR, here it is PLURAL (cf. I Cor 2:7; Heb. 1:2; 11:3). This implies that (1) there are at least two ages or (2) the PLURAL is used to accentuate and magnify the coming age—a rabbinical idiom called a "plural of majesty." This use of the PLURAL in a symbolic sense can be seen in the passages that refer to the past "ages" (cf. Rom. 10:25; I Cor. 10:11; II Tim. 1:9; Titus 1:2).

Some scholars believe this was simply a metaphor for eternity because of the way the phrase was used in secular Koine Greek and in several places in the NT (cf. Luke 1:33, 55; John 12:34; Rom. 9:5; Gal. 1:5; I Tim. 1:17).

} **"He might show"** This is an AORIST MIDDLE SUBJUNCTIVE. God clearly manifested His own character (cf. 1:5-7). This term means "to publicly display" (cf. Rom. 9:17,22). God's mercy and purpose in Christ are clearly manifested to the angels by His treatment of fallen mankind (cf. 3:10; I Cor. 4:9; I Pet. 1:12).

} **"surprising"** *Huperballō*. See Special Topic: Paul's Use of *Huper* Compounds at 1:19.

2:8 "For by grace" Salvation is by the "grace" of God (cf. Eph. 1:3-14). The character of God is revealed through His mercy (cf. vv. 4-6). Believers are the trophies of His love. Grace is best defined as the unmerited, undeserved love of God. It flows from God's nature through Christ and is irrespective of the worth or merit of the one loved.

} **"you have been saved"** This is a PERFECT PASSIVE PERIPHRASTIC PARTICIPLE which is parallel with v. 5. Its thrust is that "believers have been and continue to be" saved by God.

In the OT the term "save" spoke of "physical deliverance" (cf. James 5:15). In the NT this meaning has taken on a spiritual dimension. God delivers believers from the results of sin and gives them eternal life.

} **"through faith"** Faith receives God's free gift in Christ (cf. Rom. 3:22,25; 4:5; 9:30; Gal. 2:16; I Pet. 1:5). Mankind must respond to God's offer of grace and forgiveness in Christ (cf. John 1:12; 3:16-17,36; 6:40; 11:25-26; Rom. 10:9-13).

God deals with fallen mankind by means of a covenant. He always takes the initiative (cf. John 6:44, 65) and sets the agenda and the boundaries (cf. Mark 1:51; Acts 3:16,19; 20:21). He allows fallen mankind to participate in their own salvation by responding to His covenant offer. The mandated response is initial and continuing faith, repentance, obedience, service, worship, and perseverance.

The term "faith" in the OT is a metaphorical extension of a stable stance. It came to denote that which is sure, trustworthy, dependable and faithful. None of these describe even redeemed fallen mankind. It is not mankind's trustworthiness, or faithfulness or dependability, but God's. We trust in His trustworthy promises, not our trustworthiness! Covenant obedience flows from gratitude! The focus has always been on His faithfulness, not the believers' faith! Faith cannot save anyone. Only grace saves, but it is received by faith. The focus is never on the amount of faith (cf. Matt. 17:20), but on its object (Jesus).

} **"and that"** This is the Greek DEMONSTRATIVE PRONOUN *(touto)*, which is NEUTER in GENDER. The closest NOUNS, "grace" and "faith," are both FEMININE in GENDER. Therefore, this must refer to the whole process of our salvation in the finished work of Christ.

There is another possibility based on a similar grammatical construction in Phil. 1:28. If this is the case then this adverbial phrase relates to faith, which is also a gift of God's grace! Here is the mystery of God's sovereignty and human free will.

} **"not of yourselves"** This is the first of three phrases which clearly show that salvation is not based on human performance: (1) "not of yourselves," v. 8 (2) "gift of God" v. 8 and (3) "not as a result of works," v. 9.

} **"the gift of God"** This is the essence of grace—love with no strings attached (cf. Rom. 3:24; 6:23). The paradox of salvation as both a free gift and a mandated covenant response are difficult to grasp. Yet both are true! Salvation is truly free, yet costs everything. Most biblical doctrines are presented as tension-filled pairs of truths (security vs. perseverance, faith vs. works, God's sovereignty vs. human free will, predestination vs. human response and transcendence vs. immanence).

SPECIAL TOPIC: NEW TESTAMENT EVIDENCE FOR ONE'S SALVATION

1. It is based on the character of the Father (cf. John 3:16), the work of the Son (cf. II Cor. 5:21), and the ministry of the Spirit (cf. Rom. 8:14-16), not on human performance, not wages due for obedience, not just a creed.
2. It is a gift (cf. Rom. 3:24; 6:23; Eph. 2:5,8-9).
3. It is a new life, a new world-view (cf. James and I John).
4. It is knowledge (the gospel), fellowship (faith in and with Jesus), and a new lifestyle (Spirit- led Christlikeness) all three, not just any one by itself.

2:9 "not as a result of works," Salvation is <u>not</u> by merit (cf. Rom. 3:20, 27-28; 9:11, 16; Gal. 2:16; Phil 3:9; II Tim. 1:9; Titus 3:5). This is in direct contrast to the false teachers.

☞ **"so that no one may boast"** Salvation is by God's grace, not human effort, so there is no room for human glorying (cf. Rom. 3:27; 4:2). If believers boast, let them boast in Christ (cf. I Cor. 1:31, which is a quote from Jer. 9:23-24).

SPECIAL TOPIC: BOASTING

These Greek terms *kauchaomai*, *kauchēma*, and *kauchēsis* are used about thirty-five times by Paul and only twice in the rest of the NT (both in James). Its predominate use is in I and II Corinthians.

There are two main truths connected to boasting.

1. no flesh shall glory/boast before God (cf. I Cor. 1:29; Eph. 2:9)
2. believers should glory in the Lord (cf. I Cor. 1:31; II Cor. 10:17, which is an allusion to Jer.9:23-24)

Therefore, there is appropriate and inappropriate boasting/glorying (i.e., pride).

1. appropriate
   a. in the hope of glory (cf. Rom. 4:2)
   b. in God through the Lord Jesus (cf. Rom. 5:11)
   c. in the cross of the Lord Jesus Christ (i.e., Paul's main theme, cf. I Cor. 1:17-18; Gal. 6:14)
   d. Paul boasts in
      (1) his ministry without compensation (cf. I Cor. 9:15,16; II Cor. 10:12)
      (2) his authority from Christ (cf. II Cor. 10:8,12)
      (3) his not boasting in other men's labor (as some at Corinth were, cf. II Cor. 10:15)
      (4) his racial heritage (as others were doing at Corinth, cf. II Cor. 11:17; 12:1,5,6)
      (5) his churches
         (a) Corinth (II Cor. 7:4,14; 8:24; 9:2; 11:10)
         (b) Thessalonika (cf. II Thess. 1:4)
      (6) his confidence in God's comfort and deliverance (cf. II Cor. 1:12)

```
2.   inappropriate
     a.   in relation to Jewish heritage (cf. Rom. 2:17,23; 3:27; Gal. 6:13)
     b.   some in the Corinthian church were boasting
          (1)   in men (cf. I Cor. 3:21)
          (2)   in wisdom (cf. I Cor. 4:7
          (3)   in freedom (cf. I Cor. 5:6)
     c.   false teachers tried to boast in the church at Corinth (cf. II Cor. 11:12)
```

2:10 "we are His workmanship," The English word "poem" comes from this Greek term (*poi'ma*). This word is used only two times in the NT, here and Rom. 1:20. This is the believers' position in grace. They are paradoxically His finished product which is still in process!

} "created in Christ Jesus" This is an AORIST PASSIVE PARTICIPLE. The Spirit forms believers through Christ's ministry by the will of the Father (cf. 1:3-14). This act of a new spiritual creation is described in the same terms used of the initial creation in Genesis (cf. 3:9; Col. 1:16).

} "for good works" Believers' lifestyles after they meet Christ are an evidence of their salvation (cf. James and I John). They are saved by grace through faith unto works! They are saved to serve! Faith without works is dead, as are works without faith (cf. Matt. 7:21-23 and James 2:14-26). The goal of the Father's choice is that believers be "holy and blameless" (cf. 1:4).

Paul was often attacked for his radically free gospel because it seemed to encourage godless living. A gospel so seemingly unconnected to moral performance must lead to abuse. Paul's gospel was free in the grace of God, but it also demanded an appropriate response, not only in initial repentance, but in ongoing repentance. Godly living is the result, not lawlessness. Good works are not the mechanism of salvation, but the result. This paradox of a completely free salvation and a cost-everything response is difficult to communicate, but the two must be held in a tension-filled balance.

American individualism has distorted the gospel. Humans are not saved because God loves them so much individually, but because God loves fallen mankind, mankind made in His image. He saves and changes individuals to reach more individuals. The ultimate focus of love is primarily corporate (cf. John 3:16), but it is received individually (cf. John 1:12; Rom. 10:9-13; I Cor. 15:1).

} "which God prepared beforehand" This strong term (*pro* + *hetoimos*, " to prepare before") relates to the theological concept of predestination (cf. 1:4-5,11) and is used only here and in Rom. 9:23. God chose a people to reflect His character. Through Christ, the Father has restored His image in fallen mankind (cf. Gen. 1:26-27).

[11]Therefore remember that formerly you, the Gentiles in the flesh, who are called "Uncircumcision" by the so-called "Circumcision," which is performed in the flesh by human hands—[12]*remember* that you were at that time separate from Christ, excluded from the commonwealth of Israel, and strangers to the covenants of promise, having no hope and without God in the world. [13]But now in Christ Jesus you who formerly were far off have been brought near by the blood of Christ. [14]For He Himself is our peace, who made both *groups into* one and broke down the barrier of the dividing wall, [15]by abolishing in His flesh the enmity, *which is* the Law of commandments *contained* in ordinances, so that in Himself He might make the two into one new man, *thus* establishing peace, [16]and might reconcile them both in one body to God through the cross, by it having put to death the enmity. [17]AND HE CAME AND PREACHED PEACE TO YOU WHO WERE FAR AWAY, AND PEACE TO THOSE WHO WERE NEAR; [18]for through Him we both have our access in one Spirit to the Father. [19]So then you are no longer strangers and aliens, but you are fellow citizens with the saints, and are of God's household, [20]having been built on the foundation of the apostles and prophets, Christ Jesus Himself being the corner *stone*, [21]in whom the whole building, being fitted together, is growing into a holy temple in the Lord, [22]in whom you also are being built together into a dwelling of God in the Spirit.

2:11 "Therefore" This could refer to (1) vv. 1-10, or (2) 1:3-2:10. Paul often uses this word to start a new literary unit by building on the combined truths of previous units (cf. Rom. 5:1; 8:1; 12:1).

This is the third major truth of Paul's doctrinal section (chapters 1-3). The first was God's eternal choice based on His gracious character, the second was the hopelessness of fallen humanity, saved by God's gracious acts through Christ which must be received and lived out by faith. Now the third, God's will has always been the salvation of all humans (cf. Gen. 3:15), both Jew and Gentile (cf. 2:11-3:13). No human intellect (i.e., Gnostics) understood these revealed truths.

⸢ "remember" This is a PRESENT ACTIVE IMPERATIVE. These Gentiles are commanded to continue to remember their previous alienation from God, vv. 11-12.

⸢ "that formerly you, the Gentiles in the flesh" This is literally "nations" (*ethnos*). It refers to all peoples who are not of the line of Jacob. In the OT the term "nations" (*go'im*) was a derogatory way of referring to all non-Jews.

⸢ "who are called Uncircumcision" Even in the OT, this rite was an outward sign of inner faith (cf. Lev. 26:41-42; Deut. 10:16; Jer. 4:4). The "Judaizers" of Galatians claimed that this was still God's will and was indispensable for salvation (cf. Acts 15:1ff; Gal. 2:11-12). Be careful not to confuse the symbol with the spiritual reality for which it stands (cf. Acts 2:38 for another example).

2:12

NASB	"separate from Christ"
NKJV, NRSV	"without Christ"
TEV	"apart from Christ"
NJB	"you had no Christ"

This is literally "on separate foundations." These next few phrases (i.e., v. 12), like vv. 1-3, show the helplessness and hopelessness of the Gentiles without Christ.

} NASB, NJB	"excluded"
NKJV, NRSV	"being aliens"
TEV	"foreigners"

This is a PERFECT PASSIVE PARTICIPLE meaning "have been and continued to be excluded." In the OT this term referred to resident non-citizens with limited rights (aliens). The Gentiles had been and continued to be separated, alienated from the Covenant of YHWH.

} **"the commonwealth of Israel"** This is literally "citizenship" (*politeia*). This word came into English as "politics." It refers to the chosen descendants of Abraham. Their benefits are enumerated in Romans 9:4-5.

} **"to the covenants of promise,"** The NT can refer to the OT as one covenant or as several covenants. This theological tension can be viewed as one faith covenant expressed in differing requirements. God confronted OT persons in different ways. His word to Adam was about things in the garden of Eden, to Noah about the ark, to Abraham about a son and a place to live, to Moses about leading the people, etc. But to all it was obedience to the word of God! Some groups (dispensationalists) focus on the differentness. Other groups (Calvinists) focus on the unifying faith aspect. Paul focused on the covenant of Abraham (cf. Romans 4) as setting the pattern for all faith relationships.

The New Covenant is like the old covenants in their demand for obedience and personal faith in God's revelation. It is different in content (cf. Jer. 31:31-34). The Mosaic covenant focused on human obedience and performance, while the NT focuses on the obedience and performance of Christ. This new covenant is God's way of uniting Jews and Gentiles by faith in Christ (cf. 2:11-3:13).

The New Covenant, like the old, is both unconditional (God's promise) and conditional (human response). It reflects both the sovereignty of God (predestination) and the free choices of mankind (faith, repentance, obedience, perseverance).

SPECIAL TOPIC: COVENANT

The OT term *berith*, covenant, is not easy to define. There is no matching VERB in Hebrew. All attempts to derive an etymological or cognate definition have proved unconvincing. However, the obvious centrality of the concept has forced scholars to examine the word usage in order to determine its functional meaning.

Covenant is the means by which the one true God deals with His human creation. The concept of covenant, treaty, or agreement is crucial in understanding the biblical revelation. The tension between God's sovereignty and human free-will is clearly seen in the concept of covenant. Some covenants are based completely on God's character, actions, and purposes.

1. creation itself (cf. Genesis 1-2)
2. the call of Abraham (cf. Genesis 12)
3. the covenant with Abraham (cf. Genesis 15)
4. the preservation and promise to Noah (cf. Genesis 6-9)

However, the very nature of covenant demands a response

1. by faith Adam must obey God and not eat of the tree in the midst of Eden (cf. Genesis 2)
2. by faith Abraham must leave his family, follow God, and believe in future descendants (cf. Genesis 12,15)
3. by faith Noah must build a huge boat far from water and gather the animals (cf. Genesis 6-9)
4. by faith Moses brought the Israelites out of Egypt and received specific guidelines for religious and social life with promises of blessings and cursings (cf. Deuteronomy 27-28)

This same tension involving God's relationship to humanity is addressed in the "new covenant." The tension can be clearly seen in comparing Ezek. 18 with Ezek. 36:27-37. Is the covenant based on God's gracious actions or mandated human response? This is the burning issue between the Old Covenant and the New. The goals of both are the same: (1) the restoration of fellowship lost in Genesis 3 and (2) the establishment of a righteous people who reflect God's character.

The new covenant of Jer. 31:31-34 solves the tension by removing human performance as the means of attaining acceptance. God's law becomes an internal desire instead of an external performance. The goal of a godly, righteous people remains the same, but the methodology changes. Fallen mankind proved themselves inadequate to be God's reflected image (cf. Rom. 3:9-18). The problem was not the covenant, but human sinfulness and weakness (cf. Romans 7; Galatians 3).

The same tension between OT unconditional and conditional covenants remains in the NT. Salvation is absolutely free in the finished work of Jesus Christ, but it requires repentance and faith (both initially and continually). It is both a legal pronouncement and a call to Christlikeness, an indicative statement of acceptance and an imperative to holiness! Believers are not saved by their performance, but unto obedience (cf. Eph. 2:8-10). Godly living becomes the evidence of salvation, not the means of salvation. This tension is clearly seen in the NT books of James and I John.

} **"having no hope and without God in the world"** If there is truly one creator God and Israel was His chosen people, the Gentiles were cut off without any hope, lost in idolatry and paganism (cf. I Thess. 4:13 and Rom. 1:18-2:16).

2:13 "But now" There is a contrast between the hopeless past of the Gentiles, vv. 11-12, and their great hope in the gospel, vv. 13-22.

} **"you who formerly were far off have been brought near"** This same concept is repeated in v. 17, where Isa. 57:14-19 is quoted. In Isaiah this text referred to Jewish exiles, but here in Ephesians it refers to Gentiles. This is one example of Paul's typological use of OT passages. The NT Apostles have universalized the OT hope. As the exiled Jews were apart from God, so too, the Gentiles were alienated from God.

} **"by the blood of Christ"** This referred to the vicarious, substitutionary atonement of Christ (cf. 1:7; Rom. 3:25; 5:6-10; II Cor. 5:21; Col. 1:20; Heb. 9:14,28; I Pet. 1:19; Rev. 1:5). God's family is no longer national, but spiritual (cf. Rom. 2:28-29; 4:16-25).

The blood of Christ was a sacrificial metaphor (cf. Leviticus 1-2) for the death of the Messiah (cf. TEV). John the Baptist said of Jesus, "Behold, the lamb of God who takes away the sin of the world" (cf. John 1:29). Jesus came to die (cf. Gen. 3:15; Isa. 53; Mark 15:53; 10:45).

2:14 This verse has three VERBALS. The first is a PRESENT INDICATIVE. Jesus continues to be and to provide our peace. The second and third are AORIST ACTIVE PARTICIPLES; all that is necessary has been accomplished to unite Jews and Gentiles into one new entity (the church).

Peace between Jew and Gentile is the focus of this literary unit 2:11-3:13. This was the mystery of the gospel hidden in ages past. The term "peace" refers to (1) peace between God and mankind (cf. John 14:27; 16:33; Rom. 5:1-11; Phil. 4:7,9) and (2) peace between Jew and Gentile, vv. 14, 15, 17 (cf. Gal. 3:28; Col. 3:11).

} **"He Himself is our peace"** "He Himself" (*autos*) is emphasized. The term "peace" means to "restore that which was broken" (reconciliation). Jesus the Messiah is called the Prince of Peace (cf. Isa. 9:6 and Zech. 6:12-13). God's peace in Christ has several aspects. See Special Topics: Peace and The Christian and Peace at Col. 1:20.

} NASB	"who made both *groups into* one"
NKJV	"who has made both one"
NRSV	"he has made both groups into one"
TEV	"by making Jews and Gentiles one people"
NJB	"has made the two into one"

Believers are no longer Jew or Gentile, but Christian (cf. 1:15; 2:15; 4:4; Gal. 3:28; Col. 3:11).

This was the mystery of God as revealed in Ephesians. This has always been God's plan (Gen. 3:15). God chose Abraham to choose a people, to choose a world (Gen. 12:3; Exod. 19:5-6). This is the unifying theme of the Old and New Covenants (Testaments).

} NASB	"the barrier of the dividing wall"
NKJV	"the middle wall of division"
NRSV	"the dividing wall"
TEV	"the wall that separated"
NJB	"the barrier which used to keep them apart"

This is literally "the middle wall of partition." This was a rare term. In context it obviously refers to the Mosaic law (cf. v.15).

Some commentators have asserted that it was an allusion to the wall in Herod's Temple between the court of the Gentiles and the court of the Women, which separated Jewish and Gentile worshipers. This same symbolism of the removal of barriers is seen in the veil of the Temple rent from top to bottom at Jesus' death (cf. Matt. 27:51). Unity is now possible. Unity is now the will of God (cf. Eph. 4:1-10).

In Gnosticism this term referred to a barrier between heaven and earth, which may be alluded to in Eph. 4:8-10.

2:15
NASB	**"abolishing"**
NKJV	**"having abolished"**
NRSV	**"has abolished"**
TEV	**"abolished"**
NJB	**"destroying"**

The term "abolish" is a favorite of Paul's (cf. Rom. 3:31; 6:6; Col. 2:14). It literally means "to make null and void" or "to bring to no effect." It is an AORIST ACTIVE PARTICIPLE. Jesus has totally eliminated the death sentence of the OT Law (cf. v. 16; Col. 2:14; Heb. 8:13).

This does not mean to imply that the OT is not inspired and important revelation for the NT believer (cf. Matt. 5:17-19). It does mean that the Law is not the means of salvation (cf. Acts 15; Romans 4; Galatians 3; Hebrews). The New Covenant (Jer. 31:31-34; Ezek. 36:22-36) is based on a new heart and a new spirit, not human performance of a legal code. Believing Jews and believing Gentiles now have the same standing before God—the imputed righteousness of Christ.

SPECIAL TOPIC: NULL AND VOID (*KATARGEŌ*)

This (*katargeō*) was one of Paul's favorite words. He used it at least twenty-five times, but it has a very wide semantic range.
- A. It's basic etymological root is from *argos* which meant
  1. inactive
  2. idle
  3. unused
  4. useless
  5. inoperative
- B. The compound with *kata* was used to express
  1. inactivity
  2. uselessness
  3. that which was cancelled
  4. that which was done away with
  5. that which was completely inoperative
- C. It is used once in Luke to describe a fruitless, therefore useless, tree (cf. Luke 13:7)

D. Paul uses it in a figurative sense in two primary ways.
   1. God making inoperative things which are hostile to mankind
      a. mankind's sin nature - Rom. 6:6
      b. the Mosaic law in relation to God's promise of "the seed" - Rom. 4:14; Gal. 3:17; 5:4,11; Eph. 2:15
      c. spiritual forces - I Cor. 15:24
      d. the "man of lawlessness" - II Thess. 2:8
      e. physical death - I Cor. 15:26; II Tim. 1:16 (Heb. 2:14)
   2. God replacing the old (covenant, age) for the new
      a. things related to the Mosaic Law - Rom. 3:3,31; 4:14; II Cor. 3:7,11,13,14
      b. analogy of marriage used of Law - Rom. 7:2,6
      c. the things of this age - I Cor. 13:8,10,11 d. this body - I Cor. 6:13
      e. leaders of this age - I Cor. 1:28; 2:6

This word is translated so many different ways but its main meaning is to make something useless, null and void, inoperative, powerless, but not necessarily non-existent, destroyed, or annihilated.

} *NASB, NKJV*   *"in His flesh"*
NRSV (2:14)   *"flesh"*
TEV (2:14)   *"in his own body"*
NJB (2:14)   *"in his own person"*

This emphasizes Jesus' humanity (cf. Col. 1:22) as well as His Incarnational ministry (cf. Eph. 4:8-10). The false teachers would have denied both because of their ontological dualism between spirit, which they saw as good, and matter, which they saw as evil (cf. Gal. 4:4; Col. 1:22).

} **"the enmity"** The balanced structure equates "the enmity" (cf. v. 16) with "the Law of commandment contained in the ordinances." The OT said "do and live," but fallen mankind was unable to perform the Mosaic Law. Once broken, the OT laws became a curse (cf. Gal. 3:10); "the soul that sins will surely die" (cf. Ezek. 18:4,20). The New Covenant removed the enmity by giving humans a new heart and spirit (cf. Jer. 31:31-34; Ezek. 36:26-27). Performance becomes the result, not the goal. Salvation is a gift, not a reward for work accomplished.

} **NASB**   **"the Law of commandments *contained* in ordinances"**
NKJV   **"the law of commandments continued in ordinances"**
NRSV   **"the law with its commandments and ordinances"**
TEV   **"the Jewish Law, with its commandments and rules"**
NJB   **"the rules and decrees of the Law"**

This referred to the way of salvation which was thought to be found only through performance of the Law of Moses (cf. Rom. 9:30-32; Gal. 2:15-21).

```
┌─────────────────────────────────────────────────────────────────────────┐
│                                                                           │
│     SPECIAL TOPIC: THE MOSAIC LAW AND THE CHRISTIAN                        │
│                                                                           │
│     A.   The Law is inspired Scripture and is eternal (cf. Matt. 5:17-19).│
│     B.   The Law as a way of salvation is void and has always been, but   │
│          mankind had to see that his/her own effort was futile (cf. Matt. │
│          5:20, 48; Rom. 7:7-12; Gal. 3:1ff; James 2:10).                  │
│     C.   The gospel of Christ is the only way to God (cf. John 14:6;      │
│          Rom. 3:21; Gal. 2:15-21; Heb. 8:12).                             │
│     D.   The Old Testament is still helpful to believers as God's will    │
│          for humans in society, but not as the way of salvation. The      │
│          cultus of Israel (sacrificial system, holy days, civic and       │
│          religious laws) has passed away but God still speaks through      │
│          the OT. The stipulations mentioned in Acts 15:20 refer only to   │
│          fellowship issues, not to salvation.                             │
│                                                                           │
└─────────────────────────────────────────────────────────────────────────┘
```

} **"that in Himself He might make"** The PRONOUN "Himself" is emphatic. God's eternal purpose of uniting all humans in salvation (cf. Gen. 3:15) and fellowship was accomplished exclusively through the performance of the person of the Messiah, not the Mosaic Law.

} **"one new man,"** This Greek term means "new" in kind, not time. The people of God are not Jews, not Gentiles, but Christians! The Church is a new entity, in and through and for Christ (cf. Rom. 11:36; Col. 1:16; Heb. 2:10).

} **"establishing peace"** This is a favorite term for Paul. It is used eleven times in Romans and seven times in Ephesians (cf. 1:2; 2:14,15,17; 4:3; 6:15,23). He uses it in three ways.
1.   peace between God and mankind, Col. 1:20
2.   subjective peace with God through Christ, John 14:27; 16:33; Phil. 4:27
3.   peace between peoples, Eph. 2:11-3:13.

This is a PRESENT PASSIVE PARTICIPLE. Christ continues to make peace for those fallen children of Adam who will respond by repentance and faith. Christ's peace is not automatic (AORIST SUBJUNCTIVE of v. 16), but it is available to all (cf. Rom. 5:12-21).

2:16 "might reconcile" The Greek term means to transfer someone from one state of being to another. It implies an exchange of contrasting positions (cf. Rom. 5:10-11; Col. 1:20,22; II Cor. 5:18,21). In a sense reconciliation is the removal of the curse of Genesis 3. God and mankind are restored to intimate fellowship even in this life, in this fallen world system. This reconciliation with God expresses itself in a new relationship with other humans and ultimately with nature (Isa. 11:6-9; 65:25; Rom. 8:18-23; Rev. 22:3). The reuniting of Jews and Gentiles is one beautiful example of God's unifying work in our world.

} **"in one body"** This metaphor of unity is used in several different ways in Paul's writings: (1) the physical body of Christ (cf. Col. 1:22) or the body of Christ, the church (cf. Col. 1:23; 4:12; 5:23,30); (2) the new humanity of both Jew and Gentile (cf. 2:16); or (3) a way of referring to the unity and diversity of spiritual gifts (cf. I Cor. 12:12-13,27). In a sense they are all related to #1.

} **"through the cross"** The Jewish leaders meant Christ's cross to be a curse (cf. Deut. 21:23). God used it as a means of redemption (cf. Isa. 53). Jesus became "the curse" for us (cf. Gal. 3:13)! It became His victory chariot (cf. Col. 2:14-15), giving believers victory over (1) the OT curse; (2) the evil powers; and (3) the enmity between Jew and Gentile.

} NASB	"by it having put to death the enmity"
NKJV	"thereby putting to death the enmity"
NRSV	"thus putting to death that hostility through it"
TEV	"Christ destroyed the enmity"
NJB	"in his own person he killed the hostility"

The English translations show that this phrase can be understood in two ways. This is because the SINGULAR PRONOUN can be a DATIVE MASCULINE (TEV, NJB) or DATIVE NEUTER (NASB, NRSV). In context either is possible. The emphasis of the larger context is on Christ's finished redemptive work.

2:17 This is an allusion to Isa. 57:19 or possibly 52:7. The rabbis, going back to Isa. 56:6, used this phrase to refer to Gentile proselytes.

2:18 The work of the Trinity is clearly stated in this book (cf. 1:3-14,17; 2:18; 4:4-6). Although the term "trinity" is not a biblical word, the concept surely is (cf. Matt. 3:16-17; 28:19; John 14:26; Acts 2:33-34,38-39; Rom. 1:4-5; 5:1,5; 8:9-10; I Cor. 12:4-6; II Cor. 1:21-22; 13:14; Gal. 4:4-6; Eph. 1:3-14; 2:18; 3:14-17; 4:4-6; I Thess. 1:2-5; II Thess. 2:13; Titus 3:4-6; I Pet. 1:2; Jude 20-21). See Special Topic at 1:3.

} **"we both have our access"** This is a PRESENT ACTIVE INDICATIVE meaning "we continue to have access." This is the concept of Jesus personally bringing believers into the presence of God and giving them a personal introduction (cf. Rom. 5:2; it is also used in the sense of confidence in Heb. 4:16; 10:19,35).

} **"in one Spirit"** This is also emphasized in Ephesians 4:4. The false teachers were causing disunity, but the Spirit brought unity (not uniformity)!

2:19 The Gentiles who were estranged (vv. 11-12) are now fully included. This is clearly stated by the use of four common biblical metaphors: (1) fellow citizens (city); (2) saints (holy nation set apart for God); (3) God's household (family members); and (4) a spiritual building (temple, vv. 20-22a).

} **"saints"** See Special Topic at Col. 1:2.

2:20 "having been built upon" This is an AORIST PASSIVE PARTICIPLE. The foundation of our faith has been fully, finally, and completely laid by the Triune God. God's good news was proclaimed by the Apostles and prophets (cf. 3:5).

} **"the foundation of the apostles and prophets"** Jesus laid the foundation of the gospel (cf. I Cor. 3:11). The OT prophesied the coming Kingdom of God, Jesus' Spirit-led life, death, and resurrection accomplished it, and the Apostles preached its reality. The only question is, to whom does the term "prophets" refer? Are they OT prophets or NT prophets (cf. 3:5; 4:1)? The order of the terms implies NT prophets (cf. vv. 3:5; 4:11), but the OT Messianic allusion to the "cornerstone" implies OT prophecy.

The reason for the distinction between OT and NT prophets is the issue of revelation. OT prophets wrote Scripture. They were God's instrument of inspired self-disclosure. However, prophecy is an ongoing gift in the NT (I Cor. 12:28; Eph. 4:11). Does Scripture writing continue? There must be a distinction drawn between inspiration (Apostles and OT prophets) and illumination and spiritual giftedness (NT gifted believers).

} **"the cornerstone"** This is an OT Messianic metaphor (cf. Isa. 28:16; Ps. 118:22; I Pet. 2:4-8). In the OT God's stability, strength, and perseverance are often visualized in "Rock" as a title (cf. Deut. 32:4, 15, 18, 30; Ps. 18:2, 31, 46; 28:1; 33:3; 42:9; 71:3; 78:15).

The metaphor of Jesus as a stone
1. a rejected stone - Ps. 118:22
2. a building stone - Ps. 118:22; Isa. 28:16
3. a stone to stumble over - Isa. 8:14-15
4. an overcoming and conquering stone (kingdom) - Dan. 2:45
5. Jesus used these passages to describe Himself (cf. Matt. 21:40; Mark 12:10; Luke 20:17)

He was the key construction item who was ignored in OT ritualism and legalism (cf. Isa. 8:14).

SPECIAL TOPIC: CORNERSTONE

I. **OT Usages**
    A. The concept of a stone as a hard durable item which made a good foundation was used to describe YHWH (cf. Ps. 18:1).
    B. It then developed into a Messianic title (cf. Gen. 49:24; Ps. 118:22; Isa. 28:16).
    C. It came to represent a judgment from YHWH by the Messiah (cf. Isa. 8:14; Dan. 2:34-35,44-45).
    D. This developed into a building metaphor.
        1. a foundation stone, the first placed, which was secure and set the angles for the rest of the building, called "the cornerstone"

        2. it could also refer to the final stone put in place, which holds the walls together (cf. Zech. 4:7; Eph. 2:20,21), called "the capstone" from the Hebrew *rush* (i.e., head)
        3. it could refer to the "keystone," which is in the center of the doorway arch and holds the weight of the entire wall

---

II. NT Usages

A. Jesus quoted Psalm 118 several times in reference to Himself (cf. Matt. 21:41-46; Mark 12:10-11; Luke 20:17)

B. Paul uses Psalm 118 in connection with YHWH's rejection of faithless, rebellious Israel (cf. Rom. 9:33)

C. Paul uses the concept of a "capstone" in Eph. 2:20-22 in reference to Christ

D. Peter uses this concept of Jesus in I Pet. 2:1-10. Jesus is the cornerstone and believers are the living stones (i.e., believers as temples, cf. I Cor. 6:19), built on Him (i.e., Jesus is the new Temple, cf. Mark 14:58; Matt. 12:6; John 2:19-20). The Jews rejected the very foundation of their hope when they rejected Jesus as Messiah.

III. Theological Statements

A. YHWH allowed David/Solomon to build a temple. He told them that if they kept the covenant He would bless them and be with them (cf. II Sam. 7), but if they did not the temple would be in ruins (cf. I Kgs. 9:1-9)!

B. Rabbinical Judaism focused on form and ritual and neglected the personal aspect of faith (this is not a blanket statement; there were godly rabbis). God seeks a daily, personal, godly relationship with those created in His image (cf. Gen. 1:26-27). Luke 20:17-18 contains frightening words of judgment.

C. Jesus used the concept of a temple to represent His physical body (cf. John 2:19-22). This continues and expands the concept of personal faith in Jesus as the Messiah as key to a relationship with YHWH.

D. Salvation is meant to restore the image of God in human beings so that fellowship with God is possible. The goal of Christianity is Christlikeness now. Believers are to become living stones (i.e., little temples built on/patterned after Christ).

E. Jesus is the foundation of our faith and the capstone of our faith (i.e., the Alpha and Omega); yet also the stone of stumbling and the rock of offense. To miss Him is to miss everything. There can be no middle ground here!

2:21-22 The collective or corporate idea of God's people seen in v. 19 (twice), 21 and 22 was expressed in the PLURAL "saints." To be saved is to be part of a family, a building, a body, a temple.

The concept of the church as a temple is expressed in I Cor. 3:16-17. This is an emphasis on the corporate nature of the church. The individual aspect was expressed in I Cor. 6:16. Both are true!

The VERBS in vv. 21-22 also have a corporate focus. They have the compound *syn*, which means "joint participation with." They are both PRESENT PASSIVE. God is continuing to build/add to His church.

There is a Greek manuscript problem connected with the phrase "the whole building." The ancient uncial manuscripts א*, B, D, F and G have no ARTICLE, while אᶜ, A, C, and P do. The question is, was Paul referring to one large building (NASB, NKJV, NRSV, NIV, TEV, REB) or to several smaller buildings (ASV, NJB, Phillips) united in some way?

The United Bible Society's 4th Edition Greek text gives a "B" rating to the ANARTHROUS construction, which indicates they are "almost certain" that it refers to one building. This one building is not finished. It is in the process of growing. The building metaphor alluded to the spiritual temple (the people of God).

SPECIAL TOPIC: EDIFY

This term *oikodomeō* and its other forms are used often by Paul. Literally it means "to build a house" (cf. Matt. 7:24), but it came to be used metaphorically for:
1.   Christ's body, the church, I Cor. 3:9; Eph. 2:21; 4:16;
2.   building up
   a.   weak brothers, Rom. 15:1
   b.   neighbors, Rom. 15:2
   c.   one another, Eph. 4:29; I Thess. 5:11
   d.   the saints for ministry, Eph. 4:11
3.   we build up or edify by
   a.   love, I Cor. 8:1; Eph. 4:16
   b.   limiting personal freedoms, I Cor. 10:23-24
   c.   avoiding speculations, I Tim. 1:4
   d.   limiting speakers in worship services (singers, teachers, prophets, tongue speakers, and interpreters), I Cor. 14:3-4,12
4.   all things should edify
   a.   Paul's authority, II Cor. 10:8; 12:19; 13:10
   b.   summary statements in Rom. 14:19 and I Cor. 14:26

DISCUSSION QUESTIONS

This is a study <u>guide</u> commentary, which means that you are responsible for your own interpretation of the Bible. Each of us must walk in the light we have. You, the Bible, and the Holy Spirit are priority in interpretation. You must not relinquish this to a commentator.

These discussion questions are provided to help you think through the major issues of this section of the book. They are meant to be thought provoking, not definitive.

1.   Are all humans really estranged from God?

2.   Do humans have a significant part in their own salvation?

3.   Why is the union of Jew and Gentile so significant?

4.   How did Jesus make the Law "null and void"?

5.   Is the Law of God eternal? How do Christians relate to the Mosaic Law and the entire Old Testament?

6.   Why does Paul emphasize the building metaphor in vv. 19-23?

ROMANS 5

PARAGRAPH DIVISIONS OF MODERN TRANSLATIONS

UBS[4]	NKJV	NRSV	TEV	JB
Results of Justification	Faith Triumphs in Trouble	Consequences of Justification	Right With God	Faith Guarantees
5:1-11	5:1-5	5:1-5	5:1-5	5:1-11
	Christ in Our Place			
	5:6-11	5:6-11	5:6-11	
Adam and Christ	Death in Adam, Life in Christ	Adam and Christ; Analogy & Contrast	Adam and Christ	Adam & Jesus Christ
5:12-14	5:12-21	5:12-14	5:12-14b	5:12-14
			5:14c-17	
5:15-21		5:15-17		5:15-21
		5:18-21	5:18-19	
			5:20-21	

READING CYCLE THREE
FOLLOWING THE ORIGINAL AUTHOR'S INTENT AT THE PARAGRAPH LEVEL

This is a study guide commentary, which means that you are responsible for your own interpretation of the Bible. Each of us must walk in the light we have. You, the Bible, and the Holy Spirit are priority in interpretation. You must not relinquish this to a commentator.

Read the chapter in one sitting. Identify the subjects. Compare your subject divisions with the five translations above. Paragraphing is not inspired, but it is the key to following the original author's intent, which is the heart of interpretation. Every paragraph has one and only one subject.

1. First paragraph

2. Second paragraph

3. Third paragraph

4. Etc.

CONTEXTUAL INSIGHTS

A. Verses 1-11 are one sentence in Greek. They develop Paul's pivotal concept of "Justification by Faith" (cf. 3:21-4:25).

B. Possible outlines of vv. 1-11:

Verses 1-5	Verses 6-8	Verses 9-11
The Benefits of Salvation	The Basis for Salvation	The Future Certainty of Salvation
Subjective Experiences of Justification	Objective Facts of Justification	Future Certainty of Justification
Justification	Progressive Sanctification	Glorification
Anthropology	Theology	Eschatology

C. Verses 12-21 are a discussion of Jesus as the second Adam (cf. I Cor. 15:21-22, 45-49; Phil. 2:6-8). It gives emphasis to the theological concept of both individual sin and corporate guilt. Paul's development of mankind's (and creation's) fall in Adam was so unique and different from the rabbis, while his view of corporality was very much in line with rabbinical teaching. It showed Paul's ability under inspiration to use, or supplement, the truths he was taught during his training in Jerusalem under Gamaliel (cf. Acts 22:3).

The Reformed Evangelical doctrine of original sin from Genesis 3 was developed by Augustine and Calvin. It basically asserts that humans are born sinful (total depravity). Often Psalm 51:5; 58:3; and Job 15:14; 25:4 are used as OT proof-texts. The alternate theological position that humans are progressively morally and spiritually responsible for their own choices and destiny was developed by Pelagius and Arminius. There is some evidence for their view in Deut. 1:39; Isa. 7:15; and Jonah 4:11; John 9:41; 15:22,24; Acts 17:30; Rom. 4:15. The thrust of this theological position would be that children are innocent until an age of moral responsibility (for the rabbis this was 13 years old for boys and 12 years old for girls).

There is a mediating position in which both an innate evil propensity and an age of moral responsibility are both true! Evil is not only corporate, but a developing evil of the individual self to sin (life progressively more and more apart from God). The wickedness of humanity is not the issue (cf. Gen. 6:5,11-12,13; Rom. 3:9-18,23), but the when, at birth or later in life?

D. There have been several theories about the implications of v. 12
  1. all people die because all people choose to sin (Pelagius)
  2. Adam's sin affected the entire creation and, thereby, all die (vv. 18-19, Augustine)
  3. in reality it is probably a combination of original sin and volitional sin
E. Paul's comparison "just as" begun in v. 12 is not finished until v. 18. Verses 13-17 form a parenthesis which is so characteristic of Paul's writings.
F. Remember Paul's presentation of the gospel, 1:18-8:39 is one sustained argument. The whole must be seen in order to properly interpret and appreciate the parts.
G. Martin Luther has said of chapter 5, "In the whole Bible there is hardly another chapter which can equal this triumphant text."

WORD AND PHRASE STUDY

NASB (UPDATED) TEXT: 5:1-5

¹Therefore, having been justified by faith, we have peace with God through our Lord Jesus Christ, ²through whom also we have obtained our introduction by faith into this grace in which we stand; and we exult in hope of the glory of God. ³And not only this, but we also exult in our tribulations, knowing that tribulation brings about perseverance; ⁴and perseverance, proven character; and proven character, hope; ⁵and hope does not disappoint, because the love of God has been poured out within our hearts through the Holy Spirit who was given to us.

5:1 "therefore" This word often signaled (1) the summary of the theological argument up to this point; (2) the conclusions based on this theological presentation; and (3) the presentation of new truth (cf. 5:1; 8:1; 12:1).

⊢ "having been justified" This is an AORIST PASSIVE PARTICIPLE; God has justified believers. This is placed first in the Greek sentence (vv. 1-2) for emphasis. There seems to be a time sequence in vv. 1-11: (1) vv. 1-5, our current experience of grace; (2) vv. 6-8, Christ's finished work on our behalf; and (3) vv. 9-11, our future hope and assurance of salvation. See outline, B. in Contextual Insights.

The OT background of the term "justified" (*dikaioç*) was a "straight edge" or "measuring reed." It came to be used metaphorically of God Himself. See Special Topic: Righteousness at 1:17. God's character, holiness, is the only standard of judgment (cf. LXX of Lev. 24:22; and theologically in Matt. 5:48). Because of Jesus' sacrificial, substitutionary death, believers have a legal (forensic) positional standing before God (see note at 5:2). This does not imply the believer's lack of guilt, but rather something like amnesty. Someone else has paid the penalty (cf. II Cor. 5:21). Believers have been declared forgiven (cf. vv. 9,10).

⊢ "by faith" Faith is the hand that accepts the gift of God (cf. v. 2; Rom. 4:1ff). Faith does not focus on the degree or intensity of the believer's commitment or resolve (cf. Matt. 17:20), but on the character and promises of God (cf. Eph. 2:8-9). The OT word for "faith" originally referred to one in a stable standing posture. It came to be used metaphorically for someone who was loyal, dependable and trustworthy. Faith does not focus on our faithfulness or trustworthiness, but on God's. See Special Topic: Faith at 4:5.

⊢ "we have peace" There is a Greek manuscript variant here. This VERB is either a PRESENT ACTIVE SUBJUNCTIVE (*echÇmen*) or a PRESENT ACTIVE INDICATIVE (*echomen*). This same grammatical ambiguity is found in vv. 1, 2 & 3. The ancient Greek manuscripts seem to support the SUBJUNCTIVE (cf. MSS ℵ*, A, B*, C, D). If it is the SUBJUNCTIVE it would be translated "let us continue enjoying peace" or "keep on enjoying peace." If it is the INDICATIVE, then it would be translated "we have peace."

The context of vv. 1-11 is not exhortation, but declaration of what believers already are and have through Christ. Therefore, the VERB is probably PRESENT ACTIVE INDICATIVE, "we have peace." The USB[4] gives this option an "A" rating (certain).

Many of our ancient Greek manuscripts were produced by one person reading a text and several others making copies. Words that were pronounced alike were often confused. Here is where context and sometimes the writing style and usual vocabulary of the author helps make the translation decision easier.

SPECIAL TOPIC: PEACE

This Greek term originally meant "binding together that which was broken" (cf. John 14:27; 16:33; Phil. 4:7). There are three ways the NT speaks of peace:
1. as objective aspect of our peace with God through Christ (cf. Col. 1:20)
2. as subjective aspect of our being right with God (cf. John 14:27; 16:33; Phil. 4:7)
3. that God has united into one new body, through Christ, both believing Jew and Gentile (cf.

Eph. 2:14-17; Col. 3:15). Once we have peace with God, it must issue in peace with others! The vertical must become the horizontal.

Newman and Nida, *A Translator's Handbook on Paul's Letter to the Romans*, p. 92, has a good comment about "peace."

"Both in the Old Testament and in the New Testament the term <u>peace</u> has a wide range of meaning. Basically it describes the total well-being of a person's life; it was even adopted among the Jews as a formula of greeting. This term had such a profound meaning that it could also be used by the Jews as a description of the Messianic salvation. Because of this fact, there are times when it is used almost synonymously with the term rendered 'to be in a right relation with God.' Here the term appears to be used as a description of the harmonious relation established between man and God on the basis of God's having put man right with himself" (p. 92).

⊦ **"with God through our Lord Jesus Christ"** Jesus is the agency which brings peace with God. Jesus is the only way to peace with God (cf. John 10:7-8; 14:6; Acts 4:12; I Tim. 2:5). For the terms in the title Jesus Christ see notes at 1:4.

5:2 "we have obtained our introduction" This is PERFECT ACTIVE INDICATIVE; it speaks of a past act which has been consummated and now results in a state of being. The term "introduction" literally meant "access" or "admission" (*prosagÇge*, cf. Eph. 2:18; 3:12). It came to be used metaphorically for (1) being personally introduced to royalty or (2) being brought safely into a harbor.

This phrase contains a Greek manuscript variant. Some ancient manuscripts added "by faith" (cf. ℵ[*,2], C as well as some old Latin, Vulgate, Syriac, and Coptic versions). Other manuscripts add a PREPOSITION to "by faith" (cf. ℵ[1], A, and some Vulgate versions). However, the uncial manuscripts B, D, F, and G omit it altogether. It seems that scribes simply filled out the parallelism of 5:1 and 4:16 (twice), 19, and 20. "By faith" is Paul's recurrent theme!

⤷ "into this grace" This term (*charis*) meant God's undeserved, no-strings-attached, unmerited love (cf. Eph. 2:4-9). It is clearly seen in Christ's death on behalf of sinful mankind (cf. v. 8).

⤷ "in which we stand" This is another PERFECT ACTIVE INDICATIVE; literally "we stand and continue to stand." This reflects believers' theological position in Christ and their commitment to remain in the faith, which combines the theological paradox of God's sovereignty (cf. I Cor. 15:1) and human's free will (cf. Eph. 6:11,13,14).

SPECIAL TOPIC: STAND (*HISTĒMI*)

This common term is used in several theological senses in the New Testament
1. to establish
    a. the OT Law, Rom. 3:31
    b. one's own righteousness, Rom. 10:3
    c. the new covenant, Heb. 10:9
    d. a charge, II Cor. 13:1
    e. God's truth, II Tim. 2:19
2. to resist spiritually
    a. the devil, Eph. 6:11
    b. the day of judgment, Rev. 6:17
3. to resist by standing one's ground
    a. military metaphor, Eph. 6:14
    b. civil metaphor, Rom. 14:4
4. a position in truth, John 8:44
5. a position in grace
    a. Rom. 5:2
    b. I Cor. 15:1
    c. I Pet. 5:12
6. a position in faith
    a. Rom. 11:20
    b. I Cor. 7:37
    c. I Cor. 15:1
    d. II Cor. 1:24
7. a position of arrogance, I Cor. 10:12

This term expresses both the covenantal grace and mercy of a sovereign God and the fact that believers need to respond to it and cling to it by faith! Both are biblical truths. They must be held together!

⤷ "we exult" This grammatical form can be understood as (1) a PRESENT MIDDLE (deponent) INDICATIVE, "we exult" or (2) a PRESENT MIDDLE (deponent) SUBJUNCTIVE, "let us exult." Scholars are split on these options. If one takes "we have" in v. 1 as an INDICATIVE then the translation should be consistent through v. 3.

The root of the word "exult" is "boasting" (NRSV, JB). See Special Topic at 2:17. Believers do not exult in themselves (cf. 3:27), but in what the Lord has done for them (cf. Jer. 9:23-24). This same Greek root is repeated in vv. 3 and 11.

} **"in hope of"** Paul often used this term in several different but related senses. See note at 4:18. Often it was associated with the consummation of the believer's faith. This can be expressed as glory, eternal life, ultimate salvation, Second Coming, etc. The consummation is certain, but the time element is future and unknown. It was often associated with "faith" and "love" (cf. I Cor. 13:13; Gal. 5:5-6; Eph. 4:2-5; I Thess. 1:3; 5:8).

A partial list of some of Paul's uses follows.
1.   The Second Coming, Gal. 5:5; Eph. 1:18; Titus 2:13
2.   Jesus is our hope, I Tim 1:1
3.   The believer to be presented to God, Col. 1:22-23; I Thess. 2:19
4.   Hope laid up in heaven, Col. 1:5
5.   Ultimate salvation, I Thess. 4:13
6.   The glory of God, Rom. 5:2; II Cor. 3:12; Col. 1:27
7.   Assurance of salvation, I Thess. 5:8-9
8.   Eternal life, Titus 1:2; 3:7
9.   Results of Christian maturity, Rom. 5:2-5
10. Redemption of all creation, Rom. 8:20-22
11. A title for God, Rom. 15:13
12. Adoption's consummation, Rom. 8:23-25
13. OT as guide for NT believers, Rom. 15:4

} **"glory of God"** This phrase is an OT idiom for the personal presence of God. This referred to the believer's standing before God in the faith-righteousness provided by Jesus on Resurrection Day (cf. II Cor. 5:21). It is often called by the theological term "glorification" (cf. vv. 9-10; 8:30). Believers will share the likeness of Jesus (cf. I John 3:2; II Pet. 1:4).
See Special Topic: Glory at 3:23.

5:3	NASB	"and not only this, but"
	NKJV	"and not only *that*, but"
	NRSV	"and not only that, but"
	TEV	–omit–
	NJB	"not only that"

Paul uses this combination of terms several times (cf. 5:3,11; 8:23; 9:10, and II Cor. 8:19).

}	NASB	"we also exult in our tribulations"
	NKJV	"we also glory in tribulations"
	NRSV	"we also boast in our sufferings"
	TEV	"we also boast in our troubles"
	NJB	"let us exult, too, in our hardships"

If the world hated Jesus, it will hate His followers (cf. Matt. 10:22; 24:9; John 15:18-21). Jesus was matured, humanly speaking, by the things He suffered (cf. Heb. 5:8). Suffering produces righteousness, which is the plan of God for every believer (cf. 8:17-19; Acts 14:22; James 1:2-4; I Pet. 4:12-19).

➥ **"knowing"** This is a PERFECT PARTICIPLE, of *oida*. It is PERFECT in form, but it functions as a PRESENT TENSE. Believers' understanding of the truths of the gospel as they relate to suffering allows them to face life with a joy and confidence which is not dependent on circumstances, even during persecution (cf. Phil. 4:4; I Thess. 5:16,18).

SPECIAL TOPIC: TRIBULATION 5:3 "tribulation"

There needs to be a theological distinction between Paul's use of this term (*thlipsis*) and John's:

I. Paul's usage (which reflects Jesus' usage)
    A.   problems, sufferings, evil involved in a fallen world
        1.   Matt. 13:21
        2.   Rom. 5:3
        3.   I Cor. 7:28
        4.   II Cor. 7:4
        5.   Eph. 3:13
    B.   problems, sufferings, evil caused by unbelievers
        1.   Rom. 5:3; 8:35; 12:12
        2.   II Cor. 1:4,8; 6:4; 7:4; 8:2,13
        3.   Eph. 3:13
        4.   Phil. 4:14
        5.   I Thess. 1:6
        6.   II Thess. 1:4
    C.   problems, sufferings, evil of the end-time
        1.   Matt. 24:21,29
        2.   Mark 13:19,24
        3.   II Thess. 1:6-9

II. John's usage
    A.   John makes a specific distinction between *thlipsis* and *orgʽ* or *thumos* (wrath) in Revelation. *Thlipsis* is what unbelievers do to believers and *orgʽ* is what God does to unbelievers
        1.   *thlipsis* - Rev. 1:9; 2:9-10,22; 7:14
        2.   *orgʽ* - Rev. 6:16-17; 11:18; 16:19; 19:15
        3.   *thumos* - Rev. 12:12; 14:8,10,19; 15:2,7; 16:1; 18:3
    B.   John also uses the term in his Gospel to reflect problems believers face in every age - John 16:33.

5:3,4 "perseverance" This term meant "voluntary," "active," "steadfast," "endurance." It was a term that related to both patience with people, as well as with circumstances. See Special Topic at 8:25.

5:4	NASB	"proven character"
	NKJV, NRSV	"character"
	TEV	"God's approval"
	NJB	"tested character"

In the LXX of Gen. 23:16; I Kgs. 10:18; I Chr. 28:18 this term was used of testing metals for purity and genuineness (cf. II Cor. 2:9; 8:2; 9:13; 13:3; Phil. 2:22; II Tim. 2:15; James 1:12). God's tests are always for strengthening (cf. Heb. 12:10-11)!

5:5 "because the love of God has been poured out within our hearts" This is a PERFECT PASSIVE INDICATIVE; literally, "God's love has been and continues to be poured out." This VERB was often used of the Holy Spirit (cf. Acts 2:17,18,33; 10:45 and Titus 3:6), which may reflect Joel 2:28-29.

The GENITIVE PHRASE, "the love of God" grammatically can refer to (1) our love for God; or (2) God's love for us (cf. II Cor. 5:14). Number two is the only contextual option.

} "the Holy Spirit that was given to us" This is an AORIST PASSIVE PARTICIPLE. The PASSIVE VOICE

is often used to express God's agency. This implies that believers do not need more of the Spirit. They either have the Spirit or they are not Christians (cf. 8:9). The giving of the Spirit was the sign of the New Age (cf. Joel 2:28-29), the New Covenant (cf. Jer. 31:31-34; Ezek. 36:22-32).

} Notice the presence of the three persons of the Trinity in this paragraph.
1. God, vv. 1,2,5,8,10
2. Jesus, vv. 1,6,8,9,10
3. the Spirit, v, 5

NASB (UPDATED) TEXT: 5:6-11

[6]For while we were still helpless, at the right time Christ died for the ungodly. [7]For one will hardly die for a righteous man; though perhaps for the good man someone would dare even to die.

[8]But God demonstrates His own love toward us, in that while we were yet sinners, Christ died for us. [9]Much more then, having now been justified by His blood, we shall be saved from the wrath *of God* through Him. [10]For if while we were enemies we were reconciled to God through the death of His Son, much more, having been reconciled, we shall be saved by His life. [11]And not only this, but we also exult in God through our Lord Jesus Christ, through whom we have now received the reconciliation.

5:6

NASB	"for while we were still helpless"
NKJV	"for when we were still without strength"
NRSV	"for while we were still weak"
TEV	"for when we were still helpless"
NJB	"when we were still helpless"

This VERB is a PRESENT PARTICIPLE. This referred to mankind's fallen Adamic nature. Humans are powerless against sin. The PRONOUN "we" explains and parallels the descriptive NOUN in v. 6b "ungodly," v. 8 "sinners," and v. 10 "enemies." Verses 6 and 8 are theologically and structurally parallel.

}	**NASB, NRSV**	**"at the right time"**
	NKJV	**"in due time"**
	TEV	**"at the time that God chose"**
	JB	**"at his appointed moment"**

This could refer historically to (1) the Roman peace allowing free travel; (2) the Greek language allowing cross cultural communication; and (3) the demise of the Greek and Roman gods producing an expectant, spiritually hungry world (cf. Mark 1:15; Gal. 4:4; Eph. 1:10; Titus 1:3). Theologically the incarnation was a planned, divine event (cf. Luke 22:22; Acts 2:23; 3:18; 4:28; Eph. 1:11).

5:6,8,10 "died for the ungodly" This is an AORIST ACTIVE INDICATIVE. It viewed Jesus' life and death as a unified event. "Jesus paid a debt He did not owe and we owed a debt we could not pay" (cf. Gal. 3:13; I John 4:10).

The death of Christ was a recurrent theme in Paul's writings. He used several different terms and phrases to refer to Jesus' substitutionary death:
1. "blood" (cf. 3:25; 5:9; I Cor. 11:25,27; Eph. 1:7; 2:13; Col. 1:20)
2. "gave Himself up" (cf. Eph. 5:2,25)
3. "delivered up" (cf. Rom. 4:25; 8:32)
4. "sacrifice" (cf. I Cor. 5:7)
5. "died" (cf. Rom. 5:6; 8:34; 14:9,15; I Cor. 8:11; 15:3; II Cor. 5:15; Gal. 5:21; I Thess. 4:14; 5:10)
6. "cross" (cf. I Cor. 1:17-18; Gal. 5:11; 6:12-14; Eph. 2:16; Phil. 2:8; Col. 1:20; 2:14)
7. "crucifixion" (cf. I Cor. 1:23; 2:2; II Cor. 13:4; Gal. 3:1) Does the PREPOSITION *huper* in this context mean
   1. representation, "on our behalf"
   2. substitution, "in our place"

Normally the basic meaning of *huper* with the GENITIVE is "on behalf of" (Louw and Nida). It expresses some advantage that accrues to persons (*The New International dictionary of New Testament Theology*, vol. 3, p. 1196). However, *huper* does have the sense of *anti*, which denotes "in the place of" thereby theologically referring to a vicarious substitutionary atonement (cf. Mark 10:45; John 11:50; 18:14; II Cor. 5:14; I Tim. 2:6). M. J. Harris (NIDOTTE, vol. 3, p. 1197) says, "but why does Paul never say that Christ died *anti hēmōn* (I Tim. 2:6 is the nearest he comes– *antilutron huper pantōn*)? Probably because the PREPOSITION *huper*, unlike *anti*, could simultaneously express representation and substitution."

M. R. Vincent, *Word Studies*, vol. 2, says

> "It is much disputed whether *huper*, on behalf of, is ever equivalent to *anti*, instead of. The classical writers furnish instances where the meanings seem to be interchanged. . The meaning of this passage, however, is so uncertain that it cannot fairly be cited in evidence. The preposition may have a local meaning, *over* the dead. None of these passages can be regarded as decisive. The most that can be said is that *huper* borders on the meaning of *anti*.
>
> *Instead of* is urged largely on dogmatic grounds. In the great majority of passages the sense is clearly *for the sake of, on behalf of*. The true explanation seems to be that, in the passages principally in question, those, namely, relating to Christ's death, as here, Gal. 3:13; Rom. 14:15; I Pet. 3:18, *huper* characterizes the more indefinite and general

proposition–Christ died on behalf of–leaving the peculiar sense of in behalf of undetermined, and to be settled by other passages. The meaning *instead of* may be included in it, but only inferentially" (p. 692).

5:7 This verse shows human love while verse 8 shows God's love!

}	NASB, NKJV,	
	TEV	"for a righteous man"
	NRSV	"for a righteous person"
	JB	"for a good man"

This term was used in the same sense as Noah and Job were righteous or blameless men. They followed the religious requirements of their day. It does not imply sinlessness.
See special topic at 1:17.

5:8 "God demonstrates His own love" This is a PRESENT ACTIVE INDICATIVE (cf. 3:5). The Father sent the Son (cf. 8:3,32; II Cor. 5:19). God's love is not sentimental, but action-oriented (cf. John 3:16; I John 4:10) and <u>constant</u>.

5:9 "much more" This was one of Paul's favorite expressions (cf. vv. 10,15,17). If God loved believers so much while they were yet sinners, how much more does He love them now that they are His children (cf. 5:10; 8:22).

} **"having now been justified"** This is an AORIST PASSIVE PARTICIPLE, which emphasized justification as a completed act accomplished by God. Paul is repeating the truth of v. 1. Also note the parallelism between the terms "justified" (v. 9) and "reconciled" (vv. 10-11).

} **"by His blood"** This was a reference to Christ's sacrificial death" (cf. 3:5; Mark 10:45; II Cor. 5:21). This concept of sacrifice, an innocent life given in place of a guilty life, goes back to Lev. 1-7 and possibly Exod. 12 (the Passover lamb), and was theologically applied to Jesus in Isa. 53:4-6. It is developed in a Christological sense in the book of Hebrews. Hebrews in effect compares the Old and New Testament at a number of points.

} **"we shall be saved"** This is FUTURE PASSIVE INDICATIVE (cf. v. 10). This referred to our ultimate salvation, which is called "glorification" (cf. v. 2; 8:30, I John 3:2).

The NT describes salvation in all VERB tenses:
1. a completed act (AORIST), Acts 15:11; Rom. 8:24; II Tim. 1:9; Titus 3:5
2. past act resulting in a present state (PERFECT), Eph. 2:5,8
3. progressive process (PRESENT), I Cor. 1:18; 15:2; II Cor. 2:15; I Thess. 4:14; I Pet. 3:21
4. future consummation (FUTURE), Rom. 5:9,10; 10:9.
See Special Topic at 10:13.

Salvation starts with an initial decision but progresses into a relationship that will one day be consummated. This concept is often described by the three theological terms: justification, which means "being delivered from the penalty of sin"; sanctification, which means "being delivered from the power of sin"; and glorification, which means "being delivered from the presence of sin."

It is worth noting that justification and sanctification are both gracious acts of God, given to the believer through faith in Christ. However the NT also speaks of sanctification as an ongoing process of Christlikeness. For this reason theologians speak of "positional sanctification" and "progressive sanctification." This is the mystery of a free salvation linked to a godly life!

⊱ "from the wrath *of God*" This is an eschatological context. The Bible tells of God's great, undeserved, unmerited love, but also clearly tells of God's settled opposition to sin and rebellion. God has provided a way of salvation and forgiveness through Christ, but those who reject Him are under wrath (cf. 1:18-3:20). This is an anthropomorphic phrase, but it expresses a reality. It is a terrible thing to fall into the hands of an angry God (Heb. 10:31).

5:10 "if" This is a FIRST CLASS CONDITIONAL SENTENCE which is assumed true from the writer's perspective or for his literary purposes. Humanity, God's ultimate creation, became enemies! Man (cf. Gen. 3:5) and Satan (cf. Isa. 14:14; Ezek. 28:2,12-17) had the same problem, a desire for independence, a desire for control, a desire to be gods.

⊱ "we were reconciled to God. . .having been reconciled" This is both an AORIST PASSIVE INDICATIVE and an AORIST PASSIVE PARTICIPLE. The VERB "reconciled" originally meant "to exchange." God has exchanged our sin for Jesus' righteousness (cf. Isa. 53:4-6). Peace is restored (cf. v. 1)!

⊱ "through the death of His son" The gospel of forgiveness is grounded in (1) the love of God; (2) the work of Christ; (3) the wooing of the Spirit; and (4) the faith/repentant response of an individual. There is no other way to be right with God (cf. John 14:6). Assurance of salvation is based on the character of the Triune God, not human performance! The paradox is that human performance after salvation is an evidence of a free salvation (cf. James and I John).

⊱ "we shall be saved" The NT speaks of salvation as past, present, and future. Here the future referred to our ultimate, complete salvation at the Second Coming. See note at v. 9 and Special Topic at 10:13.

⊱ "by His life" This Greek term for life is *zoa*. This term in John's writings always referred to resurrection life, eternal life, or kingdom life. Paul also used it in this theological sense. The thrust of this context is that since God paid such a high price for believers' forgiveness He will surely continue its effectiveness.

"Life" can refer to either (1) Jesus' resurrection (cf. 8:34; I Cor. 15); (2) Jesus' intercessory work (cf. 8:34; Heb. 7:25; I John 2:1); or (3) the Spirit forming Christ in us (cf. Rom. 8:29; Gal. 4:19). Paul asserted that Jesus' earthly life and death as well as His exalted life are the basis of our reconciliation.

5:11 "And not only this, but" See note at verse 3.

⊱ "we also exult" See note at 5:2. This is the third use of "exult" (boast) in this context.
1. exult in the hope of glory, v. 2
2. exult in tribulation, v. 3
3. exult in reconciliation, v. 11

Negative boasting is seen in 2:17 and 23!

} **"we have now received the reconciliation"** This is an AORIST ACTIVE INDICATIVE, a completed act. Believers' reconciliation is also discussed in v. 10 and II Cor. 5:18-21; Eph. 2:16-22; Col. 1:19-23. In this context "reconciliation" is the theological synonym of "justification."

NASB (UPDATED) TEXT: 5:12-14

[12]Therefore, just as through one man sin entered into the world, and death through sin, and so death spread to all men, because all sinned— [13]for until the Law sin was in the world, but sin is not imputed when there is no law. [14]Nevertheless death reigned from Adam until Moses, even over those who had not sinned in the likeness of the offense of Adam, who is a type of Him who was to come.

5:12 "Therefore" Romans has several strategically placed "therefores" (cf. 5:1; 8:1; 12:1). The interpretive question is to what they relate. They could be a way of referring to Paul's whole argument. For sure this one relates to Genesis and, therefore, probably back to Rom. 1:18-32.

} **"as through one man sin entered into the world"** All three VERBS in v. 12 are AORIST TENSE. Adam's fall brought death (cf. I Cor. 15:22). The Bible does not dwell on the origin of sin. Sin also occurred in the angelic realm (cf. Gen. 3 and Rev. 12:7-9). How and when are uncertain (cf. Isa. 14:12- 27; Ezek. 28:12-19; Job 4:18; Matt. 25:41; Luke 10:18; John 12:31; Rev. 12:7-9).
Adam's sin involved two aspects (1) disobedience to a specific commandment (cf. Gen. 2:16-17), and (2) self-oriented pride (cf. Gen. 3:5-6). This continues the allusion to Genesis 3 begun in Rom. 1:18-32.

It is the theology of sin that so clearly separates Paul from rabbinical thought. The rabbis did not focus on Genesis 3; they asserted instead, that there were two "intents" (*yetzers*) in every person. Their famous rabbinical saying "In every man's heart is a black and a white dog. The one you feed the most becomes the biggest." Paul saw sin as a major barrier between holy God and His creation. Paul was not a systematic theologian (cf. James Steward's *A Man in Christ*). He gave several origins of sin (1) Adam's fall, (2) satanic temptation, and (3) continuing human rebellion.

In the theological contrasts and parallels between Adam and Jesus two possible implications are present.

1. Adam was a real historical person.
2. Jesus was a real human being.

Both of these truths affirm the Bible in the face of false teaching. Notice the repeated use of "one man" or "the one." These two ways of referring to Adam and Jesus are used eleven times in this context.

} **"death through sin"** The Bible reveals three stages of death: (1) spiritual death (cf. Gen. 2:17; 3:1-7; Eph. 2:1); (2) physical death (cf. Gen. 5); and (3) eternal death (cf. Rev. 2:11; 20:6,14; 21:8). The one spoken of in this passage is the spiritual death of Adam (cf. Gen. 3:14-19) that resulted in the physical death of the human race (cf. Genesis 5).

} **"death spread to all men"** The major thrust of this paragraph is the universality of sin (cf. vv. 16-19; I Cor. 15:22; Gal. 1:10) and death.

} **"because all sinned"** All humans sin in Adam corporately (i.e., inherited a sinful state and a sinful propensity.) Because of this each person chooses to sin personally and repeatedly. The Bible is emphatic that all humans are sinners both corporately and individually (cf. I Kgs. 8:46; II Chr. 6:36; Ps. 14:1-2; 130:3; 143:2; Prov. 20:9; Eccl. 7:20; Isa. 9:17; 53:6; Rom. 3:9-18,23; 5:18; 11:32; Gal. 3:22; I John 1:8-10).

Yet it must be said that the contextual emphasis (cf. vv. 15-19) is that one act caused death (Adam) and one act caused life (Jesus). However, God has so structured His relationship to humanity that human response is a significant aspect of "lostness" and "justification." Humans are volitionally involved in their future destinies! They continue to choose sin or they choose Christ. They cannot affect these two choices, but they do volitionally show to which they belong!

The translation "because" is common, but its meaning is often disputed. Paul used *eph' hǪ* in II Cor. 5:4; Phil. 3:12; and 4:10 in the sense of "because." Thus each and every human chooses to personally participate in sin and rebellion against God. Some by rejecting special revelation, but all by rejecting natural revelation (cf. 1:18-3:20).

5:13-14 This same truth is taught in Rom. 4:15 and Acts 17:30. God is fair. Humans are only responsible for what is available to them. This verse is speaking exclusively of special revelation (OT, Jesus, NT), not natural revelation (Psalm 19; Rom. 1:18-23; 2:11-16).

Notice that the NKJV sees the comparison of v. 12 as separated by a long parenthesis (cf. vv. 13-17) from its conclusion in vv. 18-21.

5:14 NASB, NKJV,
JB	**"death reigned"**
NRSV	**"death exercised dominion"**
TEV	**"death ruled"**

Death reigned as a King (cf. vv. 17 and 21). This personification of death and sin as tyrants is sustained throughout this chapter and chapter 6. The universal experience of death confirms the universal sin of mankind. In verses 17 and 21, grace is personified. Grace reigns! Humans have a choice (the two OT ways): death or life. Who reigns in your life?

} **"even over those who had not sinned in the likeness of the offence of Adam"** Adam violated a stated command of God, even Eve did not sin in this same way. She heard about the tree from Adam, not from God directly. Humans from Adam until Moses were affected by Adam's rebellion! They did not violate a specific command from God, but 1:18-32, which is surely part of this theological context, expresses the truth that they did violate the light that they had from creation and are thereby responsible to God for rebellion/sin. Adam's sinful propensity spread to all of his children.

	NASB, NKJV,	
	NRSV	"who is a type of Him who was to come"
	TEV	"Adam was a figure of the one who was to come"
	JB	"Adam prefigured the One to come"

This expresses in a very concrete way the Adam-Christ typology (cf. I Cor. 15:21-22,45-49; Phil. 2:6-8). Each of them is seen as the first in a series, the origin of a race (cf. I Cor. 15:45-49). Adam is the only person from the OT specifically called a "type" by the NT. See Special Topic: Form (*Tupos*) at 6:17.

NASB (UPDATED) TEXT: 5:15-17

¹⁵But the free gift is not like the transgression. For if by the transgression of the one the many died, much more did the grace of God and the gift by the grace of the one Man, Jesus Christ, abound to the many. ¹⁶The gift is not like *that which came* through the one who sinned; for on the one hand the judgment *arose* from one *transgression* resulting in condemnation, but on the other hand the free gift *arose* from many transgressions resulting in justification. ¹⁷For if by the transgression of the one, death reigned through the one, much more those who receive the abundance of grace and of the gift of righteousness will reign in life through the One, Jesus Christ.

5:15-19 This is a sustained argument using parallel phrases. The NASB, NRSV, and TEV divide the paragraph at verse 18. However UBS⁴, NKJV, and JB translate it as a unit. Remember the key to interpretation of the original author's intent is one main truth per paragraph. Notice that the term "many," vv. 15 & 19, is synonymous with "all" in vv. 12 and 18. This is also true in Isa. 53:11-12 and v. 6. No theological distinctions (Calvin's elect versus non-elect) should be made based on these terms!

5:15 "the free gift" There are two different Greek words for "gift" used in this context—*charisma*, vv. 15,16 (6:23) and *dorea/dorama*, vv. 15, 16, 17 (see note at 3:24)—but they are synonymous. This is really the Good News about salvation. It is a free gift from God through Jesus Christ (cf. 3:24; 6:23; Eph. 2:8,9) to all who believe in Christ.

} **"if"** This is a FIRST CLASS CONDITIONAL SENTENCE which is assumed to be true from the author's perspective or for his literary purposes. Adam's sin brought death to all humans. This is paralleled in v. 17.

} **"abound"** See Special Topic at 15:13.

5:16 "condemnation. . .justification" Both of these are forensic, legal terms. Often the OT presented the prophet's message as a court scene. Paul uses this form (cf. Rom. 8:1, 31-34).

5:17 "if" This is another FIRST CLASS CONDITIONAL SENTENCE which is assumed to be true from the author's perspective or for his literary purposes. The transgression of Adam did result in the death of all humans.

} "much more those who receive" Verses 18-19 are not exactly theologically balanced. This phrase cannot be removed from the context of Romans 1-8 and used as a proof-text for universalism (that all will be saved eventually). Humans must receive (v. 17b) God's offer in Christ. Salvation is available to all, but must be accepted individually (cf. John 1:12; 3:16; Rom. 10:9-13).

Adam's one act of rebellion issued in the total rebellion of all humans. The one sinful act is magnified! But in Christ one righteous sacrifice is magnified to cover the many individual sins as well as the corporate affect of sin. The "much more" of Christ's act is emphasized (cf. vv. 9,10,15,17). Grace abounds!

5:17,18 "the gift of righteousness will reign in life. . .justification of life" Jesus is God's gift and provision for all of fallen mankind's spiritual needs (cf. I Cor. 1:30). These parallel phrases can mean (1) sinful mankind is given right standing with God through Christ's finished work which results in a "godly life" or (2) this phrase is synonymous to "eternal life." The context supports the first option. For a word study on righteousness see special topic at 1:17.

SPECIAL TOPIC: REIGNING IN THE KINGDOM OF GOD

The concept of reigning with Christ is part of the larger theological category called "the Kingdom of God." This is a carry-over from the OT concept of God as the true king of Israel (cf. I Sam. 8:7). He symbolically reigned (I Sam. 8:7; 10:17-19) through a descendant from the tribe of Judah (cf. Gen. 49:10) and the family of Jesse (cf. II Sam. 7).

Jesus is the promised fulfillment of OT prophecy concerning the Messiah. He inaugurated the Kingdom of God with His incarnation at Bethlehem. The Kingdom of God became the central pillar of Jesus' preaching. The Kingdom had fully come in Him (cf. Matt: 10:7; 11:12; 12:28; Mark 1:15; Luke 10:9,11; 11:20; 16:16; 17:20-21).

However, the Kingdom was also future (eschatological). It was present, but not consummated (cf. Matt. 6:10; 8:11; 16:28; 22:1-14; 26:29; Luke 9:27; 11:2; 13:29; 14:10-24; 22:16,18). Jesus came the first time as a suffering servant (cf. Isa. 52:13-53:12), as humble (cf. Zech. 9:9), but He will return as King of Kings (cf. Matt. 2:2; 21:5; 27:11-14). The concept of "reigning" is surely a part of this "kingdom" theology. God has given the kingdom to Jesus' followers (see Luke 12:32).

The concept of reigning with Christ has several aspects and questions:
1. Do the passages which assert that God has given believers "the kingdom" through Christ refer to "reigning" (cf. Matt. 5:3,10; Luke 12:32)?
2. Do Jesus' words to the original disciples in the first century Jewish context refer to all believers (cf. Matt. 19:28; Luke 22:28-30)?
3. Does Paul's emphasis on reigning in this life now contrast or complement the above texts (cf. Rom. 5:17; I Cor. 4:8)?
4. How are suffering and reigning related (cf. Rom. 8:17; II Tim. 2:11-12; I Pet. 4:13; Rev. 1:9)?
5. The recurrent theme of Revelation is sharing the glorified Christ's reign a. earthly, 5:10
   b. millennial, 20:5,6
   c. eternal, 2:26; 3:21; 22:5 and Dan. 7:14,18,27

---

[18]So then as through one transgression there resulted condemnation to all men, even so through one act of righteousness there resulted justification of life to all men. [19]For as through the one man's disobedience the many were made sinners, even so through the obedience of the One

the many will be made righteous. [20]The Law came in so that the transgression would increase; but where sin increased, grace abounded all the more, [21]so that, as sin reigned in death, even so grace would reign through righteousness to eternal life through Jesus Christ our Lord.

5:18
NASB "even so through one act of righteousness there resulted justification of life to all men"
NKJV "even so through one Man's righteous act the free gift came to all men"
NRSV "so one man's act of righteousness leads to justification and life for all"
TEV "in the same way the one righteous act set all men free and gives them life"
JB "so the good act of one man brings everyone life and makes them justified"

This is not saying that everyone will be saved (universalism). This verse can not be interpreted apart from the message of the book of Romans and the immediate context. This is referring to the potential salvation of all humans through Jesus' life/death/resurrection. Mankind must respond to the gospel offer by repentance and faith (cf. Mark 1:15; Acts 3:16,19; 20:21).

God always takes the initiative (cf. John 6:44,65), but He has chosen that each individual must respond personally (cf. Mark 1:15; John 1:12; and Rom. 10:9-13). His offer is universal (cf. I Tim. 2:4,6; II Pet. 3:9; I John 2:2), but the mystery of iniquity is that many say "no."

The "act of righteousness" is either (1) Jesus' entire life of obedience and revelation of the Father or (2) specifically His death on sinful mankind's behalf. As one man's life affected all (Jewish corporality, cf. Josh. 7), so too, one innocent life affected all. These two acts are parallel, but not equal. All are affected by Adam's sin, but all are only potentially affected by Jesus' life—only believers who receive the gift of justification. Jesus' act also affects all human sin, for those who believe and receive, past, present, and future!

5:18-19 "condemnation to all men. . .justification of life to all men. . .the many were made sinners... the many will be made righteous" These are parallel phrases which show that the term "many" is not restrictive, but inclusive. This same parallelism is found in Isa. 53:6 "all" and 53:11,12 "many." The term "many" cannot be used in a restrictive sense to limit God's offer of salvation to all mankind (Calvin's elect versus non-elect).

Notice the PASSIVE VOICE of the two VERBS. They refer to the activity of God. Humans sin in relationship to God's character and they are justified in relation to His character.

5:19 "one man's disobedience. . .the obedience of the One" Paul was using the theological concept of Old Testament corporality. One person's acts affected the whole community (cf. Achan in Josh. 7). Adam and Eve's disobedience brought about the judgment of God on all creation (cf. Gen. 3). All creation has been affected by the consequences of Adam's rebellion (cf. 8:18-25). The world is not the same. Humans are not the same. Death became the end of all earthly life (cf. Gen. 5). This is not the world that God intended it to be!

In this same corporate sense Jesus' one act of obedience, Calvary, resulted in (1) a new age, (2) a new people, and (3) a new covenant. This representative theology is called "the Adam-Christ typology" (cf. Phil. 2:6). Jesus is the second Adam. He is the new beginning for the fallen human race.

} **"made righteous"** See Special Topic at 1:17.

5:20

NASB	**"And the Law came in that the transgression might increase"**
NKJV	**"Moreover the law entered that the offense might abound"**
NRSV	**"But law came in, with the result and the trespass multiplied"**
TEV	**"Law was introduced in order to increase wrongdoing"**
JB	**"When law came, it was to multiply the opportunities of falling"**

The purpose of the Law was never to save mankind, but to show fallen mankind's need and helplessness (cf. Eph. 2:1-3) and thereby bring them to Christ (cf. 3:20; 4:15; 7:5; Gal. 3:19, 23-26). The Law is good, but mankind is sinful!

} **"grace abounded all the more"** This was Paul's main thrust in this section. Sin is horrible and pervasive, but grace abounds and exceeds its deadly influence! This was a way to encourage the first century fledgling church. They were overcomers in Christ (cf. 5:9-11; 8:31-39; I John 5:4). This is not a license to sin more! See Special Topic: Paul's Use of *Huper* Compounds at 1:30.

5:21 Both "sin" and "grace" are personified as kings. Sin reigned by the power of universal death (vv. 14, 17). Grace reigns through the power of imputed righteousness through the finished work of Jesus Christ and believers' personal faith and repentant response to the gospel.

As God's new people, as Christ's body, Christians also reign with Christ (cf. 5:17; II Tim. 2:12; Rev. 22:5). This can be seen as an earthly or millennial reign (cf. Rev. 5:9-10; 20). The Bible also speaks of the same truth by asserting that the Kingdom has been given to the saints (cf. Matt. 5:3,10; Luke 12:32; Eph. 2:5-6). See Special Topic: Reigning in the Kingdom of God at 5:17.

DISCUSSION QUESTIONS

This is a study <u>guide</u> commentary, which means that you are responsible for your own interpretation of the Bible. Each of us must walk in the light we have. You, the Bible, and the Holy Spirit are priority in interpretation. You must not relinquish this to a commentator.

These discussion questions are provided to help you think through the major issues of this section of the book. They are meant to be thought-provoking, not definitive.

1.   Define God's "righteousness."

2.   What is the theological distinction between "positional sanctification" and "progressive possession"?

3.   Are we saved by grace or faith (cf. Eph. 2:8-9)?

4.   Why do Christians suffer?

5.   Are we: saved or being saved or will be saved?

6.   Are we sinners because we sin, or do we sin because we are sinners?

7.   How are the terms "justified," "saved" and "reconciled" related in this chapter?

8.   Why does God hold me responsible for another man's sin who lived thousands of years ago (vv.12-21)?

9.   Why did everyone die between Adam and Moses if sin was not counted during this period (vv. 13-14)?

10.   Are the terms "all" and "many" synonymous (vv. 18-19, Is. 53:6, 11-12)?

ROMANS 6

PARAGRAPH DIVISIONS OF MODERN TRANSLATIONS

UBS4	NKJV	NRSV	TEV	JB
Dead to Sin But Alive in Christ	Dead to Sin, Alive to God	Dying and Rising With Christ	Dead to Sin But Alive in	Baptism Christ Christ
6:1-11	6:1-14	6:1-4	6:1-4	6:1-7
		6:5-11	6:5-11	
				6:8-11
				Holiness, Not Sin to be Master
6:12-14		6:12-14	6:12-14	6:12-14
Slaves of Righteousness	From Slaves of Sin to Slaves of God	The Two Slaveries	Slaves of Righteousness	The Christian is From the Slavery of Sin
6:15-23	6:15-23	6:15-19	6:15-19	6:15-19
				The Reward of Sin and the Reward of Holiness
		6:20-23	6:20-23	6:20-23

READING CYCLE THREE
FOLLOWING THE ORIGINAL AUTHOR'S INTENT AT THE PARAGRAPH LEVEL

This is a study guide commentary, which means that you are responsible for your own interpretation of the Bible. Each of us must walk in the light we have. You, the Bible, and the Holy Spirit are priority in interpretation. You must not relinquish this to a commentator.

Read the chapter in one sitting. Identify the subjects. Compare your subject divisions with the five translations above. Paragraphing is not inspired, but it is the key to following the original author's intent, which is the heart of interpretation. Every paragraph has one and only one subject.

1. First paragraph

2. Second paragraph

3. Third paragraph

4. Etc.

CONTEXTUAL INSIGHTS

A. Chapters 6:1-8:39 form a unit of thought (literary unit) that deals with the Christian's relationship to sin. This is a very important issue because the gospel is based on the free unmerited grace of God through Christ (3:21-5:21) so, therefore, how does sin affect the believer? Chapter 6 is based on two supposed questions, vv. 1 and 15. Verse 1 relates to 5:20, while v. 15 relates to 6:14. The first is related to sin as a lifestyle (PRESENT TENSE), the second to individual acts of sin (AORIST TENSE). It is obvious also that vv. 1-14 deal with believers' freedom from sin's domination, while vv. 15-23 deal with believers freedom to serve God as they previously served sin—totally, completely and whole-heartedly.

B. Sanctification is both
   1. a position (imputed like justification at salvation, 3:21-5:21)
   2. a progressing Christlikeness
      a. 6:1-8:39 express this truth theologically
      b. 12:1-15:13 express it practically
(See Special Topic at 6:4)

C. Often commentators must theologically split the subject of justification and positional sanctification to help grasp their biblical meanings. In reality they are simultaneous acts of grace (positional, I Cor. 1:30; 6:11). The mechanism for both is the same—God's grace demonstrated in Jesus' life and death which is received by faith (cf. Eph. 2:8-9).

D. This chapter teaches the potential full maturity (sinlessness, cf. I John 3:6,9; 5:18) of God's children in Christ. Chapter 7 and I John 1:8-2:1 show the reality of believers' continuing sinfulness.
   Much of the conflict over Paul's view of forgiveness was related to the issue of morality. The Jews wanted to assure godly living by demanding that new converts conform to the Mosaic law. It must be admitted that some did and do use Paul's views as a license to sin (cf. vv. 1,15; II Pet. 3:15-16). Paul believed that the indwelling Spirit, not an external code, would produce godly Christlike followers. In reality this is the difference between the Old Covenant (cf. Deuteronomy 27-28) and the New Covenant (cf. Jer. 31:31-34; Ezek. 36:26-27).

E. Baptism is simply a physical illustration of the spiritual reality of justification/sanctification. In Romans the twin doctrines of positional sanctification (justification) and experiential sanctification (Christlikeness) are both stressed. Being buried with Him (v. 4) is parallel with "be crucified with Him" (v. 6).

F. The keys to overcoming temptation and sin in the Christian's life are
   1. Know who you are in Christ. Know what He has done for you. You are free from sin! You are dead to sin!
   2. Reckon/count your position in Christ into your daily life situations.
   3. We are not our own! We must serve/obey our Master. We serve/obey out of gratitude and love to the One who loved us!

4. The Christian life is a supernatural life. It, like salvation, is a gift from God in Christ. He initiates it and provides its power. We must respond in repentance and faith, both initially and continually.
5. Don't play around with sin. Label it for what it is. Turn from it; flee from it. Don't put yourself into the place of temptation.
6. Sin is an addiction that can be broken, but it takes time, effort, and volition.

WORD AND PHRASE STUDY

NASB (UPDATED) TEXT: 6:1-7

[1]What shall we say then? Are we to continue in sin so that grace may increase? [2]May it never be! How shall we who died to sin still live in it? [3]Or do you not know that all of us who have beenbaptized into Christ Jesus have been baptized into His death? [4]Therefore we have been buried with Him through baptism into death, so that as Christ was raised from the dead through the glory of the Father, so we too might walk in newness of life. [5]For if we have become united with *Him* in the likeness of His death, certainly we shall also be *in the likeness* of His resurrection, [6]knowing this, that our old self was crucified with *Him*, in order that our body of sin might be done away with, so that we would no longer be slaves to sin; [7]for he who has died is freed from sin.

6:1

NASB	"Are we to continue to sin that grace might increase"
NKJV	"Shall we continue in sin that grace may abound"
NRSV	"Should we continue in sin in order that grace may abound"
TEV	"That we should continue to live in sin so that God's grace will increase"
JB	"Does it follow that we should remain in sin so as to let grace have greater scope"

This is a PRESENT ACTIVE SUBJUNCTIVE. It literally asks the question, are Christians "to abide with" or "to embrace" sin? This question looks back to 5:20. Paul used a hypothetical objector (diatribe) to deal with the potential misuse of grace (cf. I John 3:6,9; 5:18). God's grace and mercy are not meant to give a license for rebellious living.

Paul's gospel of a free salvation as the gift of God's grace through Christ (cf. 3:24; 5:15,17; 6:23) raised many questions about life style righteousness. How does a free gift produce moral uprightness? Justification and sanctification must not be separated (cf. Matt. 7:24-27; Luke 8:21; 11:28; John 13:17; Rom. 2:13; James1:22-25; 2:14-26).

On this point let me quote F. F. Bruce in *Paul: Apostle of the Heart Set Free*,
"The baptism of Christians constituted the frontier between their old unregenerate existence and their new life in Christ:
it marked their death to the old order, so that for a baptized Christian to go on in sin was as preposterous as it would be for an emancipated slave to remain in bondage to his former owner (cf. Rom. 6:1-4, 15- 23) or for a widow to remain subject to 'the law of her husband,'" pp. 281-82 (cf. Rom. 7:1-6).

In James S. Stewart's book, *A Man in Christ*, he writes:
"The *locus classicus* for all this side of the apostles' thought is to be found in Romans 6. There Paul, with magnificent vigor and effort, drives home to heart and conscience the lesson that to be united with Jesus in His death means for the believer a complete and drastic break with sin," pp. 187-88.

6:2 "may it never be" This is a rare OPTATIVE form which was a grammatical mood or mode used of a wish or prayer. It was Paul's stylistic way of answering a hypothetical objector. It expressed Paul's shock and horror at unbelieving mankind's misunderstanding and abuse of grace (cf. 3:4,6).

} "we who died to sin" This is an AORIST ACTIVE INDICATIVE, meaning "we have died." The SINGULAR "sin" is used so often throughout this chapter. It seems to refer to our "sin nature" inherited from Adam (cf. Rom. 5:12-21; I Cor. 15:21-22). Paul often uses the concept of death as a metaphor to show the believer's new relationship to Jesus. They are no longer subject to sin's mastery.

} "still live in it" This is literally "walk." This metaphor was used to stress either our lifestyle faith (cf. Eph. 4:1; 5:2,15) or lifestyle sin (cf. v. 4). Believers cannot be happy in sin!

6:3-4 "have been baptized. . .have been buried" These are both AORIST PASSIVE INDICATIVES. This grammatical form emphasized a completed act accomplished by an outside agent, here the Spirit. They are parallel in this context.

SPECIAL TOPIC: BAPTISM

Curtis Vaughan, *Acts*, has an interesting footnote on p. 28.

"The Greek word for 'baptized' is a third person imperative; the word for 'repent,' a second person imperative. This change from the more direct second person command to the less direct third person of 'baptized' implies that Peter's basic primary demand is for repentance."

This follows the preaching emphasis of John the Baptist (cf. Matt. 3:2) and Jesus (cf. Matt. 4:17). Repentance seems to be a spiritual key and baptism is an outward expression of this spiritual change. The New Testament knew nothing of unbaptized believers! To the early church baptism was the public profession of faith. It is the occasion for the public confession of faith in Christ, not the mechanism for salvation! It needs to be remembered that baptism is not mentioned in Peter's second sermon, though repentance is (cf. 3:19; Luke 24:17). Baptism was an example set by Jesus (cf. Matt. 3:13-18). Baptism was commanded by Jesus (cf. Matt. 28:19). The modern question of the necessity of baptism for salvation is not addressed in the New Testament; all believers are expected to be baptized. However, one must also guard against a sacramental mechanicalism! Salvation is a faith issue, not a right-place, right-words, right-ritual act issue!

⟩ **"into Christ Jesus"** The use of *eis* (into) parallels the Great Commission of Matt. 28:19, where new believers are baptized *eis* (into) the name of the Father and the Son and the Holy Spirit. The PREPOSITION is also used to describe the believers being baptized by the Spirit into the body of Christ in I Cor. 12:13. *Eis* in this context is synonymous with *en* (in Christ) in v. 11, which is Paul's favorite way to denote believers. It is a LOCATIVE OF SPHERE. Believers live and move and have their being in Christ. These PREPOSITIONS express this intimate union, this sphere of fellowship, this vine and branch relationship. Believers identify with and join with Christ in His death (cf. v. 6; 8:17), in His resurrection (cf. v. 5), in His obedient service to God, and in His Kingdom!

⟩ **"into His death. . .we have been buried with Him"** Baptism by immersion illustrates death and burial (cf. v. 5 and Col. 2:12). Jesus used baptism as a metaphor for His own death (cf. Mark 10:38-39; Luke 12:50). The emphasis here is not a doctrine of baptism, but of the Christian's new, intimate relationship to Christ's death and burial. Believers identify with Christ's baptism, with His character, with His sacrifice, with His mission. Sin has no power over believers!

6:4 "we have been buried with Him through baptism into death" In this chapter, as is characteristic of all of Paul's writing, he uses many *sun* (with) compounds (e.g. Eph. 2:5-6).
1. *sun* + *thaptō* = co-buried, v. 4; Col. 2:12; also note v. 8
2. *sun* + *stauroō* = co-planted, v. 5
3. *sun* + *azō* = co-exist, v. 8; II Tim. 2:11 (he also has co-died and co-reign)

⟩ **"so we too might walk in newness of life"** This is an AORIST ACTIVE SUBJUNCTIVE. The expected result of salvation is sanctification. Because believers know God's grace through Christ, their lives must be different. Our new life does not bring us salvation, but it is the result of salvation (cf. vv. 16, 19; and Eph. 2:8-9,10; James 2:14-26). This is not an either/or question, faith or works, but there is a sequential order.

SPECIAL TOPIC: SANCTIFICATION

The NT asserts that when sinners turn to Jesus in repentance and faith, they are instantaneously justified and sanctified. This is their new position in Christ. His righteousness has been imputed to them (Rom. 4). They are declared right and holy (a forensic act of God).

But the NT also urges believers on to holiness or sanctification. It is both a theological position in the finished work of Jesus Christ and a call to be Christlike in attitude and actions in daily life. As salvation is a free gift and a cost-everything lifestyle, so too, is sanctification.

Initial Response	**A Progressive Christlikeness**
Acts 20:23; 26:18	Romans 6:19
Romans 15:16	II Corinthians 7:1
I Corinthians 1:2-3; 6:11	I Thessalonians 3:13; 4:3-4,7; 5:23
II Thessalonians 2:13	I Timothy 2:15
Hebrews 2:11; 10:10,14; 13:12	II Timothy 2:21
I Peter 1:1	Hebrews 12:14
	I Peter 1:15-16

} **"Christ was raised"** In this context the Father's acceptance and approval of the Son's words and works are expressed in two great events.
1. Jesus' resurrection from the dead
2. Jesus' ascension to the Father's right hand

} **"the glory of the Father"** For "glory" see Special Topic at 3:23.
For "Father" see Special Topic at 1:7.

6:5 "if" This is a FIRST CLASS CONDITIONAL SENTENCE, which is assumed to be true from the writer's perspective or for his literary purposes. Paul assumed his readers were believers.

} **"we have become united with *Him*"** This is a PERFECT ACTIVE INDICATIVE, which could be translated "have been and continue to be joined together," or "have been or continue to be planted together with." This truth is theologically analogous to "abiding" in John 15. If believers have been identified with Jesus' death (cf. Gal. 2:19-20; Col. 2:20; 3:3-5), theologically they should be identified with His resurrection life (cf. v. 10).

This metaphorical aspect of baptism as death was meant to show (1) we have died to the old life, the old covenant, (2) we are alive to the Spirit, the new covenant. Christian baptism is, therefore, not the same as the baptism of John the Baptist, who was the last OT prophet. Baptism was the early church's opportunity for the new believer's public profession of faith. The earliest baptismal formula, to be repeated by the candidate, was "I believe Jesus is Lord" (cf. Rom. 10:9-13). This public declaration was a formal, ritual act of what had happened previously in experience. Baptism was not the mechanism of forgiveness, salvation, or the coming of the Spirit, but the occasion for their public profession and confession (cf. Acts 2:38). However, it also was not optional. Jesus commanded it (cf. Matt. 28:19-20) and exemplified it (cf. Matt. 3; Mark 1; Luke 3) and it became part of the Apostolic sermons and procedures of Acts.

6:6
NASB "knowing this, that our old self was crucified with Him"
NKJV "knowing this, that our old man was crucified with him"
NRSV "We know that our old self was crucified with him"
TEV "And we know this: our old being has been put to death with Christ on his cross"
JB "We must realize that our former selves have been crucified with him"

This is an AORIST PASSIVE INDICATIVE meaning "our old self has been once for all crucified by the Spirit." This truth is crucial to victorious Christian living. Believers must realize their new relationship to sin (cf. Gal. 2:20; 6:14). Mankind's old fallen self (Adamic nature) has died with Christ (cf. v. 7; Eph. 4:22 and Col. 3:9). As believers we now have a choice about sin as Adam originally did.

} NASB, NKJV   "that our body of sin might be done away with"
  NRSV   "so that the body of sin might be destroyed"
  TEV   "in order that the power of the sinful self might be destroyed"
  JB   "to destroy the sinful body"

Paul uses the word "body" (*soma*) with several GENITIVE phrases.
1. body of (the) sin, Rom. 6:6
2. body of this death, Rom. 7:24
3. body of the flesh, Col. 2:11

Paul is speaking of the physical life of this age of sin and rebellion. Jesus' new resurrection body is the body of the new age of righteousness (cf. II Cor. 5:17). Physicalness is not the problem (Greek philosophy), but sin and rebellion. The body is not evil. Christianity affirms the belief in a physical body in eternity (cf. I Corinthians 15). However, the physical body is the battle ground of temptation, sin, and self.

This is an AORIST PASSIVE SUBJUNCTIVE. The phrase "done away with" meant "made inoperative," "made powerless," or "made unproductive," not "destroyed." This was a favorite word with Paul, used over twenty-five times. See special topic at 3:3. Our physical body is morally neutral, but it is also the battleground for the continuing spiritual conflict (cf. vv. 12-13; 5:12-21; 12:1-2).

6:7 "he who has died is freed from sin" This is an AORIST ACTIVE PARTICIPLE and a PERFECT PASSIVE INDICATIVE, meaning "he who has died has been and continues to be free from sin." Because believers are new creations in Christ they have been and continue to be set free from the slavery of sin and self inherited from Adam's fall (cf. 7:1-6).

The Greek term translated here as "freed" is the term translated elsewhere in the opening chapters as "justified" (ASV). In this context "freed" makes much more sense (similar to its use in Acts 13:39). Remember, context determines word meaning, not a dictionary or preset technical definition. Words only have meaning in sentences and sentences only have meaning in paragraphs.

NASB (UPDATED) TEXT: 6:8-11

[8]Now if we have died with Christ, we believe that we shall also live with Him, [9]knowing that Christ, having been raised from the dead, is never to die again; death no longer is master over Him. [10]For the death that He died, He died to sin once for all; but the life that He lives, He lives to God. [11]Even so consider yourselves to be dead to sin, but alive to God in Christ Jesus.

6:8 "If" This is a FIRST CLASS CONDITIONAL SENTENCE which is assumed to be true from the writer's perspective or for his literary purposes. Believer's baptism visually exemplifies one's death with Christ.

⁂ "we shall also live with Him" This context demands a "here and now" orientation (cf. I John 1:7), not an exclusively future setting. Verse 5 speaks of our sharing Christ's death, while verse 8 speaks of our sharing His life. This is the same tension inherent in the biblical concept of the Kingdom of God. It is both here and now, yet future. Free grace must produce self-control, not license.

6:9 "having been raised from the dead" This is an AORIST PASSIVE PARTICIPLE (see 6:4, AORIST PASSIVE INDICATIVE).

The NT affirms that all three persons of the Trinity were active in Jesus' resurrection: (1) the Spirit (cf. Rom. 8:11); (2) the Son (cf. John 2:19-22; 10:17-18); and most frequently (3) the Father (cf. Acts 2:24,32; 3:15,26; 4:10; 5:30; 10:40; 13:30,33,34,37; 17:31; Rom. 6:4,9). The Father's actions were confirmation of His acceptance of Jesus' life, death, and teachings. This was a major aspect of the early preaching of the Apostles.

} NASB	"death no longer is master over Him"
NKJV, NRSV	"Death no longer has dominion over Him"
TEV	"death will no longer rule over him"
NJB	"Death has no power over him anymore"

The VERB *kurieuō* is from the term *kurios*, which means "owner," "master," "husband," or "lord," Jesus is now lord over death (cf. Rev. 1:18). Jesus is the first to break the power of death (cf. I Corinthians 15)!

6:10 "for the death that He died, He died to sin" Jesus lived in a sinful world and although He never sinned, the sinful world crucified Him (cf. Heb. 10:10). Jesus' substitutionary death on mankind's behalf canceled the Law's requirements and consequences over them (cf. Gal. 3:13; Col 2:13-14).

} "once for all" In this context Paul is emphasizing the crucifixion of Jesus. His one-time death <u>for</u> sin has affected His followers' death <u>to sin.</u>

The book of Hebrews also emphasizes the ultimacy of Jesus' once-given sacrificial death. This once- done salvation and forgiveness are forever accomplished (cf. "once" [*ephapax*], 7:27; 9:12; 10:10 and "once for all" [*hapax*], 6:4; 9:7,26,27,28; 10:2; 12:26,27). This is the recurrent accomplished sacrificial affirmation.

} "but the life that He lives, He lives to God" The two AORISTS of v. 10a are contrasted with two PRESENT ACTIVE INDICATIVES in v. 10b. Believers died with Christ; believers live to God, through Christ. The goal of the gospel is not forgiveness only (justification), but service to God (sanctification). Believers are saved to serve.

6:11 "Even so consider yourselves to be dead to sin," This is a PRESENT MIDDLE (deponent) IMPERATIVE. This is an ongoing, habitual command for believers. Christians' knowledge of Christ's work on their behalf is crucial for daily life. The term "consider" (cf. 4:4,9) was an accounting term that meant "carefully add it up" and then act on that knowledge. Verses 1-11 acknowledged one's position in Christ (positional sanctification), while 12-13 emphasized walking in Him (progressive sanctification). See Special Topic at v. 4.

¹²Therefore do not let sin reign in your mortal body so that you obey its lusts, ¹³and do not go on presenting the members of your body to sin as instruments of unrighteousness; but present yourselves to God as those alive from the dead, and your members *as* instruments of righteousness to God. ¹⁴For sin shall not be master over you, for you are not under law but under grace.

6:12 "Therefore do not let sin reign in your mortal body" This is a PRESENT ACTIVE IMPERATIVE with the NEGATIVE PARTICLE, which usually meant to stop an act already in process. The term "reign" relates to 5:17-21 and 6:23. Paul personifies several theological concepts: (1) death reigned as king (cf. 5:14,17; 6:23); (2) grace reigned as king (cf. 5:21); and (3) sin reigned as king (cf. 6:12,14). The real question is who is reigning in your life? The believer has the power in Christ to choose! The tragedy for the individual, the local church, and the Kingdom of God is when believers choose self and sin, even while claiming grace!

6:13 "do not go on presenting the members of your body to sin" This is a PRESENT ACTIVE IMPERATIVE with the NEGATIVE PARTICLE which usually meant to stop an act already in process. This shows the potential for sin in the lives of believers (cf. 7:1ff; I John 1:8-2:1). But the necessity of sin has been eliminated in the believer's relationship with Christ, vv. 1-11.

⟩ "as instruments" This term referred to "a soldier's weapons." Our physical body is the battleground for temptation (cf. vv. 12-13; 12:1-2; I Cor. 6:20; Phil. 1:20). Our lives publicly display the gospel.

⟩ "but present yourselves to God" This is an AORIST ACTIVE IMPERATIVE which was a call for a decisive act (cf. 12:1). Believers do this at salvation by faith, but they must continue to do this throughout their lives.
Notice the parallelism of this verse.
1. same VERB and both IMPERATIVES
2. battle metaphors
   a.   weapons of unrighteousness
   b.   weapons of righteousness
3. believers can present their bodies to sin or themselves to God
Remember, this verse is referring to believers—the choice continues; the battle continues!

6:14 "For sin shall not be master over you" This is a FUTURE ACTIVE INDICATIVE (cf. Ps. 19:13) functioning as an IMPERATIVE, "sin must not be master over you!" Sin is not master over believers because it is not master over Christ, (cf. v. 9; John 16:33).

```
┌────────────────────────────────────────────────────────────────────┐
│                                                                      │
│     NASB (UPDATED) TEXT: 6:15-19                                     │
│                                                                      │
│     ¹⁵What then? Shall we sin because we are not under law but       │
│   under grace? May it never be!                                      │
│     ¹⁶Do you not know that when you present yourselves to            │
│   someone as slaves for obedience, you are slaves of the one whom    │
│   you obey, either of sin resulting in death, or of obedience        │
│   resulting in righteousness? ¹⁷But thanks be to God that though     │
│   you were slaves of sin, you became obedient from the heart to      │
│   that form of teaching to which you were committed, ¹⁸and having    │
│   been freed from sin, you became slaves of righteousness. ¹⁹I am    │
│   speaking in human terms because of the weakness of your flesh.     │
│   For just as you presented your members as slaves to impurity and   │
│   to lawlessness, resulting in further lawlessness, so now present   │
│   your members as slaves to righteousness, resulting in              │
│   sanctification.                                                    │
│                                                                      │
└────────────────────────────────────────────────────────────────────┘
```

6:15 This second supposed question (diatribe) is much like 6:1. Both answer different questions about the Christian's relation to sin. Verse 1 deals with grace not being used as a license to sin while v. 15deals with the Christian's need to fight, or resist, individual acts of sin. Also, at the same time the believer must serve God now with the same enthusiasm with which he previously served sin (cf. 6:14).

> **NASB, NKJV,**
> **TEV**   **"Shall we sin"**
> **NRSV**   **"Should we sin"**
> **JB**   **"that we are free to sin"**

The Williams and Phillips translations both translate this AORIST ACTIVE SUBJUNCTIVE as a PRESENT ACTIVE SUBJUNCTIVE similar to v. 1. This is not the proper focus. Notice the alternate translations (1) KJV, ASV, NIV - "shall we sin?"; (2) The Centenary Translation - "Shall we commit an act of sin?"; (3) RSV - "are we to sin?" This question is emphatic in Greek and expected a "yes" answer. This was Paul's diatribe method of communicating truth. This verse expresses false theology! Paul answered this by his characteristic "May it never be." Paul's gospel of the radical free grace of God was misunderstood and abused by many false teachers.

6:16 The question expects a "yes" response. Humans serve something or someone. Who reigns in your life, sin or God? Who humans obey shows who they serve (cf. Gal. 6:7-8).

6:17 "But thanks be to God" Paul often breaks out into praise to God. His writings flow from his prayers and his prayers from his knowledge of the gospel. See Special Topic: Paul's Prayer, Praise, and Thanksgiving to God at 7:25.

> **"you were. . .you became"** This is the IMPERFECT TENSE of the VERB, "to be," which described their state of being in the past (slaves of sin), followed by an AORIST TENSE, which asserts that their state of rebellion has ceased.

} **"You became obedient from your heart to that form of teaching"** In context, this refers to their justification by faith, which must lead to daily Christlikeness. The term "teaching" referred to Apostolic teaching or the gospel.

} **"heart"** See Special Topic: Heart at 1:24.

} NASB **"that form of teaching to which you were committed"**
NKJV **"that form of doctrine to which you were delivered"**
NRSV, NIV **"to the form of teaching to which you were entrusted"**
TEV **"the truth found in the teaching you received"**
NJB **"to the pattern of teaching** to which you were introduced"

SPECIAL TOPIC: FORM (*TUPOS*)

The problem is the word *tupos*, which has a variety of uses.
1. Moulton and Milligan, *The Vocabulary of the Greek New Testament*, p. 645
    a. pattern
    b. plan
    c. form or manner of writing
    d. decree or rescript
    e. sentence or decision
    f. model of human body as votive offerings to the healing god
    g. verb used in the sense of enforcing the precepts of the law
2. Louw and Nida, *Greek-English Lexicon*, vol. 2, p. 249
    a. scar (cf. John 20:25) b. image (cf. Acts 7:43) c. model (cf. Heb. 8:5)
    d. example (cf. I Cor. 10:6; Phil. 3:17)
    e. archetype (cf. Rom. 5:14)
    f. kind (cf. Acts 23:25)
    g. contents (cf. Acts 23:25)
3. Harold K. Moulton, *The Analytical Greek Lexicon Revised*, p. 411
    a. a blow, an impression, a mark (cf. John 20:25)
    b. a delineation
    c. an image (cf. Acts 7:43)
    d. a formula, scheme (cf. Rom. 6:17)
    e. form, purport (cf. Acts 23:25)
    f. a figure, counterpart (cf. I Cor. 10:6)
    g. an anticipative figure, type (cf. Rom. 5:14; I Cor. 10:11)
    h. a model pattern (cf. Acts 7:44; Heb. 8:5)
    i. a moral pattern (cf. Phil. 3:17; I Thess. 1:7; II Thess. 3:9; I Tim. 4:12; I Pet. 5:3)

In this context # I above seems best. The gospel has both doctrine and lifestyle implications. The free gift of salvation in Christ also demands a life like Christ!

6:18 "having been freed from sin" This is an AORIST PASSIVE PARTICIPLE. The gospel has freed believers by the agency of the Spirit through the work of Christ. Believers have been freed both from the penalty of sin (justification) and the tyranny of sin (sanctification, cf. vv. 7 and 22).

} "you became the slaves of righteousness" This is an AORIST PASSIVE INDICATIVE, "you became enslaved to righteousness." See special topic at 1:17. Believers are freed from sin to serve God (cf. vv. 14,19,22; 7:4; 8:2)! The goal of free grace is a godly life. Justification is both a legal pronouncement and an impetus for personal righteousness. God wants to save us and change us so as to reach others! Grace does not stop with us!

6:19 "I am speaking in human terms because of the weakness of your flesh" Paul is addressing the believers at Rome. Is he addressing a local problem he had heard about (jealousy among Jewish believers and Gentile believers) or is he asserting a truth about all believers? Paul used this phrase earlier in Rom. 3:5, as he does in Gal. 3:15.

Verse 19 is parallel to v. 16. Paul repeats his theological points for emphasis.

Some would say this phrase means that Paul was apologizing for using a slave metaphor. However, "because of the weakness of your flesh" does not fit this interpretation. Slavery was not viewed as an evil by first century society, especially in Rome. It was simply the culture of its day.

} "flesh" See Special Topic at 1:3.

} "resulting in sanctification" This is the goal of justification (cf. v. 22). The NT used this term in two theological senses related to salvation (1) positional sanctification, which is the gift of God (objective aspect) given at salvation along with justification through faith in Christ (cf. Acts 26:18; I Cor. 1:2; 6:11; Eph. 5:26-27; I Thess. 5:23; II Thess. 2:13; Heb. 10:10; 13:12; I Pet. 1:2) and (2) progressive sanctification which is also the work of God through the Holy Spirit whereby the believer's life is transformed into the image and maturity of Christ (subjective aspect, cf. II Cor. 7:1; I Thess. 4:3,7; I Tim. 2:15; II Tim. 2:21; Heb. 12:10,14). See Special Topic: Sanctification at 6:4.

It is both a gift and a command! It is a position (OBJECTIVE) and an activity (SUBJECTIVE)! It is an INDICATIVE (a statement) and an IMPERATIVE (a command)! It comes at the beginning, but does not mature until the end (cf. Phil. 1:6; 2:12-13).

NASB (UPDATED) TEXT: 6:20-23

[20]For when you were slaves of sin, you were free in regard to righteousness. [21]Therefore what benefit were you then deriving from the things of which you are now ashamed? For the outcome of those things is death. [22]But now having been freed from sin and enslaved to God, you derive your benefit, resulting in sanctification, and the outcome, eternal life. [23]For the wages of sin is death, but the free gift of God is eternal life in Christ Jesus our Lord.

6:20-21 This is simply stating the opposite of vv. 18 and 19. Believers can only serve one master (cf. Luke 16:13).

6:22-23 These verses form a logical progression of the wages paid by whom one serves. Thank God this discussion of sin and the believer ends on a grace focus! First is the gift of salvation through our cooperation, and then the gift of the Christian life, also through our cooperation. Both are gifts received through faith and repentance.

6:22 "you derive your benefit, resulting in sanctification, and the outcome, eternal life" The term "benefit," literally "fruit," is used in v. 21 to speak of the consequences of sin, but in v. 22 it speaks of the consequences of serving God. The immediate benefit is the believer's Christlikeness. The ultimate benefit is being with Him and like Him eternally (cf. I John 3:2). If there is no immediate result (changed life, cf. James 2) the ultimate result can be legitimately questioned (eternal life, cf. Matt. 7). "No fruit, no root!"

6:23 This is the summary of the entire chapter. Paul painted the choice in black and white. The choice is ours—sin and death or free grace through Christ and eternal life. It is very similar to the "two ways" of OT wisdom literature (Psalm 1; Prov. 4; 10-19; Matt. 7:13-14).

} **"the wages of sin"** Sin is personified as (1) a slave owner, (2) a military general, or (3) a king who pays wages (cf. 3:9; 5:21; 6:9,14,17).

} **"the free gift of God is eternal life"** This word, translated "free gift" (*charisma*) was from the root for grace (*charis*, cf. 3:24; 5:15, 16, 17; Eph. 2:8-9). See note at 3:24.

DISCUSSION QUESTIONS

This is a study <u>guide</u> commentary, which means that you are responsible for your own interpretation of the Bible. Each of us must walk in the light we have. You, the Bible, and the Holy Spirit are priority in interpretation. You must not relinquish this to a commentator.

These discussion questions are provided to help you think through the major issues of this section of the book. They are meant to be thought-provoking, not definitive.

1. How are good works related to salvation (cf. Eph. 2:8-9,10)?

2. How is continual sin in the life of the believer related to salvation (cf. I John 3:6,9)?

3. Does the chapter teach "sinless perfection?"

4. How is chapter 6 related to chapters 5 and 7?

5. Why is baptism discussed here?

6. Do Christians retain their old nature? Why?

7. What is the implication of PRESENT TENSE VERBALS dominating v. 1-14 and AORIST TENSE VERBALS in 15-23?

APPENDIX ONE

OLD TESTAMENT AS HISTORY

I. **Christianity and Judaism are historical faiths**.

They base their faith on historical events (accompanied by their interpretations). The problem comes in trying to define or describe what is "history" or "historical study." Much of the problem in modern theological interpretation rests on modern literary or historical assumptions projected back onto ancient Near Eastern biblical literature. Not only is there not a proper appreciation of the temporal and cultural differences, but also of the literary differences. As modern western people we simply do not understand the genres and literary techniques of ancient Near Eastern writings, so we interpreted them in light of western literal genres.

The nineteenth century's approach to biblical studies atomized and depreciated the books of the Old Testament as historical, unified documents. This historical scepticism has affected hermeneutics and historical investigation of the Old Testament. The current trend toward "canonical hermeneutics" (Brevard Childs) has helped focus on the current form of the Old Testament text. This, in my opinion, is a helpful bridge over the abyss of German higher criticism of the nineteenth century. We must deal with the canonical text that has been given us by an unknown historical process whose inspiration is assumed. Many scholars are returning to the assumption of the historicity of the OT. This is surely not meant to deny the obvious editing and updating of the OT by later Jewish scribes, but it is a basic return to the OT as a valid history and the documentation of true events (with their theological interpretations).

A quote from R. K Harrison in *The Expositor's Bible Commentary*, vol. 1, in the article, "Historical and Literary Criticism of the Old Testament" is helpful.

"Comparative historiographic studies have shown that, along with the Hittites, the ancient Hebrews were the most accurate, objective, and responsible recorders of Near Eastern history.

Form-critical studies of books such as Genesis and Deuteronomy, based on specific types of tablets recovered from sites that include Mari, Nuzu, and Boghazköy, have shown that the canonical material has certain nonliterary counterparts in the cultures of some Near Eastern peoples. As a result, it is possible to view with a new degree of confidence and respect those early traditions of the Hebrews that purport to be historiographic in nature" (p. 232).

I am especially appreciative of R. K. Harrison's work because he makes it a priority to interpret the Old Testament in light of contemporary events, cultures and genres.

II. In my own classes on early Jewish literature (Genesis - Deuteronomy and Joshua), I try to establish a credible link with other ancient Near Eastern literature and artifacts.
A. Genesis literary parallels from the ancient Near East
    1. Earliest known literary parallel of the cultural setting of Genesis 1-11 is the Ebla cuniform tablets from northern Syria dating about 2500 B.C., written in Akkadian.

    2. Creation
        a. The closest Mesopotamian account dealing with creation, *Enuma Elish*, dating from about 1900-1700 B.C., was found in Ashurbanipal's library at Nineveh and several other places. There are seven cuniform tablets written in Akkadian which describe creation by Marduk.
            1) the gods, *Apsu* (fresh water-male) & *Tiamat* (salt water-female) had unruly, noisy children. These two gods tried to silence the younger gods.
            2) one of the god's children, *Marduk*, helped defeat *Tiamat*. He formed the earth from her body.
            3) *Marduk* formed humanity from another defeated god, *Kingu*, who was the male consort of *Tiamat* after the death of *Apsu*. Humanity came from *Kingu's* blood.
            4) *Marduk* was made chief of the Babylonian pantheon.
        b. "The creation seal" is a cuniform tablet which is a picture of a naked man and woman beside a fruit tree with a snake wrapped around the tree's trunk and positioned over the woman's shoulder as if talking to her.
    3. Creation and Flood - *The Atrahasis Epic* records the rebellion of the lesser gods because of overwork and the creation of seven human couples to perform the duties of these lesser gods. Because of (1) over population and (2) noise, human beings were reduced in number by a plague, two famines and finally a flood, planned by *Enlil*. These major events are seen in the same order in Gen. 1-8. This cuniform composition dates from about the same times as *Enuma Elish* and the *Gilgamesh Epic*, about 1900-1700 B.C. All are in Akkadian.
    4. Noah's flood
        a. A Summerian tablet from Nippur, called *Eridu Genesis*, dating from abut 1600 B.C., tells about *Zivsudra* and a coming flood.
           1) *Enka*, the water god, warned of a coming flood
           2) *Zivsudra*, a king-priest, saved in a huge boat
           3) The flood lasted seven days
           4) *Zivsudra* opened a window on the boat and released several birds to see if dry land had appeared
           5) He also offered a sacrifice of an ox and sheep when he left the boat
        b. A composite Babylonian flood account from four Summerian tales, known as the *Gilgamesh Epic*, originally dating from about 2500-2400 B.C., although the written composite form was cuniform Akkadian, is much later. It tells about a flood survivor, *Utnapishtim*, who tells *Gilgamesh*, the king of *Uruk* how he survived the great flood and was granted eternal life.

1) *Ea*, the water god, warns of a coming flood and tells *Utnapishtim* (Babylonian form of *Zivsudra*) to build a boat
2) *Utnapishtim* and his family, along with selected healing plants, survived the flood
3) The flood lasted seven days
4) The boat came to rest in northeast Persia, on Mt. Nisir
5) He sent out three different birds to see if dry land had yet appeared

5. The Mesopotamian literature which describes an ancient flood draws from the same source.
   The names often vary, but the plot is the same. An example is that *Zivsudra*, *Atrahasis*, and *Utnapishtim* are all the same human king.

6. The historical parallels to the early events of Genesis can be explained in light of man's pre- dispersion (Genesis 10-11) knowledge and experience of God. These true historical core memories have been elaborated and mythologicalized into the current flood accounts common throughout the world. The same can also be said of: creation (Gen. 1-2) and human and angelic unions (Genesis 6).

7. Patriarch's Day (Middle Bronze)
   a. Mari tablets - cuniform legal (Ammonite culture) and personal texts written in Akkadian from about 1700 B.C.
   b. Nuzi tablets - cuniform archives of certain families (Horite or Hurrian culture) written in Akkadian from about 100 miles SE of Nineveh about 1500-1300 B.C. They record family and business procedures. For further specific examples, see Walton, pp. 52-58.
   c. Alalak tablets - cuniform texts from Northern Syria from about 2000 B.C.
   d. Some of the names found in Genesis are named as place names in the Mari Tablets: Serug, Peleg, Terah, Nahor. Other biblical names were also common: Abraham, Isaac, Jacob, Laban, and Joseph.

8. "Comparative historiographic studies have shown that, along with the Hittites, the ancient Hebrews were the most accurate, objective and responsible recorders of Near Eastern history," R. K Harrison in *Biblical Criticism*, p. 5.

9. Archaeology has proven to be so helpful in establishing the historicity of the Bible. However, a word of caution is necessary. Archaeology is not an absolutely trustworthy guide because of
   a. poor techniques in early excavations,
   b. various, very subjective interpretations of the artifacts that have been discovered,
   c. no agreed-upon chronology of the Ancient Near East (although one is being developed from tree rings)

B. Egyptian creation accounts can be found in John W. Walton's, *Ancient Israelite Literature in Its Cultural Context*. Grand Rapids, MI: Zondervan, 1990. pp. 23-34, 32-34.
   1. In Egyptian literature creation began with an unstructured, chaotic, primeval water. Creation was seen as developing structure out of watery chaos.
   2. In Egyptian literature from Memphis, creation occurred by the spoken word of Ptah.

C. Joshua literary parallels from the ancient Near East
   1. Archaeology has shown that most of the large walled cities of Canaan were destroyed and rapidly rebuilt about 1250 B.C.
      a. Hazor
      b. Lachish
      c. Bethel
      d. Debir (formerly called Kerioth Sepher, 15:15)
   2. Archaeology has not been able to confirm or reject the biblical account of the fall of Jericho (cf. Joshua 6). This is because the site is in such poor condition:
      a. weather/location
      b. later rebuildings on old sites using older materials
      c. uncertainty as to the dates of the layers
   3. Archaeology has found an altar on Mt. Ebal that might be connected to Joshua 8:30-31 (Deuteronomy. 27:2-9). It is very similar to a description found in the Mishnah (Talmud).
   4. The Ras Shamra texts found at Ugarit show Canaanite life and religion of 1400's B.C.:
      a. polytheistic nature worship (fertility cult)
      b. El was chief deity
      c. El's consort was Asherah (later she is consort to Ba'al) who was worshiped in the form of a carved stake or live tree, which symbolized "the tree of life"
      d. their son was Ba'al (Haddad), the storm god
      e. Ba'al became the "high god" of the Canaanite pantheon. Anat was his consort
      f. ceremonies similar to Isis and Osiris of Egypt
      g. Ba'al worship was focused on local "high places" or stone platforms (ritual prostitution)
      h. Ba'al was symbolized by a raised stone pillar (phallic symbol)
   5. The accurate listing of the names of ancient cities fits a contemporary author, not later editor(s):
      a. Jerusalem called Jebus, 15:8; 18:16,28 (15:28 said the Jebusites still remained in part of Jerusalem)
      b. Hebron called Kiriath-arba, 14:15; 15:13,54; 20:7; 21:11
      c. Kiriath-jearim is called Baalah, 15:9,10
      d. Sidon is referred to as the major Phoenician city, not Tyre, 11:8; 13:6; 19:28, which later became the chief city

APPENDIX TWO

OT HISTORIOGRAPHY COMPARED WITH CONTEMPORARY NEAR EASTERN CULTURES

I. **Mesopotamian sources**
   A. Like most ancient literature the subject is usually the king or some national hero. B. The events are often embellished for propaganda purposes.
   C. Usually nothing negative is recorded.
   D. The purpose was to support current status quo institutions or explain the rise of new regimes.
   E. The historical distortions involve
      1. embellished claims of great victories
      2. earlier achievements presented as current achievements
      3. only positive aspects recorded
   F. The literature served not only a propagandistic function, but was also a didactic function

II. **Egyptian sources**
   A. They support a very static view of life, which was not affected by time.
   B. The king and his family are the object of much of the literature.
   C. It, like Mesopotamian literature, is very propagandistic.
      1. no negative aspects
      2. embellished aspects

III. **Rabbinical sources (later)**
   A. Attempt to make Scripture relevant by Midrash, which moves from the faith of the interpreter to text and does not focus on authorial intent nor historical setting of the text
      1. *Halakha* deals with truths or rules for life
      2. *Haggada* deals with application and encouragement for life
   B. Pesher - later development seen in Dead Sea Scrolls. It used a typological approach to see the prophetic fulfillment of past events in the current setting. The current setting was the prophesied eschaton (coming new age).

IV. It is obvious that ancient Near Eastern genres and later Jewish literature are different from Old Testament Scripture.

In many ways the genres of the Old Testament, though often sharing characteristics of contemporary literature, are unique, especially in their depiction of historical events. The closest to Hebrew historiography is the Hittite literature.

It must be acknowledged how different ancient historiography is from modern, western historiography. Herein lies the problem for interpretation.

Modern historiography attempts to be objective (non-propaganda, if this is possible) and to document and record in chronological sequence what "really happened!" It attempts to document "cause and effect" of historical events. It is characterized by details!

Just because Near Eastern histories are not like modern histories does not make them wrong, inferior, or untrustworthy. Western modern histories reflect the biases (presuppositions) of their writers. Biblical history is by its very nature (inspiration) different. There is a sense in which biblical history is seen through the eyes of the faith of the inspired author and for the purposes of theology, but it is still a valid historical account.

This historicity of the Old Testament is important to me as a way of advocating my faith to others. If the Bible can be demonstrated to be historical then its faith claims have stronger appeal to non- believers. My faith does not rest on the historical confirmation of archaeology and anthropology, but these help to introduce the message of the Bible, and to give it a credibility that otherwise it would not have.

To summarize then, historicity does not function in the area of inspiration, but in the area of apologetics and evangelism.

APPENDIX THREE

HEBREW HISTORICAL NARRATIVE

I. **OPENING STATEMENTS**
   A. The relationship between the OT and other ways of the chronicling of events
      1. Other ancient Near Eastern literature is mythological
         a. polytheistic (usually humanistic gods reflecting the powers of nature but using interpersonal conflict motifs)
         b. based on the cycles of nature (dying and rising gods)
      2. Greco-Roman is for entertainment and encouragement rather than the recording of historical events per se (Homer in many ways reflects Mesopotamian motifs)
   B. Possibly the use of three German terms illustrates the difference in types or definitions of history
      1. "Historie," the recording of events (bare facts)
      2. "Geschichte," the interpretation of events showing their significance to mankind
      3. "Heilsgeschichte" refers uniquely to God's redemptive plan and activity within the historical process
   C. The OT and NT narratives are "Geschichte" which leads to an understanding of Heilgeschichte
      They are selected theologically oriented historical events
      1. selected events only
      2. chronology not as significant as theology
      3. events shared to reveal truth
   D. Narrative is the most common genre in the OT. It has been estimated that 40% of the OT is narrative. Therefore, this genre is useful to the Spirit in communicating God's message and character to fallen mankind. But, it is done, not propositionally (like the NT Epistles), but by implication, summation or selected dialog/monolog. One must continue to ask why this is recorded. What is it trying to emphasize? What is its theological purpose?
   This in no way is meant to depreciate the history. But, it is history as the servant and channel of revelation.

II. **Biblical Narratives**
   A. God is active in His world. Inspired Bible authors chose certain events to reveal God. God is the major character of the OT.
   B. Every narrative functions in several ways:
      1. who is God and what is He doing in His world
      2. mankind is revealed through God's dealing with individuals and national entities
      3. as an example specifically notice Joshua's military victory linked to covenant performance (cf. 1:7-8; 8:30-35).
   C. Often narratives are strung together to make a larger literary unit which reveals a single theological truth.

III.   Interpretive principles of OT narratives

A.   The best discussion I have seen about interpreting OT narratives is by Douglas Stuart in How to Read the Bible For All Its Worth, pp. 83-84
1.   An OT narrative usually does not directly teach a doctrine.
2.   An OT narrative usually illustrates a doctrine or doctrines taught propositionally elsewhere.
3.   Narratives record what happened—not necessarily what should have happened or what ought to happen every time. Therefore, not every narrative has an individual identifiable moral of the story.
4.   What people do in narratives is not necessarily a good example for us. Frequently, it is just the opposite.
5.   Most of the characters in OT narratives are far from perfect, and their actions also
6.   We are not always told at the end of a narrative whether what happened was good or bad. We are expected to be able to judge that on the basis of what God has taught us directly and categorically elsewhere in the Scripture.
7.   All narratives are selective and incomplete. Not all the relevant details are always given (cf. John 21:25). What does appear in the narrative is everything that the inspired author thought important for us to know.
8.   Narratives are not written to answer all our theological questions. They have particular, specific, limited purposes and deal with certain issues, leaving others to be dealt with elsewhere, in other ways.
9.   Narratives may teach either explicitly (by clearly stating something) or implicitly (by clearly implying something without actually stating it).
10.   In the final analysis, God is the hero of all biblical narratives.

B.   Another good discussion on interpreting narratives is in Walter Kaiser's *Toward Exegetical* Theology:

"The unique aspect of the narrative portions of Scripture is that the writer usually allows the words and actions of the people in his narrative to convey the main thrust of his message. Thus, instead of addressing us through direct statements, such as are found in doctrinal or teaching portions of Scripture, the writer tends to remain instead somewhat in the background as far as direct teaching or evaluative statements are concerned. Consequently, it becomes critically important to recognize the larger context in which the narrative fits and to ask why the writer used the specific selection of events in the precise sequence in which he placed them. The twin clues to meaning now will be arrangement of episodes and selection of detail from a welter of possible speeches, persons, or episodes. Furthermore, the divine reaction to and estimate of these people and events must often be determined from the way the author allows one person or a group of people to respond at the climax of the selected sequence of events; that is, if he has not interrupted the narration to give his own (in this instance, God's) estimate of what has taken place" (p. 205).

C.   In narratives, the truth is found in the whole literary unit and not the details. Beware of proof- texting or using OT narratives as a precedent for your life.

IV.   Two levels of interpretation

A.   YHWH's redemptive, revelatory acts for Abraham's seed
B.   YHWH's will for every believer's life (in every age)
C.   The first focuses on "knowing God (salvation); the second on serving Him (the Christian life of faith, cf. Rom. 15:4; I Cor. 10:6,11)

APPENDIX FOUR

HEBREW PROPHECY

I.   **Introduction**
    A.   Opening Statements
        1.   The believing community does not agree on how to interpret prophecy. Other truths have been established as to an orthodox position throughout the centuries, but not this one.
        2.   There are several well defined stages of OT prophecy
            a.   premonarchial (before King Saul)
                (1) individuals called prophets
                    (a) Abraham - Gen. 20:7
                    (b) Moses - Num. 12:6-8; Deut. 18:15; 34:10
                    (c) Aaron - Exod. 7:1 (spokesman for Moses)
                    (d) Miriam - Exod. 15:20
                    (e) Medad and Eldad - Num. 11:24-30
                    (f) Deborah - Jdgs. 4:4
                    (g) unnamed - Jdgs. 6:7-10
                    (h) Samuel - I Sam. 3:20
                (2) references to prophets as a group - Deut. 13:1-5; 18:20-22
                (3) prophetic groups or guilds - I Sam. 10:5-13; 19:20; I Kgs. 20:35,41; 22:6,10-13; II Kgs. 2:3,7; 4:1,38; 5:22; 6:1, etc.
                (4) Messiah called prophet - Deut. 18:15-18
            b.   non-writing monarchial prophets (they address the king)
                (1) Gad - I Sam. 7:2; 12:25; II Sam. 24:11; I Chron. 29:29
                (2) Nathan - II Sam. 7:2; 12:25; I Kgs. 1:22
                (3) Ahijah - I Kgs. 11:29
                (4) Jehu - I Kgs. 16:1,7,12
                (5) unnamed - I Kgs. 18:4,13; 20:13,22
                (6) Elijah -I Kgs. 18; II Kgs. 2
                (7) Milcaiah - I Kgs. 22 (8) Elisha - II Kgs. 2:8,13
            c.   classical writing prophets (they address the nation as well as the king): Isaiah—Malachi (except Daniel)

    B. Biblical Terms
        1.   *ro'eh* = seer, I Sam. 9:9. This reference shows the transition to the term *Nabi*, which means "prophet" and comes from the root, "to call." *Ro'eh* is from the general Hebrew term "to see." This person understood God's ways and plans and was consulted to ascertain God's will in a matter.
        2.   *hozeh* = seer, II Sam. 24:11. It is basically a synonym of *ro'eh*. It is from a rarer Hebrew term "to see in a vision." The participle form is used most often to refer to prophets.

3. *nabi'* = prophet, cognate of Akkadian verb *nabu* = "to call" and Arabic *naba'a* = "to announce." This is the most common OT term to designate a prophet. It is used over 300 times. The exact etymology is uncertain, but "to call" at present seems the best option. Possibly the best understanding comes form YHWH's description of Moses' relationship to Pharaoh through Aaron (cf. Exod. 4:10-16; 7:1; Deut. 5:5). A prophet is someone who speaks for God to His people (cf. Amos 3:8; Jer. 1:7,17; Ezek. 3:4).

4. All three terms are used of the prophet's office in I Chron. 29:29; Samuel - *Ro'eh*; Nathan - *Nabi'*; and Gad - *Hozeh*.

5. The phrase *'ish ha - 'elohim*, "man of God," is also a broader designation for a speaker for God. It is used some 76 times in the OT in the sense of "prophet."

6. The word "prophet" is Greek in origin. It comes from (1) *pro* = "before" or "for"; (2) *phemi* = "to speak."

II. Definition of Prophecy

A. The term "prophecy" had a wider semantic field in Hebrew than in English. The Jews labeled the history books of Joshua through Kings (except Ruth) "the former prophets." Both Abraham (Gen. 20:7; Ps. 105:5) and Moses (Deut. 18:18) are designated as prophets (also Miriam, Exod. 15:20). Therefore, beware of an assumed English definition!

B. "Propheticism may legitimately be defined as that understanding of history which accepts meaning only in terms of divine concern, divine purpose, divine participation" (*Interpreter's Dictionary of the Bible*, vol. 3, p. 896).

C. "The prophet is neither a philosopher nor a systematic theologian, but a covenant mediator who delivers the word of God to His people in order to shape their future by reforming their present" ("Prophets and Prophecy," *Encyclopedia Judaica*, vol. 13, p. 1152).

III. Purpose of Prophecy

A. Prophecy is a way for God to speak to His people, providing guidance in their current setting and hope in His control of their lives and world events. Their message was basically corporate. It is meant to rebuke, encourage, engender faith and repentance, and inform God's people about Himself and His plans. Often it is used to clearly reveal God's choice of a spokesman (Deut. 13:1-3; 18:20-22). This, taken ultimately, would refer to the Messiah.

B. Often, the prophet took a historical or theological crisis of his day and projected it into an eschatological setting. This end-time view of history (teleological) is unique to Israel and her sense of divine election and covenant promises.

C. The office of prophet seems to balance (Jer. 18:18) and supplant the office of High Priest as a way of knowing God's will. The Urim and Thummim transcend into a verbal message from God's spokesman. The office of prophet seems to also have passed away in Israel after Malachi (or the writing of Chronicles). It does not appear until 400 years later with John the Baptist. It is uncertain how the New Testament gift of "prophecy" relates to the OT. New Testament prophets (Acts 11:27-28; 13:1; 14:29,32,37; 15:32; I Cor. 12:10,28-29; Eph. 4:11) are not revealers of new revelation, but forth-tellers and fore-tellers of God's will in recurrent situations.

D. Prophecy is not exclusively or primarily predictive in nature. Prediction is one way to confirm his office and his message, but it must be noted ". . .less than 2% of OT prophecy is Messianic. Less than 5% specifically describes the New Covenant Age. Less than 1% concerns events yet to come" (Fee & Stuart, *How to Read the Bible For All Its Worth*, p. 166).

E. Prophets represent God to the people, while Priests represent the people to God. This is a general statement. There are exceptions like Habakkuk, who addresses questions to God.

F. One reason it is difficult to understand the prophets is because we do not know how their books were structured. They are not chronological. They seem to be thematic, but not always the way one would expect. Often there is no obvious historical setting, time-frame, or clear division between oracles, it is difficult (1) to read the books through in one sitting; (2) to outline them by topic; and (3) to ascertain the central truth or authorial intent in each oracle.

IV. Characteristics of Prophecy

A. In the Old Testament there seems to be a development of the concept of "prophet" and "prophecy." In early Israel there developed a fellowship of prophets, led by a strong charismatic leader such as Elijah or Elisha. Sometimes the phrase "the sons of the prophets" was used to designate this group (II Kgs. 2). The prophets at times were characterized by forms of ecstasy (I Sam. 10:10-13; 19:18-24).

B. However, this period passed rapidly into the time of individual prophets. There were those prophets (both true and false) who identified with the King, and lived at the palace (Gad, Nathan). Also, there were those who were independent, sometimes totally unconnected with the status quo of Israelite society (Amos). They are both male and female (II Kgs. 22:14).

C. The prophet was often a revealer of the future, conditioned on a person's or a people's immediate response. Often the prophet's task was to unfold God's universal plan for His creation which is not affected by human response. This universal eschatological plan is unique among the prophets of Israel in the ancient Near East. Prediction and Covenant fidelity are twin foci of the prophetic messages (cf. Fee and Stuart, p. 150). This implies that the prophets were primarily corporate in focus. They usually, but not exclusively, address the nation of Israel.

D.   Most prophetic material was presented orally. It was later combined by means of theme or chronology, or other patterns of Near Eastern literature, which are lost to us. Because it was oral, it is not as structured as written prose. This makes the books difficult to read straight through and difficult to understand without a specific historical setting.

E.   The prophets use several patterns to convey their messages
   1.   Court scene - God takes His people to court; often it is a divorce case where YHWH rejects his wife (Israel) for her unfaithfulness (Hosea 4; Micah 6).
   2.   Funeral dirge - the special meter of this type of message and its characteristic "woe" sets it apart as a special form (Isaiah 5; Habakkuk 2).
   3.   Covenant blessing pronouncement - the conditional nature of the Covenant is emphasized and the consequences, both positively and negatively, are spelled out for the future (Deuteronomy 27-29).

V.   Biblical Qualifications for Verification of a True Prophet

A.   Deuteronomy 13:1-5 (predictions/signs are linked to monotheistic purity)
B.   Deuteronomy 18:9-22 (false prophets/true prophets)
C.   Both men and women are called and designated as prophets or prophetesses
   1.   Miriam - Exodus 15
   2.   Deborah - Judges 4:4-6
   3.   Huldah - II Kings 22:14-20; II Chronicles 34:22-28
D.   In the surrounding cultures prophets were verified by means of divination. In Israel they were verified by
   1.   a theological test - the use of the name of YHWH
   2.   a historical test - accurate predictions

VI.   Helpful Guidelines for Interpreting Prophecy

A.   Find the intent of the original prophet (editor) by noting the historical setting and the literary context of each oracle. Usually it will involve Israel breaking the Mosaic Covenant in some way.

B.   Read and interpret the whole oracle, not just a part; outline it as to content. See how it relates to surrounding oracles. Try to outline the whole book (by literary units and to paragraph level).

C.   Assume a literal interpretation of the passage until something in the text itself points you to figurative usage; then attempt to put the figurative language into prose.

D.   Analyze symbolic action in light of historical setting and parallel passages. Be sure to remember that this is ancient Near Eastern literature, not western or modern literature.

E. Treat predictions with care
    1. Are they exclusively for the author's day?
    2. Were they subsequently fulfilled in Israel's history?
    3. Are they yet future events?
    4. Do they have a contemporary fulfillment and yet a future fulfillment?
    5. Allow the authors of the Bible, not modern authors, to guide your answers.

F. Special concerns
    1. Is the prediction qualified by conditional response?
    2. Is it certain to whom the prophecy is addressed (and why)?
    3. Is there a possibility both biblically and/or historically for multiple fulfillments?
    4. The NT authors under inspiration were able to see the Messiah in many places in the OT that are not obvious to us. They seem to use typology or word play. Since we are not inspired, we best leave this approach to them.

VII. Helpful Books
    1. *A Guide to Biblical Prophecy* by Carl E. Armerding and W. Ward Gasque
    2. *How to Read the Bible for All Its Worth* by Gordon Fee and Douglas Stuart
    3. *My Servants the Prophets* by Edward J. Young
    4. *Plowshares and Pruning Hooks: Rethinking the Language of Biblical Prophecy and Apocalyptic* by D. Brent Sandy
    5. *Cracking the Old Testament Code*, D. Brent Sandy and Ronald L. Giese, Jr.

APPENDIX FIVE

NEW TESTAMENT PROPHECY

I.   **NT prophecy is not the same as OT** prophecy (BDB 611), which has the rabbinical connotation of inspired revelations from YHWH (cf. Acts 3:18,21; Rom. 16:26). Only prophets could write Scripture.

    A.   Moses was called a prophet (cf. Deut. 18:15-21).

    B.   History books (Joshua - Kings [except Ruth]) were called the "former prophets" (cf. Acts 3:24).

    C.   Prophets usurp the place of High Priest as the source of information from God (cf. Isaiah -Malachi)

    D.   The second division of the Hebrew canon is "the Prophets" (cf. Matt. 5:17; 22:40; Luke 16:16; 24:25,27; Rom. 3:21).

II. **In the NT the concept is used in several different ways.**

    A.   referring to OT prophets and their inspired message (cf. Matt. 2:23; 5:12; 11:13; 13:14; Rom. 1:2)

    B.   referring to a message for an individual rather than a corporate group (i.e., OT prophets spoke primarily to Israel)

    C.   referring to both John the Baptist (cf. Matt. 11:9; 14:5; 21:26; Luke 1:76) and Jesus as proclaimers of the Kingdom of God (cf. Matt. 13:57; 21:11,46; Luke 4:24; 7:16; 13:33; 24:19). Jesus also claimed to be greater than the prophets (cf. Matt. 11:9; 12:41; Luke 7:26).

    D.   other prophets in the NT
        1.   early life of Jesus as recorded in Luke's Gospel (i.e., Mary's memories)
            a.   Elizabeth (cf. Luke 1:41-42)
            b.   Zacharias (cf. Luke 1:67-79)
            c.   Simeon (cf. Luke 2:25-35)
            d.   Anna (cf. Luke 2:36)
        2.   ironic predictions (cf. Caiaphas, John 11:51)

    E.   referring to one who proclaims the gospel (the lists of proclaiming gifts in I Cor. 12:28-29; Eph. 4:11)

F. referring to an ongoing gift in the church (cf. Matt. 23:34; Acts 13:1; 15:32; Rom. 12:6; I Cor. 12:10,28-29; 13:2; Eph. 4:11). Sometimes this can refer to women (cf. Luke 2:36; Acts 2:17; 21:9; I Cor. 11:4-5).

G. referring to the apocalyptic book of Revelation (cf. Rev. 1:3; 22:7,10,18,19)

III. NT prophets

A. They do not give inspired revelation in the same sense as did the OT prophets (i.e., Scripture).
This statement is possible because of the use of the phrase "the faith" (i.e., a sense of a completed gospel) used in Acts 6:7; 13:8; 14:22; Gal. 1:23; 3:23; 6:10; Phil. 1:27; Jude 3,20.
This concept is clear from the full phrase used in Jude 3, "the faith once and for all handed down to the saints." The "once for all" faith refers to the truths, doctrines, concepts, world-view teachings of Christianity. This once-given emphasis is the biblical basis for theologically limiting inspiration to the writings of the NT and not allowing later or other writings to be considered revelatory. There are many ambiguous, uncertain, and grey areas in the NT, but believers affirm by faith that everything that is "needed" for faith and practice is included with sufficient clarity in the NT. This concept has been delineated in what is called "the revelatory triangle"
1. God has revealed Himself in time-space history (REVELATION)
2. He has chosen certain human writers to document and explain His acts (INSPIRATION)
3. He has given His Spirit to open the minds and hearts of humans to understand these writings, not definitively, but adequately for salvation and an effective Christian life (ILLUMINATION). The point of this is that inspiration is limited to the writers of Scripture.
There are no further authoritative writings, visions, or revelations. The canon is closed. We have all the truth we need to respond appropriately to God. This truth is best seen in the agreement of biblical writers versus the disagreement of sincere, godly believers. No modern writer or speaker has the level of divine leadership that the writers of Scripture did.

B. In some ways NT prophets are similar to OT prophets.
1. prediction of future events (cf. Paul, Acts 27:22; Agabus, Acts 11:27-28; 21:10-11; other unnamed prophets, Acts 20:23)
2. proclaim judgment (cf. Paul, Acts 13:11; 28:25-28)
3. symbolic acts which vividly portray an event (cf. Agabus, Acts 21:11)

C. They do proclaim the truths of the gospel sometimes in predictive ways (cf. Acts 11:27-28; 20:23; 21:10-11), but this is not the primary focus. Prophesying in I Corinthians is basically communicating the gospel (cf. 14:24,39).

D. They are the Spirit's contemporary means of revealing the contemporary and practical applications of God's truth to each new situation, culture, or time period (cf. I Cor. 14:3).

E. They were active in the early Pauline churches (cf. I Cor. 11:4-5; 12:28,29; 13:29; 14:1,3,4,5,6, 22,24,29,31, 32,37,39; Eph. 2:20; 3:5; 4:11; I Thess. 5:20) and are mentioned in the *Didache* (written in the late first century or in the second century, date uncertain) and in Montanism of the second and third centuries in northern Africa.

IV. Have the NT gifts ceased?

A. This question is difficult to answer. It helps to clarify the issue by defining the purpose of the gifts. Are they meant to confirm the initial preaching of the gospel or are they ongoing ways for the church to minister to itself and a lost world?

B. Does one look at the history of the church to answer the question or the NT itself? There is no indication in the NT that the spiritual gifts were temporary. Those who try to use I Cor. 13:8-13 to address this issue abuse the authorial intent of the passage, which asserts that everything but love will pass away.

C. I am tempted to say that since the NT, not church history, is the authority, believers must affirm that the gifts continue. However, I believe that culture affects interpretation. Some very clear texts are no longer applicable (i.e., the holy kiss, women wearing veils, churches meeting in homes, etc). If culture affects texts, then why not church history?

D. This is simply a question that cannot be definitively answered. Some believers will advocate "cessation" and others "non-cessation." In this area, as in many interpretative issues, the heart of the believer is the key. The NT is ambiguous and cultural. The difficulty is being able to decide which texts are affected by culture/history and which are for all time and all cultures (cf. Fee and Stuart's *How to Read the Bible for All Its Worth*, pp. 14-19 and 69-77). Here is where the discussions of freedom and responsibility, which are found in Rom. 14:1-15:13 and I Cor. 8-10, are crucial. How we answer the question is important in two ways.
   1. Each believer must walk in faith in the light they have. God looks at our heart and motives.
   2. Each believer must allow other believers to walk in their faith understanding. There must be tolerance within biblical bounds. God wants us to love one another as He does.

E. To sum up the issue, Christianity is a life of faith and love, not a perfect theology. A relationship with Him which impacts our relationship with others is more important than definitive information or creedal perfection.

APPENDIX SIX

HEBREW POETRY

I.   INTRODUCTION

A.   This type of literature makes up 1/3 of the Old Testament. It is especially common in the "Prophets" (all but Haggai and Malachi contain poetry) and "Writings" sections of the Hebrew canon.

B   It is very different from English poetry. English poetry is developed from Greek and Latin poetry, which is primarily sound-based. Hebrew poetry has much in common with Canaanite poetry. There are no accented lines or rhyme in Near East poetry (but there is a beat).

C.   The archaeological discovery north of Israel at Ugarit (Ras Shamra) has helped scholars understand OT poetry. This poetry from the 15th century B.C. has obvious literary connections with biblical poetry.

II. GENERAL CHARACTERISTICS OF POETRY

A.   It is very compact.

B.   It tries to express truth, feelings or experiences in imagery.

C.   It is primarily written not oral. It is highly structured. This structure is expressed in:
   1.   balanced lines (parallelism)
   2.   word plays
   3.   sound plays

III.   THE STRUCTURE   R. K. Harrison, *Introduction To The Old Testament*, pp.965-975)

A.   Bishop Robert Lowth in his book, *Lectures on the Sacred Poetry of the Hebrews* (1753) was the first to characterize biblical poetry as balanced lines of thought. Most modern English translations are formatted to show the lines of poetry.
   1.   synonymous - the lines express the same thought in different words:
      a.   Psalm 3:1; 49:1; 83:14; 103:13
      b.   Proverbs 19:5; 20:1
      c.   Isaiah 1:3,10
      d.   Amos 5:24; 8:10

2.   antithetical - the lines express opposite thoughts by means of contrast or stating the positive and the negative:
   a.   Psalm 1:6; 90:6
   b.   Proverbs 1:29; 10:1,12; 15:1; 19:4
3.   synthetic - the next two or three lines develop the thought - Ps. 1:1-2; 19:7-9; 29:1-2
4.   chiasmic - a pattern of poetry expressing the message in a descending and ascending order.
The main point is found in the middle of the pattern.

B.   A. Briggs in his book, *General Introduction to the Study of Holy Scripture* (1899) developed the next stage of analysis of Hebrew poetry:
   1.   emblematic - one clause literal and the second metaphorical, Ps. 42:1; 103:3.
   2.   climatic or stair-like - the clauses reveal truth in an ascending fashion, Ps. 19:7-14; 29:1-2; 103:20-22.
   3.   introverted - a series of clauses, usually at least four are related by the internal structure of line 1 to 4 and 2 to 3 - Ps. 30:8-10a

C.   G.B. Gray in his book, *The Forms of Hebrew Poetry* (1915) developed the concept of balanced clauses further by:
   1.   complete balance - where every word in line one is repeated or balanced by a word in line two - Psalm 83:14 and Isaiah 1:3
   2.   incomplete balance where the clauses are not the same length - Ps. 59:16; 75:6

D.   Today there is a growing recognition of literary structural pattern in Hebrew called a chiasm, which denotes an odd number of parallel lines forming an hour glass shape whereby the central line is emphasized.

E.   Type of sound patterns found in poetry in general, but not often in eastern poetry
   1.   play on alphabet (acrostic. cf. Ps. 9,34,37,119; Prov. 31:10ff; Lam. 1-4)
   2.   play on consonants (alliteration, cf. Ps. 6:8; 27:7; 122:6; Isa. 1:18-26)
   3.   play on vowels (assonance, cf. Gen. 49:17; Exod. 14:14; Ezek. 27:27)
   4.   play on repetition of similar sounding words with different meanings (paronomasia)
   5.   play on words which, when pronounced, sound like the thing they name (onomatopoeia)
   6.   special opening and close (inclusive)

F.   There are several types of poetry in the Old Testament. Some are topic related and some are form related.
   1.   dedication song - Num. 21:17-18
   2.   work songs - (alluded to but not recorded in Jdgs. 9:27); Isa. 16:10; Jer. 25:30; 48:33
   3.   ballads - Num. 21:27-30; Isa. 23:16
   4.   drinking songs - negative, Isa. 5:11-13; Amos 6:4-7 and positive, Isa. 22:13

5.   love poems - Song of Songs, wedding riddle - Jdgs. 14:10-18, wedding song - Ps. 45

6.   laments/dirge - (alluded to but not recorded in II Sam. 1:17 and II Chr. 35:25) II Sam. 3:33; Ps. 27, 28; Jer. 9:17-22; Lam.; Ezek. 19:1-14; 26:17-18; Nah. 3:15-19

7.   war songs - Gen. 4:23-24; Exod. 15:1-18,20; Num. 10:35-36; 21:14-15; Josh. 10:13; Jdgs. 5:1-31; 11:34; I Sam. 18:6; II Sam. 1:18; Isa. 47:1-15; 37:21

8.   special benedictions or blessing of leader - Gen. 49; Num. 6:24-26; Deut. 32; II Sam. 23:1-7

9.   magical texts - Balaam, Num. 24:3-9

10.   sacred poems - Psalms

11.   acrostic poems - Ps. 9,34,37,119; Prov. 31:10ff and Lamentations 1-4

12.   curses - Num. 21:22-30

13.   taunt poems - Isa. 14:1-22; 47:1-15; Ezek. 28:1-23

14.   a book of war poems (Jashar) - Num. 21:14-15; Josh. 10:12-13; II Sam. 1:18

IV.   GUIDELINE TO INTERPRETING HEBREW POETRY

A.   Look for the central truth of the stanza or strophe (this is like a paragraph in prose.) The RSV was the first modern translation to identify poetry by stanzas. compare modern translations for helpful insights.

B.   Identify the figurative language and express it in prose. Remember this type of literature is very compact, much is left for the reader to fill in.

C.   Be sure to relate the longer issue oriented poems to their literary context (often the whole book) and historical setting.

D.   Judges 4 and 5 are very helpful in seeing how poetry expresses history. Judges 4 is prose and Judges 5 is poetry of the same event (also compare Exodus 14 & 15).

E.   Attempt to identify the type of parallelism involved, whether synonymous, antithetical, or synthetic. This is very important.

APPENDIX SEVEN

HEBREW WISDOM LITERATURE

I. **THE GENRE**

A. Common Literary type in the ancient Near East ®. J. Williams, "Wisdom in the Ancient Near East," Interpreter Dictionary of the Bible, Supplement)
  1. Mesopotamia (I Kgs. 4:30-31; Isa. 47:10; Dan. 1:20; 2:2)
      a. Sumeria had a developed wisdom tradition both proverbial and epic (texts from Nippur).
      b. Babylon's proverbial wisdom was connected with the priest/magician. It was not morally focused (W. G. Lambert, *Babylonian Wisdom Literature*). It was not a developed genre like in Israel.
      c. Assyria also had a wisdom tradition; ONE EXAMPLE WOULD BE the teachings of Ahiqar. He was an advisor to Sennacherib (704-681 B.C.).
  2. Egypt (I Kgs. 4:30; Gen. 41:8; Isa. 19:11-12)
      a. "The Teaching for Vizier Ptah-hotep," written about 2450 B.C. His teachings were in paragraph, not proverbial, form. They were structured as a father to his son, so too, "The Teachings for King Meri-ka-re," about 2200 B.C. (LaSor, Hubbard, Bush, *Old Testament Survey*, p. 533).
      b. The Wisdom of Amen-em-opet, written about 1200 B.C., is very similar to Prov. 22:17-24:12.
  3. Phoenicia (Ezek. 27:8-9; 28:3-5)
      a. The discoveries at Ugarit has shown the close connection between Phoenician and Hebrew wisdom, especially the meter. Many of the unusual forms and rare words in biblical Wisdom Literature are now understandable from the archaeological discoveries at Ras Shamra (Ugarit).
      b. Song of Songs is very much like Phoenician wedding songs called *wasps* written about 600 B.C.
  4. Canaan (i.e., Edom, cf. Jer. 49:7; Obad. 8) - Albright has revealed the similarity between Hebrew and Canaanite wisdom literature especially the Ras Shamra texts from Ugarit, written about the 15th century B.C.
      a. often the same words appear as pairs
      b. presence of chiasmus
      c. have superscriptions
      d. have musical notations
  5. Biblical Wisdom Literature includes the writings of several non-Israelites:
      a. Job from Edom
      b. Agur from Massa (an Israelite kingdom in Saudi Arabia (cf. Genesis 25:14 and I Chronicles 1:30)
      c. Lemuel from Massa
  6. There are two Jewish non-canonical books that share this genre form.
      a. Ecclesiasticus (Wisdom of Ben Sirach)
      b. Wisdom of Solomon (wisdom)

B. Literary Characteristics
    1. Primarily two distinct types
        a. proverbial guidelines for a happy, successful life (originally oral, cf. Prov. 1:8; 4:1)
            (1) short
            (2) easily culturally understood (common experience)
            (3) thought provoking - arresting statements of truth
            (4) usually uses contrast
            (5) generally true but not always specifically applicable
        b. longer developed special topic, literary works (usually written) like Job, Ecclesiastes and Jonah..
            (1) monologues
            (2) dialogues
            (3) essays
            (4) they deal with life's major questions and mysteries
            (5) the sages were willing to challenge the theological status quo!
        c. personification of wisdom (always female). The term wisdom was feminine.
            (1) often in Proverbs wisdom is described as a woman (cf. 1:8-9:18)
                (a) positively
                    i   1:20-33
                    ii 4:6-9
                    iii 8:1-36 iv 9:1-6
                (b) negatively
                    i   7:1-27
                    ii 9:13-18
            (2) in Proverbs 8:22-31 wisdom is personified as the first born of creation by which God created all else (3:19-20; Ps. 104:24; Jer. 10:12). This may be the background of John's use of *logos* in John 1:1 to refer to Jesus the Messiah.
            (3) this can also be seen in Ecclesiasticus 24.
    2. This literature is unique from the Law and the Prophets (cf. Jer. 18:18) in that it addresses the individual not the nation. There are no historical or cultic allusions. It primarily focuses on daily, successful, joyful, moral living.
    3. Biblical wisdom literature is similar to that of its surrounding neighbors in its structure but not content. The One true God is the foundation on which all biblical wisdom is based (e.g., Gen. 41:38-39; Job 12:13; 28:28; Prov. 1:7; 9:10; Ps.111:10). In Babylon it was Apsu, Ea or Marduk. In Egypt it was Thoth.
    4. Hebrew wisdom was very practical. It was based on experience, not special revelation. It focused on an individual being successful in life (all of life: sacred and secular). It is divine "horse-sense."
    5. Because wisdom literature used human reason, experience and observation it was international, transcultural. It was the monotheistic religious world view which is often not stated, that made Israel's wisdom revelatory.

II.   POSSIBLE ORIGINS

A.   Wisdom Literature developed in Israel as alternative or balance to the other forms of revelation. (Jer. 18:18; Ezek. 7:26)
  1.   priest - law - form (corporate)
  2.   prophet - oracle - motive (corporate)
  3.   sage - wisdom - practical, successful daily life (individual)
  4.   As there were female prophets in Israel (Miriam, Huldah) so, too, there were female sages (cf. II Sam. 14:1-21; 20:14-22).

B.   This type of literature seemed to have developed:
  1.   as folk stories around camp fires
  2.   as family traditions passed on to the male children
  3.   written and supported by the Royal Palace:
    a.   David is connected to the Psalms
    b.   Solomon is connected to Proverbs (I Kgs. 4:29-34; Ps. 72 & 127; Prov. 1:1; 10:1; 25:1)
    c.   Hezekiah is connected to editing wisdom literature (Prov. 25:1)

III.   PURPOSE

A.   It is basically a "how to" focus on happiness and success. It is primarily individual in its focus. It is based on
  1.   the experience of previous generations
  2.   cause and effect relationships in life
  3.   trusting in God has rewards (cf. Deut. 27-29)

B.   It was society's way to pass on truth and train the next generation of leaders and citizens.

C.   OT wisdom, though not always expressing it, sees the Covenant God behind all of life. For the Hebrew there was no sharp division between the sacred and secular. All of life was sacred.

D.   It was a way to challenge and balance traditional theology. The sages were free thinkers not bound by textbook truths. They dared to ask, "Why," "How," "What if?"

IV.   KEYS TO INTERPRETATION

A.   Short proverbial statements
  1.   look for common elements of life used to express the truth.
  2.   express the central truth in a simple declarative sentence.
  3.   since context will not help look for parallel passages on the same subject.

B. Longer literary pieces
1. be sure to express the central truth of the whole.
2. do not take verses out of context.
3. check the historical occasion or reason of the writing.

C. Some common misinterpretations (Fee & Stuart, *How to Read the Bible for All Its Worth*, p. 207)
1. People do not read the whole Wisdom book (like Job and Ecclesiastes) and look for its central truth but pull parts of the book out of its context and apply it literally to modern life.
2. People do not understand the uniqueness of the literary genre. This is a highly compact and figurative Ancient Near Eastern literature.
3. Proverbs are statements of general truth. They are broad sweeps of the pen not specifically true, in every case, every time, statements of truth.

IV. **BIBLICAL EXAMPLES**

A. Old Testament
1. Job
2. Psalm 1, 19, 32, 34, 37 (acrostic), 49, 78, 104, 107, 110, 112-119 (acrostic), 127-128, 133, 147, 148
3. Proverbs
4. Ecclesiastes
5. Song of Songs
6. Lamentations (acrostic)
7. Jonah

B. Extra canonical
1. Tobit
2. Wisdom of Ben Sirach (Ecclesiasticus)
3. Wisdom of Solomon (Book of Wisdom)
4. IV Maccabees

C. New Testament
1. The proverbs and parables of Jesus
2. The book of James

APPENDIX EIGHT

APOCALYPTIC
(This special topic is taken from my commentary on Revelation.)

I. Revelation is a uniquely Jewish literary genre, apocalyptic.

It was often used in tension-filled times to express the conviction that God was in control of history and would bring deliverance to His people. This type of literature is characterized by

A.   a strong sense of the universal sovereignty of God (monotheism and determinism)

B.   a struggle between good and evil, this age and the age to come (dualism)

C.   use of secret code words (usually from the OT or intertestamental Jewish apocalyptic literature)

D.   use of colors, numbers, animals, sometimes animals/humans

E.   use of angelic mediation by means of visions and dreams, but usually through angelic mediation

F.   primarily focuses on the end-time (new age)

G.   use of a fixed set of symbols, not reality, to communicate the end-time message

H.   Some examples of this type of genre are:
   1. Old Testament
      a.   Isaiah 24-27, 56-66 b. Ezekiel 37-48
      c.   Daniel 7-12
      d.   Joel 2:28-3:21
      e.   Zechariah 1-6, 12-14
   2. New Testament
      a.   Matthew 24, Mark 13, Luke 21, and I Corinthians 15 (in some ways)
      b.   II Thessalonians 2 (in most ways)
      c.   Revelation (chapters 4-22)
   3. non-canonical (taken from D. S. Russell, *The Method and Message of Jewish Apocalyptic*, pp. 37-38)
      a.   I Enoch, II Enoch (the Secrets of Enoch)
      b.   The Book of Jubilees
      c.   The Sibylline Oracles III, IV, V
      d.   The Testament of the Twelve Patriarchs e. The Psalms of Solomon
      f.   The Assumption of Moses g. The Martyrdom of Isaiah
      h.   The Apocalypse of Moses (Life of Adam and Eve)
      i.   The Apocalypse of Abraham
      j.   The Testament of Abraham
      k.   II Esdras (IV Esdras)
      l.   Baruch II, III

I. There is a sense of duality in this genre. It sees reality as a series of dualisms, contrasts, or tensions (so common in John's writings) between:
1. heaven - earth
2. evil age (evil men and evil angels) - new age of righteousness (godly men and godly angels)
3. current existence - future existence

J. All of these are moving toward a consummation brought about by God. This is not the world God intended it to be, but He is continuing to play, work, and project His will for a restoration of the intimate fellowship begun in the Garden of Eden. The Christ event is the watershed of God's plan, but the two comings have brought about the current dualisms.

APPENDIX NINE

PARABLES

I. **PARABLES**

A. The Gospels were written many years after Jesus' life. The Gospel writers (by the aid of the Spirit) were culturally accustomed to oral tradition. The rabbis taught by oral presentation. Jesus mimicked this oral approach to teaching. To our knowledge He never wrote down any of His teachings or sermons. To aid in the memory, teaching presentations were repeated, summarized and illustrated. The Gospel writers retained these memory aids. Parables are one of these techniques. Parables are hard to define:

"Parables are best defined as stories with two levels of meaning; the story level provides a mirror by which reality is perceived and understood." taken from *Dictionary of Jesus and the Gospels*, p. 594

"A parable is a saying or story that seeks to drive home a point that the speaker wishes to emphasize by illustrating it from a familiar situation of common life." taken from *The Zondervan Pictorial Bible Encyclopedia*, p. 590

B. It is hard to define exactly what was understood by the term "parable" in Jesus' day
   1. Some say it reflects the Hebrew term *mashal* which was any kind of riddle (Mark 3:23), clever saying (Proverbs, Luke 4:23), short saying (Mark 7:15) or mysterious saying ("dark saying").
   2. Others hold to a more limited definition of a short story.

C. Depending on how one defines the term, over one-third of Jesus' recorded teachings are in parabolic form. This was a major NT literary genre. Parables are certainly authentic sayings of Jesus. If one accepts the second definition, there are still several different types of short stories
   1. simple stories (Luke 13:6-9)
   2. complex stories (Luke 15:11-32)
   3. contrasting stories (Luke 16:1-8; 18:1-8)
   4. typological/allegorical (Matt. 13:24-30, 47-50; Luke 8:4-8, 11-15; 10:25-37; 14:16-24; 20:9-19; John 10; 15:1-8)

D. In dealing with this variety of parabolic material one must interpret these sayings on several levels. The first level would be general hermeneutic principles applicable to all biblical genres. Some guidelines are
   1. identify the purpose of the entire book or at least the larger literary unit
   2. identify the original audience. It is significant that often the same parable is given to different groups, example:
      a. lost sheep in Luke 15 directed to sinners
      b. lost sheep in Matt. 18 directed toward disciples

3. be sure to note the immediate context of the parable. Often Jesus or the gospel writer tells the main point (usually at the end of the parable or immediately after it).
4. express the central intent(s) of the parable in one declarative sentence. Parables often have two or three main characters. Usually there is an implied truth, purpose or point (plot) to each character.
5. check the parallel passages in the other Gospels, then other NT books and OT books.

E. The second level of interpretive principles are those that relate specifically to parabolic material
1. Read (hear if possible) the parable again and again. These were given for oral impact, not written analysis.
2. Most parables have only one central truth which is related to the historical and literary contexts of both Jesus and/or the evangelist.
3. Be careful of interpreting the details. Often they are just part of the setting of the story.
4. Remember parables are not reality. They are life-like analogies, but often exaggerations, to drive home a point (truth).
5. Identify the main points of the story that a first century Jewish audience would have understood. Then look for the twist or surprise. Usually it comes toward the end of the story (cf. A. Berkeley Mickelsen, Interpreting the Bible, pp. 221-224).
6. All parables were given to elicit a response. That response is usually related to the concept of "the Kingdom of God." Jesus was the inaugurator of the new Messianic Kingdom (Matt. 21:31; Luke 17:21). Those who heard Him must respond to Him now!
The Kingdom was also future (Matt. 25). A person's future was dependent on how he responded to Jesus at the time. Kingdom parables described the new kingdom that had arrived in Jesus. They described its ethical and radical demands for discipleship. Nothing can be as it was. All is radically new and focused on Jesus!
7. Parables often do not express the point or central truth. The interpreter must seek the contextual keys that reveal the originally culturally obvious central truths but now obscure to us.

F. A third level that is often controversial is that of the hiddenness of parabolic truth. Jesus often spoke of the hiddenness of parables (cf. Matt. 13:9-15; Mark 4:9-13; Luke 8:8-10; Jn. 10:6; 16:25). This was related to the prophecy in Isa. 6:9-10. The heart of the hearer determines the level of understanding (cf. Matt. 11:15; 13:9,15,16,43; Mark 4:9,23,33-34; 7:16; 8:18; Luke 8:8; 9:44; 14:35).
However, it must also be stated that often the crowd (Matt. 15:10; Mark 7:14) and the Pharisees (Matt. 21:45; Mark 12:12; Luke 20:19) understood exactly what Jesus was saying but refused to respond appropriately to it by faith and repentance. In one sense this is the truth of the Parable of the Soils (Matt. 13; Mark 4; Luke 8).

The parables were a means to conceal or reveal truth (Matt. 13:16-17; 16:12; 17:13; Luke 8:10; 10:23-24).

Grant Osborne, in his Hermeneutical Spiral, p. 239, makes the point that
"Parables are an 'encounter mechanism' and function differently depending on the audience. . .Each group (leaders, crowds, disciples) is encountered differently by the parables." Often even the disciples did not understand either His parables or His teachings (cf. Matt. 15:16; Mark 6:52; 8:17-18,21; 9:32; Luke 9:45; 18:34; John 12:16)."

G.   A fourth level is also controversial. It deals with the central truth of parables. Most modern interpreters have reacted (justifiably so) to the allegorical interpretation of the parables. Allegory turned the details into elaborate systems of truth. This method of interpretation did not focus on the historical setting, literary setting or authorial intent, but presented the thought of the interpreter, not the text.
However, it must be admitted that the parables that Jesus interpreted are very close to allegorical or at least typological. Jesus used the details to convey truth (the Sower, Matt. 13; Mark 4; Luke 8 and the wicked tenants, Matt. 21; Mark 12, Luke 20).
Some of the other parables also have several main truths. A good example is the parable of the Prodigal Son (Luke 15:11-32). It is not only the love of the Father and waywardness of the younger son but the attitude of the older son that is integral to the full meaning of the parable.

A helpful quote from Linguistics and Biblical Interpretation by Peter Cotterell and Max Turner,
"It was Adulf Julicher more than any other who directed New Testament scholarship towards a decisive attempt to understand the role of parable in the teaching of Jesus. The radical allegorizing of the parables was abandoned and the search begun for a key that would enable us to penetrate their true meaning. But as Jeremias made clear, 'His efforts to free the parables from the fantastic and arbitrary interpretations of every detail caused him to fall into a fatal error.' The error was to insist not merely that a parable should be understood as conveying a single idea, but that the idea should be as general as possible" (p. 308).

Another helpful quote from *The Hermeneutical Spiral* by Grant Osborne,
"Yet I have noted many indications that the parables are indeed allegories, albeit controlled by the author's intention. Blomberg (1990) in fact argues that there are as many points as there are characters in the parables and that they are indeed allegories. While this is somewhat overstated, it is nearer the truth than the 'one point' approach" (p. 240).

H. Should parables be used to teach doctrinal truths or illuminate doctrinal truths? Most interpreters have been influenced by the abuse of the allegorical method of interpreting parables which allowed them to be used to establish doctrines that had no connection to Jesus' original intent nor that of the gospel writer. Meaning must be linked to authorial intent. Jesus and the gospel writers were under inspiration, but interpreters are not.

However badly the parables have been abused they still function as teaching vehicles of truth, doctrinal truth. Hear Bernard Ramm on this point.

"Parables do teach doctrine and the claim that they may not be used at all in doctrinal writing is improper. . .we must check our results with plain, evident teaching of our Lord, and with the rest of the New Testament. Parables with proper cautions may be used to illustrate doctrine, illuminate Christian experience and to teach practical lessons." *Protestant Biblical Interpretation*" (p. 285).

II.   **In conclusion let me give three quotes that reflect warnings in our interpretation of parables.**

    A.   Taken from *How to Read the Bible For All Its Worth* by Gordon Fee and Doug Suart: "The parables have suffered a fate of misinterpretation in the church second only to the Revelation" (p. 135).

    B.   Taken from Understanding and Applying the Bible by J. Robertson McQuilkin, "Parables have been the source of untold blessing in enlightening God's people concerning spiritual truth. At the same time, parables have been the source of untold confusion in

both doctrine and practice in the church" (p. 164).

    C.   Taken from The Hermeneutical Spiral by Grant Osborne, "Parables have been among the most written about yet hermeneutically abused portions of Scripture. . .the most dynamic yet the most difficult to comprehend of the biblical genres. The potential of the parable for communication is enormous, since it creates a comparison or story based upon everyday experiences. However, that story itself is capable of many meanings, and the modern reader has as much difficulty interpreting it as did the ancient hearers" (p. 235).

APPENDIX TEN

GLOSSARY OF TERMS OFTEN USED IN HISTORICAL, TEXTUAL, AND LEXICAL STUDIES

Adoptionism. This was one of the early views of Jesus' relation to deity. It basically asserted that Jesus was a normal human in every way and was adopted in a special sense by God at his baptism (cf. Matt. 3:17; Mark 1:11) or at His resurrection (cf. Rom. 1:4). Jesus lived such an exemplary life that God, at some point, (baptism, resurrection) adopted Him as His "son" (cf. Rom. 1:4; Phi. 2:9). This was an early church and eighth century minority view. Instead of God becoming a man (the Incarnation) it reverses this and now man becomes God!

It is difficult to verbalize how Jesus, God the Son, pre-existent deity, was rewarded or extolled for an exemplary life. If He was already God, how could He be rewarded? If He had pre-existent divine glory how could He be honored more? Although it is hard for us to comprehend, the Father somehow honored Jesus in a special sense for His perfect fulfillment of the Father's will.

Alexandrian School. This method of biblical interpretation was developed in Alexandria, Egypt in the second century A.D. It uses the basic interpretive principles of Philo, who was a follower of Plato. It is often called the allegorical method. It held sway in the church until the time of the Reformation. Its most able proponents were Origen and Augustine. See Moises Silva, *Has The Church Misread The Bible?* (Academic, 1987)

Alexandrinus. This fifth-century Greek manuscript from Alexandria, Egypt includes the Old Testament, Apocrypha, and most of the New Testament. It is one of our major witnesses to the entire Greek New Testament (except parts of Matthew, John, and II Corinthians). When this manuscript, which is designated "A," and the manuscript designated "B" (Vaticanus) agree on a reading, it is considered to be original by most scholars in most instances.

Allegory. This is a type of biblical interpretation which originally developed within Alexandrian Judaism. It was popularized by Philo of Alexandria. Its basic thrust is the desire to make the Scripture relevant to one's culture or philosophical system by ignoring the Bible's historical setting and/or literary context. It seeks a hidden or spiritual meaning behind every text of Scripture. It must be admitted that Jesus, in Matthew 13, and Paul, in Galatians 4, used allegory to communicate truth. This, however, was in the form of typology, not strictly allegory.

Analytical lexicon. This is a type of research tool which allows one to identify every Greek form in the New Testament. It is a compilation, in Greek alphabetical order, of forms and basic definitions. In combination with an interlinear translation, it allows non-Greek reading believers to analyze New Testament Greek grammatical and syntactic forms.

Analogy of Scripture. This is the phrase used to describe the view that all of the Bible is inspired by God and is, therefore, not contradictory but complementary. This presuppositional affirmation is the basis for the use of parallel passages in interpreting a biblical text.

Ambiguity. This refers to the uncertainty that results in a written document when there are two or more possible meanings or when two or more things are being referred to at the same time. It is possible that John uses purposeful ambiguity (double entendres).

Anthropomorphic. Meaning "having characteristics associated with human beings," this term is used to describe our religious language about God. It comes from the Greek term for mankind. It means that we speak about God as if He were a man. God is described in physical, sociological, and psychological terms which relate to human beings (cf. Gen. 3:8; I Kgs. 22:19-23). This, of course, is only an analogy. However, there are no categories or terms other than human ones for us to use. Therefore, our knowledge of God, though true, is limited.

Antiochian School. This method of biblical interpretation was developed in Antioch, Syria in the third century A.D. as a reaction to the allegorical method of Alexandria, Egypt. Its basic thrust was to focus on the historical meaning of the Bible. It interpreted the Bible as normal, human literature. This school became involved in the controversy over whether Christ had two natures (Nestorianism) or one nature (fully God and fully man). It was labeled heretical by the Roman Catholic Church and relocated to Persia but the school had little significance. Its basic hermeneutical principles later became interpretive principles of the Classical Protestant Reformers (Luther and Calvin).

Antithetical. This is one of three descriptive terms used to denote the relationship between lines of Hebrew poetry. It relates to lines of poetry which are opposite in meaning (cf. Prov. 10:1, 15:1).

Apocalyptic literature. This was predominantly, possibly even uniquely, a Jewish genre. It was a cryptic type of writing used in times of invasion and occupation of the Jews by foreign world powers. It assumes that a personal, redemptive God created and controls world events, and that Israel is of special interest and care to Him. This literature promises ultimate victory through God's special effort.

It is highly symbolic and fanciful with many cryptic terms. It often expressed truth in colors, numbers, visions, dreams, angelic mediation, secret code words and often a sharp dualism between good and evil.

Some examples of this genre are (1) in the OT, Ezekiel (chapters 36-48), Daniel (chapters 7-12), Zechariah; and (2) in the NT, Matt.24; Mark 13; II Thess. 2 and Revelation.

Apologist (Apologetics). This is from the Greek root for "legal defense." This is a specific discipline within theology which seeks to give evidence and rational arguments for the Christian faith.

A priori. This is basically synonymous with the term "presupposition." It involves reasoning from previously accepted definitions, principles or positions which are assumed to be true. It is that which is accepted without examination or analysis.

Arianism. Arius was a presbyter in the church at Alexandria Egypt in the third and early fourth century. He affirmed that Jesus was pre-existent but not divine (not of the same essence as the Father), possibly following Proverbs 8:22-31. He was challenged by the bishop of Alexandria, who started (A.D. 318) a controversy which lasted many years. Arianism became the official creed of the Eastern Church. The Council of Nicaea in A.D. 325, condemned Arius and asserted the full equality and deity of the Son.

Aristotle. He was one of the philosophers of ancient Greece, a pupil of Plato and teacher of Alexander the Great. His influence, even today, reaches into many areas of modern studies. This is because he emphasized knowledge through observation and classification. This is one of the tenets of the scientific method.

Autographs. This is the name given to the original writings of the Bible. These original, handwritten manuscripts have all been lost. Only copies of copies remain. This is the source of many of the textual variants in the Hebrew and Greek manuscripts and ancient versions.

Bezae. This is a Greek and Latin manuscript of the sixth century A.D. It is designated by "D." It contains the Gospels and Acts and some of the General Epistles. It is characterized by numerous scribal additions. It forms the basis for the "Textus Receptus," the major Greek manuscript tradition behind the King James Version.

Bias. This is the term used to describe a strong predisposition toward an object or point of view. It is the mindset in which impartiality is impossible regarding a particular object or point of view. It is a prejudiced position.

Biblical Authority. This term is used in a very specialized sense. It is defined as understanding what the original author said to his day and applying this truth to our day. Biblical authority is usually defined as viewing the Bible itself as our only authoritative guide. However, in light of current, improper interpretations, I have limited the concept to the Bible as interpreted by the tenets of the historical-grammatical method.

Canon. This is a term used to describe writings which are believed to be uniquely inspired. It is used regarding both the Old and New Testament Scriptures.

Christocentric. This is a term used to describe the centrality of Jesus. I use it in connection with the concept that Jesus is Lord of all the Bible. The Old Testament points toward Him and He is its fulfillment and goal (cf. Matt. 5:17-48).

Commentary. This is a specialized type of research book. It gives the general background of a biblical book. It then tries to explain the meaning of each section of the book. Some focus on application, while others deal with the text in a more technical way. These books are helpful, but should be used after one has done his own preliminary study. The commentator's interpretations should never be accepted uncritically. Comparing several commentaries from different theological perspectives is usually helpful.

Concordance. This is a type of research tool for Bible study. It lists every occurrence of every word in the Old and New Testaments. It helps in several ways: (1) determining the Hebrew or Greek word which lies behind any particular English word; (2) comparing passages where the same Hebrew or Greek word was used; (3) showing where two different Hebrew or Greek terms are translated by the same English word; (4) showing the frequency of the use of certain words in certain books or authors; (5) helping one find a passage in the Bible (cf. Walter Clark's *How to Use New Testament Greek Study Aids*, pp. 54-55).

Dead Sea Scrolls. This refers to a series of ancient texts written in Hebrew and Aramaic which were found near the Dead Sea in 1947. They were the religious libraries of sectarian Judaism of the first century. The pressure of Roman occupation and the zealot wars of the 60's caused them to conceal the scrolls in hermetically sealed pottery jars in caves or holes. They have helped us understand the historical setting of first century Palestine and have confirmed the Masoretic Text as being very accurate, at least as far back as the early B.C. era. They are designated by the abbreviation "DSS."

Deductive. This method of logic or reasoning moves from general principles to specific applications by means of reason. It is opposite from inductive reasoning, which reflects the scientific method by moving from observed specifics to general conclusions (theories).

Dialectical. This is the method of reasoning whereby that which seems contradictory or paradoxical is held together in a tension, seeking a unified answer which includes both sides of the paradox. Many biblical doctrines have dialectical pairs, predestination—free will; security—perseverance; faith—works; decision—discipleship; Christian freedom—Christian responsibility.

Diaspora. This is the technical Greek term used by Palestinian Jews to describe other Jews who live outside the geographical boundaries of the Promised Land.

Dynamic equivalent. This is a theory of Bible translation. Bible translation can be viewed as a continuum from "word to word" correspondence, where an English word must be supplied for every Hebrew or Greek word, to a "paraphrase" where only the thought is translated with less regard to the original wording or phrasing. In between these two theories is "the dynamic equivalent" which attempts to take the original text seriously, but translates it in modern grammatical forms and idioms. A really good discussion of these various theories of translations is found in Fee and Stuart's *How to Read the Bible For All Its Worth*, p. 35 and in Robert Bratcher's Introduction to the TEV.

Eclectic. This term is used in connection with textual criticism. It refers to the practice of choosing readings from different Greek manuscripts in order to arrive at a text which is supposed to be close to the original autographs. It rejects the view that any one family of Greek manuscripts captures the originals.

Eisegesis. This is the opposite of exegesis. If exegesis is a "leading out" of the original author's intent, this term implies a "leading in" of a foreign idea or opinion.

Etymology. This is an aspect of word study that tries to ascertain the original meaning of a word. From this root meaning, specialized usages are more easily identified. In interpretation, etymology is not the main focus, rather the contemporary meaning and usage of a word.

Exegesis. This is the technical term for the practice of interpreting a specific passage. It means "to lead out" (of the text) implying that our purpose is to understand the original author's intent in light of historical setting, literary context, syntax and contemporary word meaning.

Genre. This is a French term that denotes different types of literature. The thrust of the term is the division of literary forms into categories which share common characteristics: historical narrative, poetry, proverb, apocalyptic and legislation.

Gnosticism. Most of our knowledge of this heresy comes from the gnostic writings of the second century. However, the incipient ideas were present in the first century (and before).

Some stated tenets of Valentian and Cerinthian Gnosticism of the second century are: (1) matter and spirit were co-eternal (an ontological dualism). Matter is evil, spirit is good. God, who is spirit, cannot be directly involved with molding evil matter; (2) there are emanations (*eons* or angelic levels) between God and matter. The last or lowest one was YHWH of the OT, who formed the universe (*kosmos*); (3) Jesus was an emanation like YHWH but higher on the scale, closer to the true God. Some put Him as the highest but still less than God and certainly not incarnate Deity (cf. John 1:14). Since matter is evil, Jesus could not have a human body and still be Divine. He was a spiritual phantom (cf. I John 1:1-3; 4:1-6); and (4) salvation was obtained through faith in Jesus plus special knowledge, which is only known by special persons. Knowledge (passwords) was needed to pass through heavenly spheres. Jewish legalism was also required to reach God.

The gnostic false teachers advocated two opposite ethical systems: (1) for some, lifestyle was totally unrelated to salvation. For them, salvation and spirituality were encapsulated into secret knowledge (passwords) through the angelic spheres (*eons*); or (2) for others, lifestyle was crucial to salvation. They emphasized an ascetic lifestyle as evidence of true spirituality.

Hermeneutics. This is the technical term for the principles which guide exegesis. It is both a set of specific guidelines and an art/gift. Biblical, or sacred, hermeneutics is usually divided into two categories: general principles and special principles. These relate to the different types of literature found in the Bible. Each different type (genre) has its own unique guidelines but also shares some common assumptions and procedures of interpretation.

Higher Criticism. This is the procedure of biblical interpretation which focuses on the historical setting and literary structure of a particular biblical book.

Idiom. This word is used for the phrases found in different cultures which have specialized meaning not connected to the usual meaning of the individual terms. Some modern examples are: "that was awfully good," or "you just kill me." The Bible also contains these types of phrases.

Illumination. This is the name given to the concept that God has spoken to mankind. The full concept is usually expressed by three terms: (1) revelation—God has acted in human history; (2) inspiration—He has given the proper interpretation of His acts and their meaning to certain chosen men to record for mankind; and (3) illumination—He has given His Spirit to help mankind understand His self-disclosure.

Inductive. This is a method of logic or reasoning which moves from the particulars to the whole. It is the empirical method of modern science. This is basically the approach of Aristotle.

Interlinear. This is a type of research tool which allows those who do not read a biblical language to be able to analyze its meaning and structure. It places the English translation on a word for word level immediately under the original biblical language. This tool, combined with an "analytical lexicon," will give the forms and basic definitions of Hebrew and Greek.

Inspiration. This is the concept that God has spoken to mankind by guiding the biblical authors to accurately and clearly record His revelation. The full concept is usually expressed by three terms: (1) revelation—God has acted in human history; (2) inspiration—He has given the proper interpretation of His acts and their meaning to certain chosen men to record for mankind; and (3) illumination—He has given His Spirit to help mankind understand His self-disclosure

Language of description. This is used in connection with the idioms in which the Old Testament is written. It speaks of our world in terms of the way things appear to the five senses. It is not a scientific description, nor was it meant to be.

Legalism. This attitude is characterized by an over-emphasis on rules or ritual. It tends to rely on the human performance of regulations as a means of acceptance by God. It tends to depreciate relationship and elevates performance, both of which are important aspects of the covenantal relationship between a holy God and sinful humanity.

Literal. This is another name for the textually-focused and historical method of hermeneutics from Antioch. It means that interpretation involves the normal and obvious meaning of human language, although it still recognizes the presence of figurative language.

Literary genre. This refers to the distinct forms that human communication can take, such as poetry or historical narrative. Each type of literature has its own special hermeneutical procedures in addition to the general principles for all written literature.

Literary unit. This refers to the major thought divisions of a biblical book. It can be made up of a few verses, paragraphs or chapters. It is a self-contained unit with a central subject.

Lower criticism. See "textual criticism."

Manuscript. This term relates to the different copies of the Greek New Testament. Usually they are divided into the different types by (1) material on which they are written (papyrus, leather), or (2) the form of the writing itself (all capitals or running script). It is abbreviated by "MS" (singular) or "MSS" (plural).

Masoretic Text. This refers to the ninth century A.D. Hebrew manuscripts of the Old Testament produced by generations of Jewish scholars which contain vowel points and other textual notes. It forms the basic text for our English Old Testament. Its text has been historically confirmed by the Hebrew MSS, especially Isaiah, known from the Dead Sea Scrolls. It is abbreviated by "MT."

Metonymy. This is a figure of speech in which the name of one thing is used to represent something else associated with it. As an example, "the kettle is boiling" actually means "the water within the kettle is boiling."

Muratorian Fragments. This is a list of the canonical books of the New Testament. It was written in Rome before A.D. 200. It gives the same twenty-seven books as the Protestant NT. This clearly shows the local churches in different parts of the Roman Empire had "practically" set the canon before the major church councils of the fourth century.

Natural revelation. This is one category of God's self-disclosure to man. It involves the natural order (Rom. 1:19-20) and the moral consciousness (Rom. 2:14-15). It is spoken of in Ps. 19:1-6 and Rom. 1-2. It is distinct from special revelation, which is God's specific self-disclosure in the Bible and supremely in Jesus of Nazareth.

This theological category is being re-emphasized by the "old earth" movement among Christian scientists (e.g., the writings of Hugh Ross). They use this category to assert that all truth is God's truth. Nature is an open door to knowledge about God; it is different from special revelation (the Bible). It allows modern science the freedom to research the natural order. In my opinion it is a wonderful new opportunity to witness to the modern scientific western world.

Nestorianism. Nestorius was the patriarch of Constantinople in the fifth century. He was trained in Antioch of Syria and affirmed that Jesus had two natures, one fully human and one fully divine.

This view deviated from the orthodox one nature view of Alexandria. Nestorius' main concern was the title "mother of God," given to Mary. Nestorius was opposed by Cyril of Alexandria and, by implication, his own Antiochian training. Antioch was the headquarters of the historical-grammatical-textual approach to biblical interpretation, while Alexandria was the headquarters of the four-fold (allegorical) school of interpretation. Nestorius was ultimately removed from office and exiled.

Original author. This refers to the actual authors/writers of Scripture.

Papyri. This is a type of writing material from Egypt. It is made from river reeds. It is the material upon which our oldest copies of the Greek New Testament are written.

Parallel passages. They are part of the concept that all of the Bible is God-given and, therefore, is its own best interpreter and balancer of paradoxical truths. This is also helpful when one is attempting to interpret an unclear or ambiguous passage. They also help one find the clearest passage on a given subject as well as all other Scriptural aspects of a given subject.

Paraphrase. This is the name of a theory of Bible translation. Bible translation can be viewed as a continuum from "word to word" correspondence, where an English word must be supplied for every Hebrew or Greek word to a "paraphrase" where only the thought is translated with less regard to the original wording or phrasing. In between these two theories is "the dynamic equivalent," which attempts to take serious the original text but translates it in modern grammatical forms and idioms.

A really good discussion of these various theories of translations is found in Fee and Stuart's *How to Read the Bible For All Its Worth*, p. 35.

Paragraph. This is the basic interpretive literary unit in prose. It contains one central thought and its development. If we stay with its major thrust we will not major on minors or miss the original author's intent.

Parochialism. This relates to biases which are locked into a local theological/cultural setting. It does not recognize the transcultural nature of biblical truth or its application.

Paradox. This refers to those truths which seem to be contradictory, yet both are true, although in tension with each other. They frame truth by presenting if from opposite sides. Much biblical truth is presented in paradoxical (or dialectical) pairs. Biblical truths are not isolated stars, but are constellations made up of the pattern of stars.

Plato. He was one of the philosophers of ancient Greece. His philosophy greatly influenced the early church through the scholars of Alexandria, Egypt, and later, Augustine. He posited that everything on earth was illusionary and a mere copy of a spiritual archetype. Theologians later equated Plato's "forms/ideas" with the spiritual realm.

Presupposition. This refers to our preconceived understanding of a matter. Often we form opinions or judgments about issues before we approach the Scriptures themselves. This predisposition is also known as a bias, an *a priori* position, an assumption or a preunderstanding.

Proof-texting. This is the practice of interpreting Scripture by quoting a verse without regard for its immediate context or larger context in its literary unit. This removes the verses from the original author's intent and usually involves the attempt to prove a personal opinion while asserting biblical authority.

Rabbinical Judaism. This stage of the life of the Jewish people began in Babylonian Exile (586-538 B.C.). As the influence of the Priests and the Temple was removed, local synagogues became the focus of Jewish life. These local centers of Jewish culture, fellowship, worship and Bible study became the focus of the national religious life. In Jesus' day this "religion of the scribes" was parallel to that of the priests. At the fall of Jerusalem in 70 A.D. the scribal form, dominated by the Pharisees, controlled the direction of Jewish religious life. It is characterized by a practical, legalistic interpretation of the Torah as explained in the oral tradition (Talmud).

Revelation. This is the name given to the concept that God has spoken to mankind. The full concept is usually expressed by three terms:
(1)   revelation—God has acted in human history;
(2)   inspiration—He has given the proper interpretation of His acts and their meaning to certain chosen men to record for mankind; and
(3)   illumination—He has given His Spirit to help mankind understand His self-disclosure.

Semantic field. This refers to the total range of meanings associated with a word. It is basically the different connotations a word has in different contexts.

Septuagint. This is the name given to the Greek translation of the Hebrew Old Testament. Tradition says that it was written in seventy days by seventy Jewish scholars for the library of Alexandria, Egypt. The traditional date is around 250 B.C. (in reality it possibly took over one hundred years to complete). This translation is significant because (1) it gives us an ancient text to compare with the Masoretic Hebrew text; (2) it shows us the state of Jewish interpretation in the third and second century B.C.; (3) it gives us the Jewish Messianic understanding before the rejection of Jesus. Its abbreviation is "LXX."

Sinaiticus. This is a Greek manuscript of the fourth century A.D. It was found by the German scholar, Tischendorf, at St. Catherine's monastery on Jebel Musa, the traditional site of Mt. Sinai. This manuscript is designated by the first letter of the Hebrew alphabet called *"aleph"* [א]. It contains both the Old and the entire New Testaments. It is one of our most ancient uncial MSS.

Spiritualizing. This term is synonymous with allegorizing in the sense that it removes the historical and literary context of a passage and interprets it on the basis of other criteria.

Synonymous. This refers to terms with exact or very similar meanings (although in reality no two words have a complete semantic overlap). They are so closely related that they can replace each other in a sentence without loss of meaning. It is also used to designate one of the three forms of Hebrew poetic parallelism. In this sense it refers to two lines of poetry that express the same truth (cf. Ps. 103:3).

Syntax. This is a Greek term which refers to the structure of a sentence. It relates to the ways parts of a sentence are put together to make a complete thought.

Synthetical. This is one of the three terms that relates to types of Hebrew poetry. This term speaks of lines of poetry which build on one another in a cumulative sense, sometimes called "climatic" (cf. Ps. 19:7-9).

Systematic theology. This is a stage of interpretation which tries to relate the truths of the Bible in a unified and rational manner. It is a logical, rather than mere historical, presentation of Christian theology by categories (God, man, sin, salvation, etc.).

Talmud. This is the title for the codification of the Jewish Oral Tradition. The Jews believe it was given orally by God to Moses on Mt. Sinai. In reality it appears to be the collective wisdom of the Jewish teachers through the years. There are two different written versions of the Talmud: the Babylonian and the shorter, unfinished Palestinian.

Textual criticism. This is the study of the manuscripts of the Bible. Textual criticism is necessary because no originals exist and the copies differ from each other. It attempts to explain the variations and arrive (as close as possible) to the original wording of the autographs of the Old and New Testaments. It is often called "lower criticism."

Textus Receptus. This designation developed into Elzevir's edition of the Greek NT in A.D. 1633. Basically it is a form of the Greek NT that was produced from a few late Greek manuscripts and Latin versions of Erasmus (1510-1535), Stephanus (1546-1559) and Elzevir (1624-1678). In *An Introduction to the Textual Criticism of the New Testament*, p. 27, A. T. Robertson says "the Byzantine text is practically the Textus Receptus." The Byzantine text is the least valuable of the three families of early Greek manuscripts (Western, Alexandrian and Byzantine). It contains the accumulation errors of centuries of hand-copied texts. However, A.T. Robertson also says "the Textus Receptus has preserved for us a substantially accurate text" (p. 21). This Greek manuscript tradition (especially Erasmus' third edition of 1522) forms the basis of the King James Version of 1611 A.D.

Torah. This is the Hebrew term for "teaching." It came to be the official title for the writings of Moses (Genesis through Deuteronomy). It is, for the Jews, the most authoritative division of the Hebrew canon.

Typological. This is a specialized type of interpretation. Usually it involves New Testament truth found in Old Testament passages by means of an analogical symbol. This category of hermeneutics was a major element of the Alexandrian method. Because of the abuse of this type of interpretation, one should limit its use to specific examples recorded in the New Testament.

Vaticanus. This is the Greek manuscript of the fourth century A.D. It was found in the Vatican's library. It originally contained all the Old Testament, Apocrypha and New Testament. However, some parts were lost (Genesis, Psalms, Hebrews, the Pastorals, Philemon and Revelation). It is a very helpful manuscript in determining the original wording of the autographs. It is designated by a capital "B."

Vulgate. This is the name of Jerome's Latin translation of the Bible. It became the basic or "common" translation for the Roman Catholic Church. It was done in the 380's A.D.

Wisdom literature. This was a genre of literature common in the ancient near east (and modern world).
It basically was an attempt to instruct a new generation on guidelines for successful living through poetry, proverb, or essay. It was addressed more to the individual than to corporate society. It did not use allusions to history, but was based on life experiences and observation. In the Bible, Job through Song of Songs assumed the presence and worship of YHWH, but this religious world view is not explicit in every human experience every time.

As a genre it stated general truths. However, this genre cannot be used in every specific situation. These are general statements that do not always apply to every individual situation.

These sages dared to ask the hard questions of life. Often they challenged traditional religious views (Job and Ecclesiastes). They form a balance and tension to the easy answers about life's tragedies.

World picture and worldview. These are companion terms. They are both philosophical concepts related to creation. The term "world picture" refers to "the how" of creation while "worldview" relates to "the Who." These terms are relevant to the interpretation that Gen. 1-2 deals primarily with the Who, not the how, of creation.

YHWH. This is the Covenant name for God in the Old Testament. It is defined in Exod. 3:14. It is the CAUSATIVE form of the Hebrew term "to be." The Jews were afraid to pronounce the name, lest they take it in vain; therefore, they substituted the Hebrew term *Adonai*, "lord." This is how this covenant name is translated in English.

APPENDIX ELEVEN

BIBLIOGRAPHY OF CITED AND RECOMMENDED BOOKS

Barr, James. *The Semantics of Biblical Language.* Oxford: Oxford University Press, 1961

Barton, John. Holy Writings – Sacred Text: The Canon in Early Christianity. Richmond: John Knox Press, 1997

Berkhof, Louis. *Systematic Theology.* Grand Rapids: Eerdmans, 1939
Principles of Biblical Interpretation. Grand Rapids: Baker 1950

Black, David A., ed. *Rethinking New Testament Textual Criticism.* Grand Rapids: Baker Academic, 2002

Braga, James. *How to Study the Bible.* Portland: Multnomah, 1982

Bruce, F. F. *The Books and the Parchments.* Old Tappan, N. J.: Revell, 1963
New Testament History. Garden City: Doubleday, 1969
The English Bible: A History of Translations From the Earliest Versions to the New English Bible. Oxford: Oxford University Press, 1970
Answers to Questions. Grand Rapids: Zondervan, 1972
ed. *The New International Commentary on the New Testament.* Grand Rapids: Eerdmans,1955

Carson, D. A. *The King James Version Debate: A Plea for Realism,* 1979
Biblical Interpretation and the Church. Nashville: Thomas Nelson, 1984
Exegetical Fallacies. Grand Rapids: Baker, 1984

Cole, Alan. *The Epistle of Paul to the Galatians.* Grand Rapids: Eerdmans, 1964

Cotterell, Peter and Max Turner. *Linguistics and Bible Interpretation,* 1989

Dana, Harvey Eugene. *Searching the Scriptures.* Kansas City: Central Seminary, 1946

Danker, Frederick W. *Multipurpose Tools for Bible Study.* Concordia, 1970

Dembski, William A., ed. *Mere Creation.* Downers Grove: InterVarsity Press, 1998

Ehrman, Bart D. *The Orthodox Corruption of Scripture.* Oxford: Oxford University Press, 1993

Falk, Darrell R. *Coming to Peace With Science.* Downers Grove: InterVarsity Press, 2004

Fee, Gordon D. *Gospel and Spirit: Issues in New Testament Hermeneutics.* Peabody: Hendrickson, 1991

Fee, Gordon D. and Douglas Stuart. *How to Read the Bible for All Its Worth*. Grand Rapids: Zondervan, 1982
   To What End Exegesis? Grand Rapids: Eerdmans, 2001

Ferguson, Duncan S. *Biblical Hermeneutics*. Atlanta: John Knox Press, 1937

Froehlich, Karlfried. *Biblical Interpretation in the Early Church*. Philadelphia: Fortress, 1984

Gilbert, George Holley. *Interpretation of the Bible, a Short History*. New York: MacMillan, 1908

Grant, Robert M. and David Tracy. *A Short History of the Interpretation of the Bible*. Philadelphia: Fortress, 1984

Greenlee, J. Harold. *Introduction to New Testament Textual Criticism*. Grand Rapids: Eerdmans, 1972

Hayes, John H. and Carl R. Holladay. *Biblical Exegesis*. Atlanta: John Knox Press, 1934

Hendricks, Howard G. *Living By the Book*, 1991

Henricksen, Walter A. *A Layman's Guide to Interpreting the Bible*. Grand Rapids: Zondervan, 1973

Hirsch, E. D.   *Validity In Interpretation*. New Haven: Yale University, 1967
     Aims of Interpretation. New Haven: Yale University, 1978

Hooykaas, R. *Religion and the Rise of Modern Science*. Grand Rapids: Eerdmans, 1972

Jansen, John Fredrick. *Exercises in Interpreting Scripture*. Philadelphia: Geneva Press, 1968

Jeeves, Malcolm A. *The Scientific Enterprise and the Christian Faith*. Downers Grove: InterVarsity, 1969

Jensen, Irving L. *Independent Bible Study: Using the Analytical Chart and the Inductive Method*.

Chicago: Moody, 1963

Johnson, Elliott E. *Expository Hermeneutics*. Grand Rapids: Zondervan, 1990

Johnson, Phillip E. *Darwinism on Trial*. Downers Grove: InterVarsity Press, 1993

Kaiser, Otto and Werner G. Kummel. *Exegetical Method*. New York: Seabury, 1981

Kaiser, Walter C., Jr. *Towards An Exegetical Theology*. Grand Rapids: Baker, 1981

Kaiser, Walter C. Jr., Peter H. Davis, F. F. Bruce, and Manfred T. Baruch. *Hard Sayings of the Bible*. Downers Grove: InterVarsity Press, 1996

Kitchen, K. A. *Ancient Orient and the Old Testament*. Downers Grove: InterVarsity, 1966

Kubo, Sakae and Walter Specht. *So Many Versions*. Grand Rapids: Zondervan, 1983

Kuhatschek, Jack. *Apply the Bible*. Downers Grove: InterVarsity Press, 1990

Ladd, George Eldon. *A Theology of the New Testament*. Grand Rapids: Eerdmans, 1974

Liefeld, Walter L.   *New Testament Exposition*. Grand Rapids: Zondervan, 1984
            Biblical Exegesis in the Apostolic Period. Grand Rapids: Eerdmans, 1999

Longman, Tremper III. *Literary Approaches to Biblical Interpretation*, vol. 3, 1987

Marle, Rene S. J. *Introduction to Hermeneutics*. New York: Herder and Herder, 1967

Marshall, I. Howard, ed. *New Testament Interpretation*. Grand Rapids: Eerdmans, 1977

Mayhue, Richard. *How to Interpret the Bible For Yourself*. Chicago: Moody, 1986

McQuilkin, J. Robertson. *Understanding and Applying the Bible*. Chicago: Moody, 1983

Metzger, Bruce M.   *The New Testament: Its Transmission, Corruption and Restoration*. Oxford: Oxford University Press, 1964
            The New Testament: Its Background, Growth and Content. New York: Abingdon, 1965
            A Textual Commentary on the Greek New Testament. New York: United Bible Societies, 1971
            The Early Versions of the New Testament, 1977
            The Canon of the New Testament. Oxford: Clarendon Press, 1997

Mickelsen, A. Berkeley. *Interpreting the Bible*. Grand Rapids: Eerdmans, 1963

Newport, John P. and William Cannon. *Why Christians Fight Over the Bible*. Nashville: Thomas Nelson, 1974

Nida, Eugene.   *God's Word in Man's Language*. London: William Carey, 1952
            The Hermeneutical Spiral. Downers Grove: InterVarsity Press, 1991

Osborn, Grant R. and Stephen B. Woodward. *Handbook For Bible Study*. Grand Rapids: Baker, 1979

Patte, Daniel. *Early Jewish Hermeneutics in Palestine*.   Missoula, MT: Society of Biblical Literature and Scholars Press, 1975

Poe, Harry L. and Jimmy H. Davis. *Science and Faith*. Nashville: Broadman, 2000

Poythress, Vern S. *Science and Hermeneutics*. Grand Rapids: Academie, 1988

Ramm, Bernard.   *The Christian View of Science and Scripture*. Grand Rapids: Eerdmans, 1954

        Protestant Biblical Interpretation. Grand Rapids: Baker, 1970

Ratzsch, Del. *The Battle of Beginnings*. Downers Grove: InterVarsity Press, 1996

Rowley, H. H. *The Relevance of the Bible*, 1940

Sandy, D. Brent and Ronald L. Giese, Jr. *Cracking Old Testament Codes*. Nashville: Broadman, 1995

        Plowshares and Pruning Hooks: Rethinking the Language of Biblical Prophecy and Apocalyptic. Downers Grove: InterVarsity Press, 2002

Scholer, D. W.   *A Basic Bibliographic Guide for New Testament Exegesis*.   Grand Rapids: Eerdmans, 1973

Schultz, Samuel J. and Morris A. Inch, eds. *Interpreting the Word of God*. Chicago: Moody, 1976

Silva, Moises. *Biblical Words and Their Meaning*. Grand Rapids: Zondervan, 1983
        Has the Church Misread the Bible? Grand Rapids: Zondervan, 1987

Silva, Moises, ed. *Foundations of Contemporary Interpretation*. Grand Rapids: Zondervan, 1996

Sire, James W. *Scripture Twisting*. Downers Grove: InterVarsity Press, 1980

Stagg, Frank. *New Testament Theology*. Nashville: Broadman, 1962

Stein, Robert H. *A Basic Guide to Interpreting the Bible: Playing by the Rules*. Grand Rapids: Baker, 2000

Sterrett, J. Norton. *How To Understand Your Bible*. Downers Grove: InterVarsity, 1973

Stewart, Douglas. *Old Testament Exegesis*. Philadelphia: Westminster, 1980

Stewart, James S. *A Man In Christ*. New York: Harper and Row, 1935

Stibbs, Alan Marshal. *Understanding God's Word*. London: InterVarsity, 1950

Stuart, Douglas. *Old Testament Exegesis*. Philadelphia: Westminster, 1980

Tenney, Merrill C. *Galatians: The Charter of Christian Liberty*. Grand Rapids: Eerdmans, 1950

Terry, Milton. *Biblical Hermeneutics*. Grand Rapids: Zondervan, 1974

Thiselton, Anthony C. *The Two Horizons*. Grand Rapids: Eerdmans, 1980

Traina, Robert A. *Methodical Bible Study*. Grand Rapids: Zondervan, 1985

Vanhoozer, Kevin J. *Is There a Meaning in This Text*. Grand Rapids: Zondervan, 1998

Vaughn, Curtis, ed. *Twenty-Six Translations of the Bible*. Chattanooga: AMG, 1985

Vine, W. E. Vine's Expository Dictionary of New Testament Words. Westwood, N. J.: Revell, 1966

Virkler, Henry A. *Hermeneutics*. Grand Rapids: Baker, 1981

Walke, B. K., D. Guthrie, G. D. Fee and R. K. Harrison. *Biblical Criticism: Historical, Literary and Textual*, 1997

APPENDIX TWELVE

DOCTRINAL STATEMENT

I do not particularly care for statements of faith or creeds. I prefer to affirm the Bible itself. However, I realize that a statement of faith will provide those who are unfamiliar with me a way to evaluate my doctrinal perspective. In our day of so much theological error and deception, the following brief summary of my theology is offered.

1. The Bible, both the Old and New Testament, is the inspired, infallible, authoritative, eternal Word of God. It is the self-revelation of God recorded by men under supernatural leadership. It is our only source of clear truth about God and His purposes. It is also the only source of faith and practice for His church.

2. There is only one eternal, creator, redeemer God. He is the creator of all things, visible and invisible. He has revealed Himself as loving and caring although He is also fair and just. He has revealed Himself in three distinct persons: Father, Son and Spirit; truly separate and yet the same in essence.

3. God is actively in control of His world. There is both an eternal plan for His creation that is unalterable and an individually focused one that allows human free will. Nothing happens without God's knowledge and permission, yet He allows individual choices both among angels and humans. Jesus is the Father's Elect Man and all are potentially elect in Him. God's foreknowledge of events does not reduce humans to a determined pre-written script. All of us are responsible for our thoughts and deeds.

4. Mankind, though created in God's image and free from sin, chose to rebel against God. Although tempted by a supernatural agent, Adam and Eve were responsible for their willful self-centeredness. Their rebellion has affected humanity and creation. We are all in need of God's mercy and grace both for our corporate condition in Adam and our individual volitional rebellion.

5. God has provided a means of forgiveness and restoration for fallen humanity. Jesus Christ, God's unique son, became a man, lived a sinless life, and by means of his substitutionary death, paid the penalty for mankind's sin. He is the only way to restoration and fellowship with God. There is no other means of salvation except through faith in His finished work.

6. Each of us must personally receive God's offer of forgiveness and restoration in Jesus. This is accomplished by means of volitional trust in God's promises through Jesus and a willful turning from known sin.

7. All of us are fully forgiven and restored based upon our trust in Christ and repentance from sin. However, the evidence for this new relationship is seen in a changed, and changing, life. The goal of God for humanity is not only heaven someday, but Christlikeness now. Those who are truly redeemed, though occasionally sinning, will continue in faith and repentance throughout their lives.

8. The Holy Spirit is "the other Jesus." He is present in the world to lead the lost to Christ and develop Christlikeness in the saved. The gifts of the Spirit are given at salvation. They are the life and ministry of Jesus divided among His body, the Church. The gifts which are basically the attitudes and motives of Jesus need to be motivated by the fruit of the Spirit. The Spirit is active in our day as He was in the biblical times.

9. The Father has made the resurrected Jesus Christ the Judge of all things. He will return to earth to judge all mankind. Those who have trusted Jesus and whose names are written in the Lamb's book of life will receive their eternal glorified bodies at His return. They will be with Him forever. However, those who have refused to respond to God's truth will be separated eternally from the joys of fellowship with the Triune God. They will be condemned along with the Devil and his angels.

This is surely not complete or thorough but I hope it will give you the theological flavor of my heart. I like the statement:

"In essentials—unity, In peripherals—freedom, In all things—love."

A Poem

It cannot mean what it never meant
I've etched that on my brain.
And when I study Scripture
I echo that refrain.
I've studied hermeneutics and exegesis too,
So, as a consequence of this
I've somewhat changed my view.
I've learned some nomenclature
too lengthy to define
like cultural relativity and textual design.
There is so much I want to know,
How to ferret out the truth.
I hope someday that I'll become a
Bible-reading sleuth.
A new respect has taken me, for God's own holy word
inspiring me to know the truth, to hear as it was heard.
But I know I must remember,
I stepped through an open door,
and never can return again to where I was before.

Pat Bergeron
11/27/91

Made in the USA
Middletown, DE
15 August 2021